Standing My Ground

Matthew Hayden

Standing My Ground

First published in Great Britain
2011 by Aurum Press Ltd
7 Greenland Street
London NW1 0ND
www.aurumpress.co.uk

Copyright © Matthew Hayden and Robert Craddock 2010

First published in Australia by Penguin Group (Australia) 2010.

Matthew Hayden has asserted his moral right to be identified as the Author of this Work in accordance with the Copyright Designs and Patents Act 1988.

All rights reserved. No part of this book may be reproduced or utilised in any form or by any means, electronic or mechanical, including photocopying, recording or by any information storage and retrieval system, without permission in writing from Aurum Press Ltd.

Every effort has been made to trace the copyright holders of material quoted in this book. If application is made in writing to the publisher, any omissions will be included in future editions.

A catalogue record for this book is available from the British Library.

ISBN 978 1 84513 662 8

1 3 5 7 9 10 8 6 4 2
2011 2013 2015 2014 2012

Text design by Cameron Midson © Penguin Group (Australia)
Typeset in Sabon by Post Pre-Press Group, Brisbane, Queensland
Printed and bound in Great Britain by MPG Books, Bodmin, Cornwall

I wish you all well in standing your own ground
in the pursuit of happiness.

And to my dearest Kellie, Grace, Joshua and Thomas,
thank you for giving me the wings to fly to great heights,
at times far from sight but never far from mind.

Contents

Foreword

by Andrew 'Freddie' Flintoff

I knew of Matthew Hayden's reputation long before I knew the man.

In 2002–03 I toured Australia for the first time in England's Ashes squad, and Matthew's reputation preceded him. He wasn't popular among our senior players. In fact, the consensus among our entire party was that he wasn't very likeable.

I'm sure some of it was simply because he was successful – it's a very English trait not to warm to people who are. The boys also felt he played on ego. New-ball bowlers weren't used to seeing an opening batsman use his feet to fast bowling. It was easy to brand that tactic as arrogant, but I never had a problem with it. Secretly I thought it was great. It was something completely different.

I was on the field in Brisbane in 2002 when Matthew walked down the pitch and hit Craig White over mid wicket for a six. That was unheard of in Test cricket at that time. As a fieldsman I was captivated by the tactic. As a bowler I found the sight of the big fellow leaving his crease and marching down the wicket in my direction far less enjoyable.

The one thing I really struggled to come to grips with was that even when you dropped short to him after he'd done the 'Hayden shuffle', he still managed to pull and hook your best work. I'm sure I bowled bouncers to Haydos that *weren't* pulled for four or six, but I can't remember them. I always considered the bouncer one of my great weapons – but against him it was a completely meaningless ball. When one of the strengths of your game is neutralised, you have to look at different options.

Haydos was quick on the lip. I remember once walking out to bat when I was coughing so much I was almost barking like a dog, and he asked me whether I had a spare cigarette. He unashamedly used his giant frame and imposing body language to intimidate opponents. He used to stand there and puff his chest out and look around the field. He had a real presence about him. But it wasn't as if he was all brawn and body language – it took great skill to play a lot of his strokes.

At Edgbaston, during the one-day series in 2005, Simon Jones threw a ball at Haydos and hit him on the body. He and Simon shaped up and Paul Collingwood raced in as Haydos stuck his chest out and was ready for a rumble. He looked a real bruiser, so it was interesting getting to know him a few months later and discovering that he wasn't like that at all.

Haydos and I had our first beer together in the dressing-room after our First Test loss to Australia at Lord's in 2005. It was my first Ashes Test and a bad one for me – I made just 0 and 3. For the first time in my career I genuinely felt I'd bottled it. There had been plenty of chat in the middle and Haydos was always in the midst of it.

But the beer with Haydos afterwards certainly cheered me up. It was then that I learnt there were two sides to him. On the field he was a hard-edged competitor; off the field he was great company and a terrific bloke. The two teams kept up the tradition of a dressing-room beer right throughout the series and I often found myself drawn to Haydos and Justin Langer. One of my great regrets about modern cricket is that sides don't mix any more; the players just don't realise what they're missing out on.

The off-field chemistry between me and Haydos changed the nature of our on-field duels. We still went at each other like two gladiators, but there was a respectful edge to proceedings. It was a duel in the best possible sense, how the game should be played. Once when I got him out he even said, 'Well bowled.' If he played a good shot I could appreciate it. Bowling to someone of his calibre brought out the best in me.

Our tradition of off-field beers continued four years later, when we became teammates in the Chennai Super Kings in the Indian Premier League. The tournament was switched to South Africa and I only made it for a week. I played with Haydos, who charitably squeezed some cricket into his busy surfing and fishing schedule. It was very big of him. He was chosen for a random drug test one day and I stayed behind for company, ending up having my favourite night of the IPL. I think it took 10 bottles of Castle before there was movement in the drug test but the time passed quickly as we swapped stories new and old.

I only fully appreciated the impact Haydos had on Australian cricket when Marcus Trescothick was in full bloom for England. Like Haydos, he took on the bowlers with great success and made things feel so much easier for all of us down the order.

I've heard that Haydos thinks we'll have a long-term

friendship, and I am sure we will – as long as he stops telling those endless surfing stories. As I keep telling him, I'm a boy from Preston in northern England. Our idea of a giant wave is something you do when you drop the kids off at school. We're also a bit of a contrast in the kitchen: he's a champion cook while my forte has always been eating. But I will always remember Haydos as one of the best batsmen I ever bowled to. I hope you enjoy his story and admire his career as much as I do.

Australia was lucky to have him.

Andrew Flintoff

Introduction

I was born, raised and live my life as a Catholic. It's a very important part of who I am. But there is already one Saint Matthew in the Church, and I'm dead certain there won't be another one coming from the ranks of recently retired Australian cricketers.

My favourite saint has always been Saint Peter. Peter didn't always succeed – he was the man who began walking on water with Jesus, but went for a bit of a dip when his faith wavered, and he was also the one who falsely denied his association with Christ three times before the cock crowed. But although he could be uncertain at times, Peter was also full of enthusiasm, even rashness. In a religion that decrees 'thou shalt not' about so many things, Peter was someone who occasionally wondered, 'Well, why not?' I've always found great realism – and great comfort – in his story.

I know some people saw a contradiction in the way I conducted myself on the cricket field throughout my career.

I crossed myself when I reached a hundred, yet I was also at the forefront of Australia's sledging, the verbal warfare against our opposition. I can see the paradox. How did I reconcile 'God-fearing Matthew' with 'man-baiting Hayden'?

During my playing days, publicly acknowledging my faith was a personal affirmation for me. Without faith I would have felt very exposed and vulnerable. I didn't do it to seek attention, I did it for me. It was a way of saying, 'This is who I am.' In contrast, intimidating opponents was a role I played, although I played for keeps. If that meant offending someone in the process, I'd do it anyway. Away from cricket I'm different – but I played the game hard.

I am also a man who has evolved. In my early years growing up on a farm, I was a laidback country kid. My environment dictated that. But I worked on cricket – and cricket worked on me. It hardened me. It had to. If I'd been content to be a 'whatever' sort of character, I would have been a 'whatever' sort of cricketer. Bush life also gave me a deep-seated tenacity, and even when I am far away from home I can still smell the rich volcanic soil of the family farm in Kingaroy, which proved so irresistible to my great-grandfather after he arrived from England that he set root in the region. That connection to the land has flowed through four generations, and even now I sometimes think of my cricket journey through the hundreds of pairs of shoes I wore on different soils around the globe. I never met my great-grandfather but I wonder sometimes what he would have made of me and how brave he must have been to make the bold voyage by ship to Australia.

Early in my career I was full of doubt and had plenty of doubters, and I often sensed that opposition players didn't rate me – they thought I was one-dimensional and easy to work out. But one quality my detractors underestimated was my relentless desire to overcome barriers, come what may. I developed a commanding physique, and an on-field presence to match. My role became one of intimidator. And just as a good actor completely gives himself to a part, I went all the way. Apart from one incident where I kicked a dressing-room door, I didn't break the rules of the game, but I played at a time when the spirit of the game was changing, becoming more professional, psychological and physical, when teams were learning to use whatever arsenal they could find as well as the bat and the ball. I might not always have been proud of my actions, and I wasn't always popular for them, but I recognised the importance of that part of my role, which helped my team become one of the most dominant of all time. As I matured, it was this that enabled me to perform when it really counted – under pressure.

In retirement, I confront the demons of introspection. Was I a hypocrite? Maybe. But I am what I am: a man of contradictions. There's the real me, and then there's the person many people think I am.

I'm the kind of person who needs to be in control. Perhaps that's why I gravitated towards being an opening batsman. There's a degree of certainty that comes with the role. I knew I'd be facing the new ball. I knew who I'd be batting with and I loved the certainty of opening with Justin Langer and knowing Ricky Ponting would be the next man in. I knew I could get the most out of the conditions. But the other element that attracted me was the pure pleasure – I just loved batting so *much*. Why wouldn't I want to bat first? Even in my last Indian Premier League tournament, at age 38, I'd bat far longer in the nets than any teammate, then retire in a state of total exhaustion to what seemed the only cool place in steamy Chennai – a concrete dressing-room floor, on which I'd lie face-down and then flip over in an attempt to cool my overcooked body.

I suffered when I wasn't in control. It almost killed me getting on a plane to tour, leaving my family, especially after I became a father. I'd be brave right up to the point where I took my seat on the plane and started watching the movies, but then I would just break down. I'd put my head against the window and everyone would think I was asleep, but in fact I was grieving massively in my own little world. How could I not? I was leaving behind the people I love most in my life. My wife, Kellie, is not only the mother of our three beautiful children, but is truly my life partner. And she has integrated her life with mine in a very peaceful, very inclusive, incredibly generous and selfless way.

Kell is often the go-to person when I am out of contact or out of the country. There were often extended periods when I was not contactable – the dressing room, for example, was a no-go zone for mobile phones in accordance with anti-corruption policies – so Kell would field calls on my behalf from family, friends, sponsors, management, and sometimes the media. She would do her level best to help someone out and I'd wonder at times whether she would be hurt or feel a little used by people bothering her to get to me. But no, never! Amazingly, her heart seems ever open and I never heard her complain, such is her capacity to give.

Any cricket player – and any human being – needs to learn to cope with the things they can't control: the weather, the touring, the opposition, sometimes even your teammates and your own form. As I came to learn, if you worry too much about what other people are doing, or what they think of you, you will fail. You have to try to remember what's important in life, what your values are, and stand your ground no matter what adversity you are facing.

This book isn't a boundary-by-boundary account of my career. It is not a strict chronology of my life inside and outside the boundary fence. Instead, I have tried to focus on the innings and the people that mattered most – the ones that shaped me.

I am proud of my career and my journey in life. I saw the game from all angles and, thanks to the IPL, even had the chance to immerse myself in another culture. I was prepared to do things my own way, whether that meant moving forward when the textbook said to move back, or using a bowling machine when others felt they were old-fashioned, or throwing myself into activities outside the game, like cooking and surfing. I've met countless people along the way – from English royalty to beggars – and often found the ones I best connected with were those down-to-earth characters leading ordinary lives.

There were times when I felt unsupported and unrated, others when I felt I had almost too much support for my own good. I had one captain who didn't want me in his team, and others who made me feel as if they couldn't do without me. I've been a humble bench player, in shock at being given the chance to make a last-minute Test debut, and a senior player who didn't hesitate to put noses out of joint by speaking up for the team's cause. I may not have always been entirely comfortable with the reflection I saw in the mirror, but I wanted to be the best cricketer that I could be. For all Saint Peter's foibles and flaws, he came to be regarded as the 'rock' of the Church. For all my shortcomings, I wanted to be one of the rocks of the Australian cricket team. This book is about how, for better and worse, I tried.

1

Sledging

I've dished it out and I've copped it back. I've locked horns with some of the game's biggest names, and I've been on the receiving end of sledges from little old ladies, family members and even priests. In fact, one of the most memorable sledges came from someone who was both a family member *and* a priest – my mum's late brother, Father Pat Jones. Father Pat was the parish priest at Weipa when I visited the North Queensland town for a Super 8s game early in my career. After watching me play out a pretty docile first over, he roared from the bleachers, 'Do you mind playing a shot? I have to live in this town!'

Although I admit to being at the forefront of Australia's psychological warfare, I was never reported for a single offence. Of course, I tried to pick my moments and do my chirping discreetly. Even so, there were times when tempers would fray and I was warned to cool down by a variety of umpires. I sailed pretty close to the wind. But I honestly don't think that I ever contravened the law or – as I understood it – the spirit of the game in the heat of battle, despite a couple of off-field slip-ups. I've always felt that the hype around sledging was overblown – to me, it was only one of the elements I had at my disposal to perform my role in the Australian team.

I reckon teams have always had a word or two in each other's ear. And I've always believed that it's part of the game, not part of the character of the people who play it. Mum was a drama teacher, and in our family we've always had a rich appreciation of theatre. As a kid, I was passionate about drama and acting. At the tender age of two and a half I was the youngest boy in one of Mum's productions of *The King and I*. Bowing to the King was a key part of my performance, but for some reason I just wouldn't do it. My uncle Jim solved the problem by promising me three Mars Bars if I bowed. I took up the offer so enthusiastically that I bowed not once but more than ten times, as the audience chuckled at the sight of me becoming a human drawbridge . . . up, down, up, down, up, down. I loved performance and being on stage. I loved the chance to be whatever I needed to be in any given scenario. During my playing career, I was performing on some of the world's greatest sporting stages, and as my career developed, my role of intimidator became more refined. My physical presence, strength, body language, movement and intensity – especially when fielding close to the bat – became far more powerful tools than any verbal barb.

In my era, Australia's dominance of other teams was played out as much in the head as at the crease. It started with our ability to create an aura of intensity that no other side could match. Many times I'd see opposition players looking over at us in pre-match warm-ups, when we were self-contained and seemed highly purposeful, and sensed they were thinking, *What are they doing?*

It was as if we had all the answers. We didn't. We just never let anyone know that we didn't. As a consequence, we often saw the mental disintegration of players – and teams – happening before our eyes. Sometimes we annihilated teams who should have performed far better than they did, simply because they were beaten in the battle for mental supremacy, often before the match began.

Our intimidation of other teams was very much a collective effort, with players filling a range of unspoken yet clearly defined roles. Damien Martyn would never have dreamed of putting serious verbal heat on someone, partly because he would have struggled with the retaliation. But he still had a clear role – to swagger around as if he thought the opposition were schoolboys playing totally out of their league. We knew that in the opposition dressing-room they'd be saying things like, 'How about that Martyn . . . Talk about being in love with yourself,' but that only confirmed to us that he was playing his role well and getting under their skin.

Adam Gilchrist had a completely different role. My dad had a saying, 'You catch more flies with honey than vinegar,' and it always reminds me of Gilly. He wasn't your big-time sledger, but he was as competitive and intense as any of us, and his subtle messages from behind the stumps, even if they were only supporting the bowler, played their part. The contrast between my disciplinary record and Gilly's makes me smile. He had four 'code of conduct' or 'behaviour' offences, while I had no on-field bookings but was fined once for kicking and shattering a dressing-room door (against England at the SCG in 2003). That my rap sheet is shorter that Gilly's wasn't because I was better behaved – I just covered my tracks well. I tried to be subtle with my chirps, sometimes walking in the opposite direction as I spoke or covering my mouth. Gilly, a very emotional man, sometimes just let the lid fly off the saucepan. And it didn't matter to him if he was standing right next to the umpire.

Andrew Symonds was the best in the business at the short, sharp quip that could slice through his opponents' concentration like a diamond-tipped drill. Where players like Warnie and me had to curb our instinctive animation, Symo just delivered piercing lines with no change of facial expression. It kept opponents guessing as they pondered, 'Did he just say that? Is he serious?'

Ricky Ponting was a sledging ringleader in his pre-captaincy days, but he went from being a slayer to one of the slain. When there was a major code breach he'd have to nurse the ensuing hangover with match and Cricket Australia officials, and it really wore him down over time.

Glenn McGrath did a lot of his best work off the field. His targeting of opposition players in the press was as successful as it was bold. His hit-rate was extraordinary. Brian Lara, Mike Atherton, Gary Kirsten and many others felt the wrath of 'Pigeon' McGrath's 'bunny' taunts. We used to privately blow up when McGrath nominated his 'bunny' for the series because we felt there was enough pressure on the team, generated by routinely high expectations, without pushing it even further. Marto loathed it more than anyone. Punter would say, 'I spend half my life going to press conferences and trying to put out fires started by McGrath and Warne.' Our initial responses to the giant headlines (accompanied by the mandatory photo of the opposition player with a target on his head) were always annoyance and frustration. But although I can't recall anyone admitting this, our feelings would change as we saw the haunted look on the face of Pigeon's nominated bunny, and watched his spirits slip through the soles of his shoes as the series progressed. Deep, deep down, we loved it! The bunny stories gave us confidence and actually became a key weapon. Newspapers would print graphics of McGrath vs. Atherton or McGrath vs. Lara, and commentators would dwell on it. We'd be sitting in the dressing-room and the figures would flash on the television screen. It would start to seem like it wasn't just McGrath targeting the bunny, but the entire cricket world.

I always felt I was a bit of a hitman for the boys, and if I had to take on Brian Lara or Sachin Tendulkar, I would. Being a big bloke was important, but equally important was that I was prepared to cop the return fire and still perform. If I was the man to rattle someone's cage, I could do it with relish. And if they retaliated, it only spurred me on. We weren't playing tiddlywinks. I deliberately avoided getting to know Lara or Tendulkar on a personal level. I never let them into my world nor sought entrance to theirs, because I felt I couldn't afford to fraternise with them. They were a threat to us, and I thought that letting down my guard could expose some vulnerability. Even so, it killed me to distance myself – from Lara in particular – but I learned so much simply by watching them play.

Brian Lara just captivated me. Every time he took the crease it was like a batting tutorial. Being a left-hander, I was all over his every move and I absolutely loved most of what I saw. Lara shaped my thoughts and actions about playing spin bowling. If anyone has played spin better, I haven't seen him. In fact, Lara didn't so much play spin bowlers as play with them – with their minds and with their captains' minds, exploiting field placements like some wicked puppeteer. To people casually watching the game it may not have been evident, but to those trying to stop him it was obvious. He was ruthless, calculating and brutally effective. I hated it and loved it at the same time. You don't like to see your own bowlers toiling unsuccessfully, but I often became totally absorbed in what Lara was doing. We'd move a bloke on the fence 10 metres to the right and he would hit it to his left. We'd move the bloke back and he'd hit it to his right. Bring men in to stop singles and he'd hit boundaries. Stop the boundaries and he'd hit effortless singles. The short story is that 11 fieldsmen were not enough to contain Brian Lara's many and varied skills.

The foundation of his great game was a beautiful technique, including quick footwork and hands that could be as soft as rubber one minute and as hard as steel the next. His sweep shots were works of art in themselves – he could subtly adjust the stroke depending on where each ball landed and where the fieldsman was – and were a snapshot of a technique that could be as fluent as running water.

Lara was also a great example of how unpredictable the psychological aspects of the game could become. As a team, we used different strategies against him. We went through periods where we felt that chirping him wouldn't help our cause – it only fired him up and made him concentrate. In that way he was just like me. But sometimes we couldn't help ourselves. Lara never took long to come to the boil and he made no attempt to be secretive about it. He was very confrontational. Again, exactly like me. My chirps to him would seem innocent enough. I'd say something like, 'Brian, you're nothing more than another wicket to us . . . Just bat.' Then, *kaboom*! Sometimes, just giving support to our bowlers would be enough to get him going. He'd look over at us discussing tactics and I'd say, 'Brian, you don't have to worry about what we're saying,' and that would set him off. He had a huge ego, like most of the best players. Great players like Lara leave deep impressions on their peers. Sometimes you find yourself imitating them – their accents, their play, sometimes even their walk. I used to find myself occasionally practising Lara's extravagant backlift when I was in the gully.

I'd always sensed that Lara hated me, because I was the one who'd chirp him in the field and then catch him with uncanny frequency (I caught him four times in international cricket). So a year after I retired, it was nice to hear him say that this wasn't the case. 'Why would I hate Matthew Hayden?' he said, when asked about his relationship with me. 'He did what he had to do for his team, and I think we all knew that was not the real person, and there was a certain amount of role-playing. I could see through that. But we did not really connect. I found I connected to players who were like me – smaller guys who were touch players – whereas Matthew was very forceful. One way in which he was a bit like me was that when challenged, we engaged in verbal combat with the opposition. It helped me and it helped him. I know. I saw it. And Australia used him well. They put him close to the bat. A big guy like that with a big presence. You want him to be as close to the batsman as you can get. When we were batting, Matthew tried to take down key opponents and so did I. I tried to take down McGrath and Warne when I played them, because I knew most people who played them didn't. You just couldn't sit back and let them take control.'

Glenn McGrath vs. Brian Lara was one of the big-ticket rivalries in world cricket, trumpeted repeatedly through the sports pages every time there was a West Indies–Australia series. Pigeon did his best to keep his distance from Lara to enhance the impression. He liked to create a bit of mystery about himself, and particularly loved it when opposition players asked us, 'What's McGrath like?' Like me, he felt it was important not to get too close to the opposition. We'd find it hard to think of someone as a great bloke and then go out and try to destroy their self-esteem.

I preferred to invest time in getting to know my own team, and this mindset was the product of a particular era, and, to a degree, of a particular country. Allan Lamb, the former England Test star who became a great mate during my time at Northamptonshire, once said to me, 'You're missing the point. You blokes, yeah, you can be the best in the world, good on you. But the reality is you have no friends from other nations, so what's the point in being the best in the world?' But I was about to enter the heat of battle in an Ashes series, and wasn't receptive to this at all. I didn't want to be friends with the other side. We had a job to do, and I was in full combat mode. Maybe it meant too much to me.

There were some players I simply couldn't sledge because I was so fond of them. West Indian Wavell Hinds fell into this category. Wavell is a wonderful character who used the money he made from cricket to put his brother through university back home in the Caribbean. In fact, verbal intimidation was a waste of time with some of the West Indians anyway – they just danced to a different tune.

Playing in the IPL and getting to know the Indian players better has helped me to understand why they were sometimes offended by our on-field sledging. Indians generally have a softer nature than most Australians, and we definitely pushed the envelope against the Indian team. We played with the competitiveness, gusto and larrikinism that typifies our often irreverent culture. But the cricket world is changing. Indian cricket is changing with it, and the players are changing too, starting to return fire.

The Pakistanis and Sri Lankans were always incredibly combative and, for the most part, they were ready, willing and able to return fire. But the South Africans simply took our sledging on the chin. They are exactly like us. They would go into battle between 11 a.m. and 6 p.m., then have a beer at the end of the day.

The New Zealanders were challenging in a different way. I always felt we played our best against the Kiwis when we treated them with total disdain. Eventually they would wilt under the pressure, almost as if they believed they were inferior. But they were great planners and, at times, a feisty and very willing opposition. I respected Kiwi captain Stephen Fleming for many years before I played under him during his term as coach of the Chennai Super Kings, and now I respect him even more.

Because the Kiwis had limited resources, they felt they needed to squeeze absolutely everything out of what they had. I used to hate 'just getting by' against New Zealand, in the way that you'd take offence at being stretched by your little brother in the backyard. I wanted to completely destroy them because I felt there was not one area of the game where they were superior to us. I couldn't stand the grinding brand of cricket they played, so I was often the ringleader in trying to get our team to fire up and treat them with complete contempt. I really wound everyone up not so much to sledge the Kiwis verbally, but to intimidate them with constant, frenzied movement and aggressive body language, eventually overwhelming them.

The old enemy, England, was the most interesting case study

in the effectiveness of sledging. Before 2005, the English team generally lacked cohesion and went missing in action. Even when a guy like Darren Gough was trying to take the fight to us, you could sense teammates behind his back thinking, *You're carrying on like a pork chop*. Australia had quite a strategic approach to sledging, and in contrast we often sensed English sides were just struggling to breathe, never mind breathe fire.

A player like fast bowler Andy Caddick was a classic example of this. An exceptionally tall man with a high action, Caddick had immense potential as a seam bowler, but it was never fully realised. During the Ashes Test of 2002 at the Gabba, I remember crossing his path at the first drinks break and saying, 'I haven't really had a chance to say g'day . . . How are you going, Andy?' He exploded. 'How do you think I'm going?' he roared, following up with a volley of abuse that only lit a fuse inside me. It was precisely what I needed at that moment. I remember going into the dressing-room at lunch and promising myself, 'This prick is going to have bleeding feet by the end of the day, and I'm not going to talk to him for the rest of the summer!'

Maybe Caddick was suspicious of me trying to start a conversation at such a stressful time. Admittedly, it probably wasn't the best time for small talk, given Justin Langer and I had managed to stay afloat throughout the first hour. But it would have been a better tactical move for him to reply along the lines of, 'Oh, battling along . . . How hot is Brisbane in November?' Had he done that, I might just have dropped my guard against him slightly. Instead, I went back out after lunch with fierce resolve, making 197 in the first innings and 103 in the second.

It's only fair to note that I wasn't always the aggressor where sledging was concerned. Adam Gilchrist loves the story about

Holland's wicketkeeper John Smid giving me both barrels at consecutive World Cups in 2003 and 2007. I can remember him saying things like, 'We haven't flown halfway around the world to watch you. Get a single and get Gilly on strike because you are crap.' This from a Dutch wicketkeeper! Do you mind?

My all-time favourite sledge came at the SCG, in a one-day match against New Zealand during the 2004–05 season. We'd won the toss and batted first, and I had made a respectable 43 off 65 balls. Solid enough by traditional standards, but with Cyclone Gilly blowing palm trees out of the ground at the other end, it seemed like a funeral procession to the fans. Or one fan, at least. When we started fielding, I was posted to the square-leg fence, and from high up in the Doug Walters Stand I could hear a voice saying, ''Ey, 'Ayden. Yer batting is crap!' He kept asking me if I could hear him, but I didn't want to give him the satisfaction of a reply. My plan was going well until he bellowed out like a bull, 'And 'Ayden, by the way, yer chicken casserole tastes like crap!' It cracked me up. I could no longer ignore him. I spun on my heel and shouted back, 'Well, you bought the book, you mug. Thanks for the 30 bucks! I'll have a beer on you tonight.'

Steve Waugh has a theory that the further down the cricket ladder you go, the more intense the sledging becomes. He's right, of course. The most heated sledging I've ever witnessed, and by a considerable margin, was at grade level. One day at Valleys, one of our batsmen, Darren 'Hooch' Turner, was being sledged by rival keeper, Gavin 'Fatty' Fitness, a renowned chirper. Hooch spun around and said to Fatty, 'You're dead.' We didn't think anything of it until a few hours later, when Fatty was leaving the field and Hooch met him on the boundary and started throwing punches. (Fatty later confessed he had lost every fight he'd ever been in.) The sight of Hooch getting stuck into Fatty confirmed a long-held theory of mine – there'd be a lot less verbal sledging in cricket if physical contact was permitted on the field!

One of the fiercest tirades I've ever copped came not from an opposing player, but from a little old lady at the SCG. A few seasons before my retirement, I was returning through the Members Stand after being dismissed and this little old lady teed off at me in a way no one has before or since. She swore her head off, and something inside me just bristled. Television footage of me making my way back to the rooms must be comical. The force of her tirade initially made me stop and think, *I'll sort this out right now!* Then the reality of a 'Big Bad Hayden Berates Little Old Lady' headline hit me, prompting me to take several heavy, reluctant steps towards the room. Then the tiger within me stirred again. I stopped and thought, *I'm not going to cop this!* Then common sense prodded my instincts and I started walking again. Stop. Start. Stop. Start. I just didn't know how to handle the situation. I went to team manager Steve 'Brute' Bernard, who seemed indifferent to it, which only served to raise my dander further. So I finally went back out and said, 'Excuse me, ma'am, could I please get your membership number? I've been playing at this ground for nearly two decades and I want you to know that your behaviour was totally unacceptable. It's so disappointing at a ground I love and respect.'

I went ahead with the report, and I understand she claimed she suffered from Tourette's syndrome, a neurological disorder characterised by repetitive involuntary movements and vocalisations. I remain unconvinced.

2

Playing for Peanuts – Farm Life

I was raised on my parents' peanut farm in Kingaroy, a two-and-a-half-hour drive from Brisbane, and was so content there as a young boy that I could see only one area where the city had it over the country – television. You could get all four TV stations in Brisbane, and all the cartoons. Reception in the bush was not as sharp. But apart from that, my thinking as a young country kid was, *The city? You can have the joint.*

I grew up in a family that was full of love and had a strong sense of values – a connection to the land, a deep religious faith and a complete commitment to each other. Mum and Dad had a very trusting, loving parenting style and, together with my older brother Gary, I revelled in every free-spirited moment. On the farm you could live the adventure – go camping, bushwalking, learn about animal husbandry and primary production. If Mum and Dad hadn't insisted I spread my wings outside the farm, I would never have left. Our property had been passed down through three generations and I could easily have been the fourth.

I loved how close and simple country life was, how Sunday was mass time and a day to sit down as a family. Occasionally I wonder how my life has taken me so far from that simplicity.

Mum taught drama at Kingaroy State High School and had real artistic flair. A great conversationalist, she had her own show on Kingaroy radio station 4SB, playing requests and interviewing people. She tried her heart out with everything she did and the musicals she put on were always sell-outs. She'd take drama groups to Sydney (by overnight bus), where they'd go to the theatre and even sit in on the taping of *The Mike Walsh Show*. She always took the students into the streets of Sydney to admire the work of local buskers. Her passion for all things musical and dramatic knew no bounds and definitely rubbed off on to others – even if sometimes it was in the most unlikely circumstances. Once she told her school principal she was short of boys for her annual musical. Soon after, a group of hardy lads from the school's football team enlisted for the cause. Unbeknown to Mum, their participation was in fact a form of detention the principal had enforced after they'd been caught smoking. Much to their surprise, they ended up loving it.

Mum had an enormous work ethic, and it's great to run in to her former students and hear of how much she helped them with their lives. Her theatrical streak was a strong influence in my life, and I know it's from her that I inherited my love of performance. I also know it's thanks to her that I developed a passion for trying my best and being positive. I was in her drama class at school, and she would occasionally start a lesson by saying, 'Okay, tell me something positive . . . I don't want to hear the word *no*.' I called her 'Mum' in class, because it would've seemed downright silly to call her Mrs Hayden. I did do it once with a playful smirk, and soon found out it was one time too many. I copped it in the car all the way home and was sternly warned never to be disrespectful again. I never was. Of all the teachers I had, Mum was definitely number one for strictness. She had to be, teaching drama. If you haven't got total control of your drama class, you might as well not bother. But I never found it uncomfortable being taught by Mum, and I loved what she was teaching. Drama saved my English studies.

Dad has one of the most even temperaments I've ever encountered. He was always very grounded, and that's a lesson I think I've learned from him over the years. He was never one to fuss over the good times or focus on the bad ones. Another of his standout traits is his love of an old-fashioned country chinwag. Cups of tea with neighbours would sometimes last an afternoon. Dad is also an honourable man, and knowing who he is and standing up for what he believes in is so important to him. He always taught us that everyone and everything has to be respected. That was one of the inherent rules of our household.

Dad's wonderful self-discipline benefited him greatly as a farmer. People used to say there wasn't a solitary weed on the property because Dad was so meticulous. I'm sure there were one or two, but the point was well made. The only part of him that's a complete shambles is his back shed. Dad is so resourceful that for him there's no such thing as rubbish – everything has a purpose, if not now, then down the track – so his shed is one big storage room, a dumping ground for the implements of yesteryear. He was the original Mr Fixit, who saved us thousands of dollars by fixing things that would normally require a call to a tradesman. Depending on what challenge confronted him, he could be a wallpaperer, plumber, painter or builder. He could make parts and even invent ones. He could swap engines from one car to another, weld gates, and I remember him even felling and taking the bark off trees to build yards. The only thing he couldn't do was cook a roast.

My brother Gary is five years older than me. The day I was born, Dad played a joke on him, saying, 'Great news . . . you've got a little sister.' For the next 10 seconds, Gaz was shattered. All he'd ever wanted was a little brother. He wanted Mum and Dad to trade me in, until Dad told him the truth and he was overjoyed. He was a very nurturing brother and I never felt bullied. We just clicked. In the early days we did everything together. Even at night, hour after hour would pass with us mucking around and jumping on the beds, until Mum finally decided enough was enough and gave us separate bedrooms.

My brother and I were taught to look after our things ourselves – cricket bats, fishing rods, tools. I had one bat – a Gray-Nicolls – that lasted my entire childhood. I've still got it. I think Mum and Dad bought it for me when I was eight and I used it until I grew out of it at age 12. Our first cricket pitch was a homemade one in the backyard. We used to mow the pitch with a ride-on mower and we had a roller that Gaz and I would pull, but it was certainly never over-rolled. For kids, that stuff's the boring part of cricket. When we got home from school there were only two things that concerned us – batting and bowling. The wicket is still there in the backyard, flanked by a flagpole flying the Australian flag, and it is a nostalgic moment for us when we visit home and see the rusted old metal stumps hanging off the side net.

Even though the five-year difference between Gaz and me was challenging in our cricketing duels, my relationship with him, growing up, was full of fun, rivalry and respect . . . but not too much respect. In Year 7 I wrote in a school assignment, *I am very proud of my brother – he has represented South Burnett, Wide Bay and Queensland and is a prefect at Ashgrove. Am I jealous? No way, because I have done most of these myself*. It's just as well he wasn't around to read my caustic description of his home habits: *He is as unpredictable as a crocodile, as tolerant as a snake that has just been stood on, and as hard-working as a sloth!*

My primary-school days were happy ones, including some high points that country living alone can provide. While my schoolmates were eating cut sandwiches for lunch, I'd head up to my grandma Hayden's place a few hundred metres away, where she'd have cooked roast chicken and an assortment of vegetables grown in the backyard. These were the days when people used to eat big for lunch and less for dinner. I didn't realise it at the time, but the sight and smells of Grandma's magnificent roast meals and countless other delights, like her Christmas cakes, ignited the interest in cooking that eventually led to me writing three cookbooks. Even something as simple as grinding away at homegrown wheat to make porridge in the morning captivated me. As a boy I had porridge every day.

I was in Grade 6 when Gaz went to boarding school, and his departure left a giant hole in my life. I never said so to my parents, but Mum caught on one night when she found me crying in my room. About that time I found a new friend – a greyhound pup sent to me by Uncle Pat, the priest in North Queensland, who also trained greyhounds. Mum would smile through the kitchen window at the sight of the dog riding shotgun with me in the old VW as we bounced over the contours of the farm.

Our heads would be going up and down together. Sometimes the dog would be on the roof of the car. Other times he'd fall out or take off after a hare. We ended up sending him back to Uncle Pat to start his racing career, and his back legs were as thick as ham hocks after racing up and down the slopes on the farm. His racing name was Dusky Station, and he went on to win a race at Cairns. Amid all the caps and cricket trophies on display at Mum and Dad's property is a photo of Dusky Station winning for the first (and last) time. Pat had to retire him because he had some bad habits – he used to play with other dogs during the races. Apparently he'd become a bit mad after his early experiences with me!

At the same time Gaz left the farm, Mum tied a cricket ball in a stocking for me and hung it from a pepperina tree. I used to hit that ball for hours on end. My 'elbow up, through the ball' crunch, developed by hitting thousands of balls alone under the pepperina tree, stayed with me my whole career.

If you speak to Ricky Ponting or Justin Langer, they'll tell you the baggy green was their heart's desire for as long as they can remember. I was different. I was always drawn to cricket, because my big brother was so good at it, but at school, cricket was just part of my life, not an all-consuming passion.

My early interest in the game was increased when I attended one of the famous coaching camps held by former Queensland batsman Sam Trimble. The camps were held at the Gabba in Brisbane, and the minimum age for entry was 10 years, but Dad somehow managed to sneak me in when I was just seven. I suspect he did it for my own protection. When Dad was umpiring Gaz in junior cricket I would wander out on to the field pleading, 'Can I play too, Dad?' and although he liked the fact that I wanted the challenge of playing with the older boys, he was always concerned I'd get injured. The camp, he hoped, would bring me up to speed – and it did. I loved every minute of it.

Dad loved his cricket, but the amount of time he spent driving Gaz and me to our games meant he didn't get the chance to play as much as he would have liked. He was the ultimate social cricketer. Perhaps his love of a chat occasionally distracted him from the task at hand – one of my early memories of him playing was watching him go out to bat when he'd forgotten to put his pads on.

From the age of about 10, I was driving an old VW – our hunting car – around the farm and would disappear for the whole afternoon shooting. To allow a 10-year-old behind a wheel with a gun these days seems outrageous, but Mum and Dad invested a lot of time and effort in teaching me and Gary to do things properly – shooting, driving, everything. Adventurous we most certainly were. Cowboys we definitely were not. That didn't mean there weren't some challenging moments for my parents. I remember one afternoon coming home and telling Mum, 'I've just rolled the VW,' as nonchalantly as if I was telling her about a green ant bite. Mum never made me do things like make my bed because she preferred me to be outdoors running around, but both Mum and Dad where strict when it mattered. If we wanted to go to a midnight-to-dawn session at the drive-in, they had no reservations in saying, 'Nice try, darlings, but no,' because they didn't know who we would be mixing with. Yet if we wanted to go camping overnight it was, 'No problem.'

Looking back, I can see my childhood was like a decade-long mini boot camp that hardened me for challenges ahead. The farm, on the side of a huge volcanic plateau, is very hilly. Gaz and I would walk those hills nearly every day. They were steep and testing. And we'd gallop down them as well. If you shot something but didn't kill it, you would race down to finish the job, over cliffs and down sharp slopes, all the while sharpening your stamina and sense of balance. It was just about the best physical training you could have – and we didn't even know we were doing it.

Hunting turned me on because it involves such subtle skills. To track and stalk an animal well, you have to understand things like wind direction, the way sound travels and the nuances of geography. It's the ability to get yourself to a final destination, a point where you are able to rest before you can get away a clean shot. Hunting was also an important part of farm life, because if we didn't control the number of kangaroos on our land, we wouldn't have had any peanuts.

I loved living on the land but also understood that it could at times be a bit of a curse. I wish I had a dollar for every time I heard my father say, 'We need rain,' or – when there was heavy rain – 'We need it to stop.' The livelihood of our family depended on rain at the right times or rain stopping at the right times. I always felt that old poem 'Said Hanrahan' summed up farm life. By John O'Brien, it's about a group of people in a small community meeting outside church and chewing bark as they discuss how desperate they are for rain. It does eventually rain, but it rains so much that the dams burst and Hanrahan expresses his fears that 'we'll all be rooned' if the rain doesn't stop. Finally it does, and the grass grows and crops boom, but Hanrahan is still fretting and the new threat of bushfires enables him to utter his famous line, 'We'll all be rooned' one last time.

Early in my life the seasons seemed regular and more

consistent. You planted your crop at the start of the season, it rained, the peanuts matured and then the crop was harvested. But as I got older the seasons changed with the El Niño weather patterns, and the only certainty was that nothing was certain. We had next to no rain for a decade. Without underground water we'd have been in huge trouble. As it was, life was a battle. Mum's teaching income steadied the ship.

It was during my teenage years that I discovered one of the most enduring loves of my life – surfing. Though I spent most of my time on the farm or at boarding school, we always holidayed at the beach, often on the Gold Coast. I had my first surf when I was about 15, and within a few years I was hooked. It is an addictive sport because you never have a bad day. At the very least, you know you're going to get out of the water hungry, physically tired yet refreshed. There's always good company out among the other surfers, and just the sound of the waves is a high in itself. I found hitting cricket balls addictive because I loved the sensation of the bat cracking the ball. But the reality of the game is that you don't get the chance to do that very often. In surfing, you're absolutely involved all the time. I broke my nose surfing in an embarrassing moment, and I'm still having plenty of those – that's surfing. The sport was great not only for my fitness but also for my batting. Surfing is all about balance, and balance equals power – on the board and at the batting crease. Moving about the batting crease seems easy compared to moving on a board. And all the paddling involved helps your shoulders and throwing strength as well. If there's a perfect sport to help you train for cricket, I reckon it has to be surfing.

My favourite day ever in Test cricket involved a late-afternoon surf. I scored a century against South Africa in Durban in March

2006, and later that day had time for a quick surf. I was out on the waves when another surfer looked at me and said, 'Aren't you Matthew Hayden? And didn't you score a century today?' My love of South Africa deepens every time I go there, and part of the reason is the surf and its many characters. Jeffreys Bay, about an hour outside Port Elizabeth on the Eastern Cape, is the best place I've ever surfed. During the 2009 IPL tour I visited the bay with former South African batsman Jonty Rhodes, and I felt like we were brothers as together we did our best to conquer the famous swell.

As a teenager, my passion for cricket grew also. Dad reckons one of the first times he sensed I might have something special was when Gaz and I were invited to play first-grade in Kingaroy. I was only 15, and a fiery local quick called Steve Lavering decided he was going to rough me up. He thundered in and gave me a verbal spray, which got my back up. I waited for him to drop the ball in short, then pulled him through mid wicket for a boundary. As often happens in the bush, the ball just kept running and running past the line. 'Fetch that!' I said. Dad didn't say so at the time, but he liked what he saw.

Playing against the big boys drove my competitive instincts. As a youngster I used to be swarmed by close fieldsmen when I came to the crease, and I knew they were thinking, *This little bloke's no good*. I often took it as a challenge to prove otherwise, trying to slog the first ball I received. If my counter-attack worked, the fieldsmen would retreat and I'd think, *That's more like it*.

I didn't know it at the time, but I was finetuning a tactic that I'd unleash in the furnace of an Indian Test series almost two decades later. It would prove the making of my career.

3

Ashgrove – Hats Off to Helmets

Former Australian rugby union captain John Eales likes to tell the story about the time I wasn't good enough to make his 'Best XI'. It was the Marist College Ashgrove First XI of 1987. I'd just arrived at Ashgrove as a Year 11 boarder, a rotund country boy fresh out of Kingaroy. Eales, a useful left-arm swing bowler, was in Year 12 and was the captain of the First XI cricket team, as well as being a teenage rugby prodigy just about to launch one of the code's most distinguished careers. The Ashgrove First XI coach, Brian Lindsay, had a theory that anyone who wore a helmet just wasn't hard enough to be playing First XI cricket. I think his exact words were, 'Boys who wear helmets sit down to piss.'

For as long as I could remember, Mum and Dad's edict had been, 'No helmet, no game,' and once you start down that road you rarely go back. Accordingly, my helmet and I spent a prosperous season in the Second XI under Father Tom Maloney. It was the start of a wonderful friendship with Father Tom, who two decades later sent me a letter from St Joseph's Aged Care Facility in Lismore wishing me the best upon my retirement. When I'd started at Ashgrove, I thought I might have an inside running with Brian Lindsay because his son was a great mate of Gary's – they'd gone through Ashgrove five years ahead of me. But Lindsay wasn't going to budge on the helmet issue and neither was I.

The first time I donned a helmet was in the backyard with Gary. It was one of those Tony Greig-style SP helmets that made you look like a storm-trooper from *Star Wars*, but once you wore one it became part of you and you never quite felt the same without one. Given that Gaz was five years my senior and our homemade backyard pitch didn't quite have the consistency of what Kevin Mitchell might prepare at the Gabba, the helmet was a wise choice. I even wore one when I was bowling, because Gaz had a habit of dispatching my best work straight back at me or into the nearby pepperina trees, from where nesting magpies would emerge like a swarm of fighter planes if disturbed. For all the challenges of facing my older brother on a seaming deck, nothing quite matched the terror of being harassed by angry magpies in nesting season. Cricket balls may sting but at least they don't have beaks and claws.

I continued to wear a helmet for my entire cricket career – not that it protected me from every threat. Once in club cricket, on a juicy deck at district club Wynnum Manly, I received a short first ball from Eddie Marriner. Eddie was a wild and woolly fast bowler who for several seasons had a reputation as one of Queensland's quickest, with a penchant for creating physical carnage as well as taking wickets. On this occasion, I was extremely pumped – too pumped. I unleashed a spring-loaded pull shot off the front foot that had so much adrenalin running through it that it was finished by the time the ball reached me – or at least my unprotected front teeth. Instead of having a full helmet I'd only used the side protection panels – the cool choice of the day – and my decision to plump for style ahead of safety saw me lose my front teeth and a quarter of my tongue. Mum was devastated when, hours later, she turned up at the ground and was told what had happened. She found out which dentist I'd been sent to and went there immediately, feeling so strongly about me getting the best possible treatment that she entered the surgery demanding, 'Are you a good dentist?' But I learnt my lesson. I wore a grid when I played again the next day at Valleys – and I have worn one ever since.

For some time after this incident I had to wear big steel braces to strap my new top teeth in, and I've got to say they weren't the flashest chops in town. Brad Pitt would've struggled to get a date with those braces on. I did my best to try to cover them on nights out by ultra-extending my top lip – you could have mistaken me for a young John Buchanan – but whenever I was talking to a member of the fairer sex I knew once I smiled I'd soon become the loneliest guy in the room. It couldn't have been more embarrassing than if I'd scratched my head and a cheap hairpiece had fallen off. In later years, Andrew Symonds referred to my once excellent choppers as 'dead pieces of coral', claiming I had the worst fake smile on earth.

Life at Marist College Ashgrove tested me. On the farm I could roam free, and when I first moved to the city I felt as out of place as Crocodile Dundee in LA. I was pretty strong-willed, but the Marist Brothers were always going to rule with an iron fist. My life was now one of rules and protocols. And

I always seemed to learn the hard way. At home, I was used to drinking a couple of litres of milk every day. On my first morning at boarding school, I came down to the refectory before anyone else and saw a giant jug of milk in the centre of the table. I polished off the whole thing and was as happy as a fat spider, until I saw the rest of the boys file in, bang the jug suspiciously and give it the 'Where's the milk?' look. I owned up, and found myself on the outer from my first day.

As my struggles continued, I contemplated ringing Mum and Dad and saying, 'I hate it – get me out of here.' I went down to the school's famous sporting ovals – 'the Flats', as we called them – and cried the tears of a young guy totally at odds with his structured and intimidating environment. But what kept me going was the thought of the sacrifices Mum and Dad had made to send me there. I knew that for them to work so hard to fund my years at Ashgrove, they must have been convinced of the benefits. They wanted me to see life beyond the farm. I just couldn't bring myself to tell them how low I was feeling, so for the first time in my life I suffered alone. I knew I had to simply buckle down and give it a go.

School pecking orders are often decided by the strangest means. On my first weekend I went down to the common room and realised that whoever played the best game of ping-pong ruled the roost. I fancied myself a bit because we had a ping-pong table at home and I used to play Gary – who was good at it – and Mum, when Gaz wasn't around. In my first match I beat a big, fat, red-haired guy from the bush. He wasn't your classical cool dude but he was respected because he was a highly rated Second XV prop. I don't exactly recall saying, 'Next please!' although that's how I was feeling as I readied myself for the next challenger. But the big fella was having none of it and we ended up in a full-blown wrestle. It didn't help my position. The smart move would have been to lose with dignity and move on. But I was brought up to stand my ground, and that's what I did.

Being a late starter didn't help my cause either. I'm not sure what the other boys thought of me when I arrived in Year 11, but I'm sure some of it wasn't flattering. Here was this cocky upstart guzzling all the milk, wrestling the big fella, wearing a helmet and telling everyone he should be in the First XI. One of the hardest things for me was that the school had regarded Gaz as an outstanding cricketer, and according to John Eales the First XI guys were definitely aware of my reputation. Yet not even in cricket was I popular.

While I was at Ashgrove I was also playing for a club side, Valleys, and there was always an uneasy relationship between the school and Valleys. It was almost inevitable, given that one was primarily interested in me as a scholar and the other as a sportsman. The best interests of each were never going to suit the other. I'd return from Valleys training at 8.30 p.m. and would study late. I wouldn't say I was a bad student, but my retention levels weren't great and the whole experience just wasn't my cup of tea. School and study never came easily to me. Even in cricket I struggle with numbers. There's a part of my mind that finds it difficult to analyse the simple equations of a scoreboard, so I decided early in my career that I wouldn't bother looking at them. The funny thing is that at school I did a straight maths–science course – go figure.

Despite all this, I did form a strong emotional attachment to Ashgrove. I don't think I realised this until I was asked back five years after leaving the school by my former sports master,

David Meehan, to present the First XI with their caps. It struck me then that the school, which had aroused such angry instincts in me, was, in fact, very close to my heart. Perhaps because of all those times when I'd felt like I was swimming against the tide, the school played a big part in making me who I am. On the day when I stood up in front of the group of young men and their parents to present the caps, I found myself so emotional I couldn't speak. I walked in to John Williamson's 'True Blue' and that just did me in. I sobbed like a baby. When I finally gathered myself – after what seemed like an eternity but was probably only a minute – I said, 'I guess what I am trying to say is . . . I am proud to be an Ashgrovian.' I wasn't sure how the audience would receive it, but they went nuts. From then, every time I went back to Valleys to play cricket, I'd call in to the Ashgrove chapel, because no matter what challenges lay ahead, I felt grounded there.

John Eales now smiles at the thought of our experiences at Ashgrove and about me not being selected in the First XI. But he also observes that my early predicament mirrored his schoolboy rugby career at the college, when he was unable to crack the Ashgrove First XV in Year 11. He went on to become arguably the greatest Wallaby ever. Perhaps the Marist Brothers knew something we didn't, and those challenges in our early years were the making of us both.

4

Gaz

I started big-time cricket in the early 1990s, an era when it seemed every second sportsman had Greg Norman or Michael Jordan as their sporting heroes. Not me. My hero was my brother Gary.

We'd always played cricket together growing up, but on the farm there were so many other distractions that I wasn't consumed by the game. As I grew older, cricket opportunities started to open up for me. I made a Queensland Under-17 side with the likes of fast bowler Michael Kasprowicz and was soon playing first-grade. I may have been left out of the Ashgrove First XI and didn't always progress as fast as I wanted to, but still, from my mid-teens, there seemed to be a carrot around every corner.

I didn't spend much time pondering where my talents might one day take me. The big picture inspired, but didn't distract me. My life was a ball – a red ball with stitches on it. At a time when most teenagers were learning about the world through experimentation, I had found my drug of choice – cricket.

I was a crack addict – the sound of willow cracking leather was the heartbeat of my existence. Enough was never enough: net sessions, club games, even tours to obscure country venues with a Wanderers team including former Queensland players. It didn't matter who was hurling the leather – I had a habit that needed to be fed.

Gaz was a PE teacher by this stage and had studied the cutting edge of sports science in a Human Movement degree at Queensland University. I was a sponge for anything he could teach me. If he was the scientist, then I was the test tube. It even got to the stage where I would sneak up to Padua College, where Gary was teaching, so he could spend his lunchtime feeding my addiction. After leaving school I stayed in Brisbane, and Gaz and I shared a house in the north Brisbane suburb of Gordon Park, just a few kilometres away from our beloved Valleys nets.

A few years later, amidst all the cricket, my 21st birthday whizzed by with precious little fanfare. The numbers that mattered most to me had three digits, not two. I had tried studying public administration at the Queensland University of Technology, but was so consumed by cricket that I failed almost every subject in my first semester. I was there in body but not in spirit. I can still see my report card with a giant list of Ns in the results column. Don't ask me what 'N' stood for. Maybe 'Not much chop' or 'Not particularly interested'. Both were true, and I never got around to finishing that degree. I had 11 subjects still to do when I called it quits. The only saving grace was that John Forrest, a good fellow whom I now sit beside on the board of Queensland Cricket, was one of my lecturers. We talked endlessly about cricket. People who saw our chats probably thought that this was a classic case of an underachieving student trying to sweet-talk the lecturer into taking pity on him. They weren't far wrong. Somehow I always passed his subjects. I still don't know how. But there are many ways to educate yourself, and university is just one of them. Sport is another way, and it can provide a tremendous education.

Gaz was ahead of his time. Dad has a theory that because Gaz encouraged me to see scoring potential in every single ball, I developed the habit of moving forward first into the ball, which was a bit different to the norm. There was no one strand of Gaz's studies that particularly shaped our thoughts; we took a holistic approach based on the need to be healthy and fit to avoid injury, and to get my body and mind in a state of readiness for the challenge of playing first-class cricket. We'd videotape all our net sessions, then retreat home and break them down – foot movements, swing patterns, head positions. Sometimes we wouldn't cook dinner until after 9 p.m. Training always came first. Cricketers of that era were fitter than they were given credit for and they did a lot of running. I didn't feel like the odd man out doing extra training, but I did feel the video analysis gave me an edge.

Living with Gaz was a small but significant step in the development of my cooking skills. I felt that cooking him a nightly meal was the least I could do in return for his help. I had a pretty limited repertoire in those days, but I loved the challenge of making something out of nothing, which, in a house containing two young bachelors, I often had to do.

A lot of the theoretical stuff about cricket didn't resonate with me, but it didn't matter – it was all about repetition. Five nights a week, 200 balls at a time, brother against brother to the death. At least, it felt that way. There was competitive tension all the time. If I was having trouble with yorkers I'd get a volley of them. If the outswinger was troubling me then that's what I mostly got. Gaz used any method to test me. He'd cheat shamelessly and bowl from illegally wide angles or through the crease to probe any weak area he saw, and yet he never bowled so many of one ball as to make it seem unrealistic. He even studied my concentration patterns. If I was losing focus in the thirties, he'd make a note in the net session when he reckoned I had reached 30 and monitor my reactions to make sure I was switched on. *Compact*, *businesslike* and *hungry* were his three buzzwords – I was certainly the last two.

At club games he'd sit at mid-off and make the occasional hand signal, and later, when I played Sheffield Shield matches, he'd be sitting on the balcony of the old Cricketers Club beckoning me to hit the ball towards him. Hit straight. Hit straight.

In 1981–82, Gaz set a record of 402 runs at the national Under-16 championship in South Australia, in a winning Queensland side that included in its top order future rugby league legend Allan Langer as a dynamic shot-maker. There's a great photo of Gaz walking off the field after his final innings in that tournament, carrying his old-fashioned helmet. Both the photo and the helmet are now on the wall in our old bedroom at the farm.

Gaz was a conservative player with a great technique and immense patience. In coaching me there was never any suggestion he was trying to make a clone of me. In fact, we were so different it was more like the opposite. He'd suffered from negative thought processes and stroke patterns, and so deliberately tried to steer me away from them. Gaz has always reckoned he's more conservative than I am, in cricket and in life. He mentioned this to me recently, when we were swimming with the kids at Stradbroke Island and some harmless wobbegong sharks passed by. He shepherded the kids away from them, but I never felt anyone was in danger.

A number of factors led Gaz to give cricket away at an early age. He was studying for a degree and he had a girlfriend. There was a lot happening in his life and it was affecting his form, so he decided to concentrate on his studies. But he remained a cricket tragic. To coach me, he had to learn about life as a bowler, but he always remembered how a batsman thought. I ended up with the best of both worlds.

I didn't fully appreciate how much Gaz meant to me until he left Brisbane. He took a teaching post in North Queensland and moved there with his wife, Alex, in 1995, the year that Queensland finally won the Shield. Gaz and Alex had bought a beach house in Ingham, and while they were up there on holidays, a local school principal rang and asked Gaz whether he wanted a job. The principal had picked the perfect time to ring. Gaz was fishing and was actually hooked up to a small-mouthed nannygai – a beautiful reef fish closely related to the red emperor – when he picked up the phone. Given the circumstances, how could he refuse? Why wouldn't he want to stay? But I suddenly felt lost. My form wavered as my preparation for games suddenly felt wafer-thin. I'd only played one Test for Australia when Gaz moved away, and for a little while after I wondered if I'd play another.

In one way, we had the separation blues. But in another way, Gaz, in his typically selfless fashion, felt it was time for me to move on to other coaches in the state and national set-ups. He saw me very much as a work in progress. In his eyes, he'd done all he could for me and felt I could be improved by other coaches. He had certainly set the bar very high, especially with all those net sessions. One of the great frustrations of my career was that I could never get enough quality practice in the nets. I've had under-12s bowling at me when I was playing a Test for Australia the next day. By the end of my career I was so wild about it I was ruthless with whoever was going to bowl to me and would say, 'Sorry – you're out,' to anyone who was substandard. Sometimes I ran out of bowlers and my net session would be over. The absence of Gaz meant no more five sessions a week with 200 balls at a time. No more sneaky practices during lunch hour at Padua. No more home video sessions. I was even missing our talks the night before matches, which had always placed me in a calm yet aggressive frame of mind for the game. I found I was sorting out problems in the middle of the match that I'd once sorted out in net sessions with Gaz. In short, I missed my brother – and felt more grateful than ever for all he'd done for me.

Gaz made his one and only international tour with me when I was selected for the 2001 Ashes. It was his first trip abroad and he loved every minute of it, meeting all the challenges of being a first-time traveller. Gaz braced himself for a culture shock, and got one soon after he landed in Manchester. He had to get a train to London and the first person he spoke to was a local with a thick northern English accent. Gaz was sure he was speaking English, but simply couldn't understand a word of it.

Stephen Waugh enjoyed Gaz's company – and his net bowling – so much in England that when Gaz went home midway through the tour, Steve suggested they should keep Gaz and send me home instead. He claimed that not only was Gaz more useful, he was a better bloke. I don't know how serious he was, but he did get Gaz to write the foreword to his *Ashes Diary 2001*. They were quite a sight at net training. Before sending any balls down, Gaz would say to Steve, 'Where do you want them?', to which Steve would reply, 'Oh . . . anywhere . . . you know.' Gaz would come back with, 'No, no, I'm serious. Let's do it properly. *Where* do you want them?' So Steve would nominate a spot and Gaz would put a piece of string down and aim for it, ball after ball after ball. Gaz had been so pumped for that tour he'd prepared for it by bowling no less than 1700 balls to a mate in the nets, over quite a few sessions. Mum, Dad and Alex, in their separate farewells to him, all said the same thing: 'Now, don't be *too* disappointed if you don't get a bowl.' They needn't have worried.

I'd have loved to have Gaz on tour with me throughout my entire career, but with his young family it just wasn't possible. Although he did live briefly in New Zealand, Gaz never came back from North Queensland, which didn't surprise me. Most people don't – and why would they? Gaz and I still have a great connection but it isn't as intense as it used to be. Nonetheless, that 2001 Ashes tour reinforced just how much he had helped me along the way. I would never have got as far as I did in cricket if it wasn't for my brother Gary.

5

Matthew Who?

My cricket career, particularly the first half of it, was essentially a marathon game of snakes and ladders. For every ladder I climbed, there seemed to be a slippery snake waiting to take me backwards. Fate slapped me around a bit and there were plenty of jolts along the way. Adversity, however, proved to be the making of me. I can look back and honestly say I'm glad it happened the way it did.

One of the biggest jolts came reasonably early. I'd been playing Under-17 and Under-19 for Queensland, and regular first-grade, but when I was put forward to the Australian Cricket Academy in 1991 I was rejected. The 15-man 1991 intake included Adam Gilchrist, Stuart MacGill, Peter McIntyre and Richard Chee Quee, but the only one to make the cut from the six Queensland nominations was batsman Gavin Maslen. I was desperate to get to the academy because I wanted access to the best cricket coaches and to live and breathe the game. I hoped Rod Marsh (then head of the academy) might reconsider my nomination, so I found the telephone number, drew a deep breath and rang him. Rod's secretary put me through and I can still hear him saying, 'G'day,' before I said my name. He responded with two words that immediately summed up my chances: 'Matthew who?' I explained why I was calling, and he made matters clearer still by replying, 'Son, I don't know who you are, but the bottom line is we're really only after players who are going to play first-class cricket.' Uggghh. I politely thanked him for his time and the call ended.

Beneath my grudging diplomacy, a furnace had been ignited. As testosterone-charged teenagers tend to do, I swore that there would be a day of retribution. I might not have been a big name, but I was still on the list of six from Queensland and an uncapped junior member of the state squad. It wasn't as if I was trying to sneak through the tradesman's entrance to the academy from Country Week Seconds! I was filthy, and supremely motivated to prove to Rod Marsh when the day came – as surely it would – that he had made a mistake.

My chance came a few months later, ironically, when the Queensland Second XI played Marsh's academy team at leafy St Lucia, club ground of Queensland University, in Brisbane. I would have put whatever I owned on me playing well that day. For the wider world the match was one of those nondescript early-season trials consigned to small print in the morning paper. For me, it was a mini Test match. My dignity was on the line. The academy side included Gilchrist and MacGill and I made 151, batting for just under a day. It says a lot about the innings and my state of mind that my main memory was not a stroke or a milestone, but being absolutely livid I got out. I was like a hungry lion who'd just had a carcass ripped away from it – no score was ever going to be enough for me that day. I wanted to bat for more than a day so I could get a second helping and further prove my point. After the St Lucia match I told reporters, 'I have had to dig in, but it has probably been good for me to dig in because it has made me tougher. I badly want to succeed but maybe it will be better to get there slowly rather than with a big boom, then fail.'

As it happened, those throwaway lines would sum up the first decade of my first-class career. Marsh was at the game that day in St Lucia but we never spoke. I'm not even sure he knew that I was the youngster who'd rung him a few months before. That phone call motivated me for many years. Marsh and I didn't cross paths much until we had a showdown in a bar at the SCG after an Australia A game during the 1994–95 season three years later. He called me 'weak', and I gave as good as I got. Just as tempers reached boiling point, Australia A coach Greg Chappell stepped in. He told me that at any other time he'd encourage me to continue making my point, but that it wasn't the time or place. As always, Greg, for whom I have the deepest respect, was the voice of reason. I was a youngster trying to push my way into a world-beating Australian side. The last thing I needed on my resumé was a black mark for exchanging unpleasantries with a Test legend, one of the biggest cricketing voices in the country. No matter how unrepentant I felt, there was little to be gained, and luckily the incident went unreported.

Greg Chappell's support meant a lot to me. I spent many days, months and years floating on the agonising periphery of national selection, but there always seemed to be someone whose opinion I admired – a Healy, Chappell, Border, Richards or Waugh – chipping in to top up my confidence levels at crucial times.

The question of whether academy selection greased your path to national selection was a provocative one. I felt it did. At least, it certainly didn't help you if you *weren't* part of the academy. It was only natural that academy officials were keen for their own to succeed, particularly as the academy had then only been operating for three years, and some states had reservations about its role. One way the academy could trumpet its worth was by pointing to how many of its crop had gone on to the big time. And I wasn't one of them.

I'm glad to say that my feud with Rod Marsh had a happy ending. A few days after my retirement I received a lovely email from him congratulating me on my career, and saying I deserved to be ranked among the top players of my era. It was big of him to do that. I also ran into him at the *This Is Your Life* show for Adam Gilchrist and we had a good chat. I harbour no bad feelings at all towards Marsh.

During those early years I had other setbacks apart from missing out on academy selection. I was one of about 22 players sent to Adelaide for the Australian Under-19 trials for a tour of England in 1991, with 14 players to be chosen for the final squad. That squad included Damien Martyn – captain and best prospect by a street – Greg Blewett and Michael Kasprowicz . . . but no Matthew Hayden. Big Greg Hayne from NSW and Brisbane's Matthew Fraser made it ahead of me. (A little later, I actually knocked Greg over during a rare bowling stint for Queensland against NSW and can remember putting a little extra spice in my celebration.) Although omission seemed cruel, the sweetener was that I was on fire in grade cricket and felt, for all the delights I was missing in England, that runs against the 'men' would ultimately take me places quicker than runs against the 'boys'.

My name was starting to surface in the Queensland media. The first man to push my barrow in the Brisbane press was colourful Queensland University Cricket Club secretary and scorer Wep Harris. Truly one of a kind, Wep was a retired dentist who never married. Actually, he *was* married – to the Queensland University Cricket Club. No one could work out how Uni broke dead-even financially every year, until someone realised that Wep was putting in his own money to make sure the books balanced. As he scored on Saturday afternoon he'd listen to the ABC radio and shout out scores from other sporting venues ('The Broncos are in again – 16–12!').

Before making my Queensland debut in November 1991, I had a good run in grade cricket, scoring five centuries in 10 one-day games for Valleys, mustering 1418 club runs for the summer in Under-19s and Firsts, and following up with a few grade centuries at the start of the next summer. Wep told the *Courier-Mail*, 'I've been associated with grade cricket for 30 years and I can't recall anything like it. Sam Trimble put together a lot of good scores before he was selected in the state team and other players have had good runs, but nothing like this.' I didn't see the story but my family did, and very much appreciated Wep's encouragement.

When you're starting out, every supportive voice is gold. Wep might not have been the biggest name in Queensland cricket but he knew his cricket and his history, and his words gave me heart. Soon after Wep made that statement, other voices joined in. I played well in a Queensland trial match in Townsville and the influential voice of Queensland coach Jeff Thomson was chiming in with lines like, 'Just play the kid,' which heightened my anticipation that a Queensland cap might not be far away.

I realised I had to work on making myself an appealing package. Part of this meant shedding my baby fat. I was massive as a kid. Mum has often said I was 'big-boned', but these are the words of a loving mother. I felt fat. Sorry, Mum, I *was* fat. John Eales remembers me from school as a short, overweight teenager, 'someone you wouldn't describe as athletic in any way'. Thankfully, he also remembers running into me when I was playing for Valleys a couple of years later and being amazed by my transformation. I didn't start to really build my physique until I was about 19. And while I'd love to blame my former shape on genetics, I reckon a love of calorie-laden food also had something to do with it. Becoming knowledgeable about my diet and modifying certain recipes to suit my needs allowed me to recover from training and competitions more rapidly, keep my weight in check and remain healthy and happy.

Fielding was also a priority. I worked my backside off to improve, because I'd always been a lazy fieldsman and I had heard the whispers about me being cumbersome on my feet. My Valleys teammate David Cottee started to call me Arjuna Ranatunga, after the feisty Sri Lankan captain who loved to bat but wasn't that fussed with fielding. At that critical time in my development I had to work on my weaknesses more than ever before. One of my uncle Gary's favourite sayings – 'Give them reasons to pick you, not reasons to leave you out'– resonated strongly with me and became a personal motto.

6

Culture Clash – Early Years for Queensland

Memories are funny things. In my first Sheffield Shield innings on 1 November 1991, I made 149 against South Australia at the Gabba, yet my strongest memory of the occasion isn't of the innings itself. It's of the spray from my brother that followed.

That night, I went to a function for our sponsors, Power's, at a tavern on the north side of Brisbane. The function was to promote its Big Red beer, which I discovered had a kick to it as powerful as one of the giant kangaroos that shared its name. Certainly that's how it affected me. I didn't destroy myself that night, but I was a cock-a-hoop 20-year-old, high on life after a big debut and definitely in the mood for a celebration.

I got home around 11 p.m. As soon as I walked in, Gary said, 'So how many have you had?' I replied, 'Oh, four or five.' I may have been unwittingly using a system Warnie often used in which you double or halve the amount you've actually had, depending on what makes you look better at the time. The correct number was probably closer to eight. Gaz's reply was as stern as it was sobering: 'If you do this again, I will *never* bowl to you in the nets again.' I'd hadn't ever received a bollocking like this from him and it stung me to the core. In the second innings the next day I made just 5, which did not lighten Gaz's mood at all. He was not a happy camper and, as I look back, I'm grateful he felt that way because I learned an important lesson early. My preparation for the first innings had been as thorough as I could make it, and then I'd strayed a bit. A few beers and an 11 p.m. bedtime was hardly a blazing bender, but it was no way to behave when I still had an innings to play.

When I started playing for Queensland in 1991, we were a team with an agonising history that tormented every cricket-loving Queenslander. In over 60 years of competition, we had never won the Sheffield Shield. Queensland had tried importing players like Viv Richards, Wes Hall and, just before I arrived, Graeme Hick, but could never get over the line. Often the team would surge to a convincing lead in the competition up to Christmas, then fade on the road in the new year. It's not as if we didn't have quality players. In the 1980s, when Queensland finished second five times in seven seasons, we had a team that could have beaten some Test nations.

Queensland cricket – and Australian cricket in general – had a poor culture when I began playing at state level. The Queensland team was hopeless away from home and the party culture of touring games didn't help. We had almost total freedom to do whatever we wanted. When cigarettes supplied by our sponsor arrived in the dressing-room, the boys swooped on them like seagulls descending on fish bones tossed off a trawler. There was even a joke that a carton of smokes was kept aside as a sweetener for whoever was going to be dropped at the end of the game.

The press used to bag us mercilessly about our away record, and so they should have. It wasn't pretty. Over the years, we'd just had too many good-time boys in the team. I came in during a transitional era, when full-time cricketers such as Allan Border, Greg Ritchie and Ian Healy were teammates of part-timers such as Dirk Tazelaar (a builder), Carl Rackemann (our famous farmer), Dirk Wellham (a school teacher) and Paul Jackson (a banker). Training used to start around 4 p.m. and you'd often see Jacko ripping off his tie and unbuttoning his business shirt as he rushed to the dressing-room after work in the hope of squeezing in a decent bowl or bat before sunset.

You might think I'm about to suggest the part-time boys treated the game less seriously than the professionals, but you'd be wrong. I couldn't fault the commitment of players like Jacko or Carl. In fact, when Ian Botham went missing for a lot of training sessions during his solo season with Queensland in the mid-1980s, it was apparently Carl who said to him firmly, 'You simply have to attend training . . . not for you but for the rest of us.'

I reckon I witnessed the shift between eras in one dramatic afternoon, when a long-standing, deep-seated culture of reckless indulgence gave way to one of professionalism and increased commitment. It was during Jeff Thomson's final years as coach and one day he invited the Brisbane Broncos' team fitness trainer, Kelvin Giles, down to training. Giles was a hard-arsed Englishman who'd been head coach of England's Olympic athletics team before being lured to Australia to coach at the newly formed Australian Institute of Sport in 1980. (Australia had been embarrassed at winning no gold medals at the 1976 Montreal Olympics and thus committed to an institute – and hard men like Giles – to improve its Olympic returns.)

Giles was hard all right. He helped drive the Broncos to their first two premierships in 1992 and 1993. Picture Sean Connery and you've just about got him – a physically robust man with a proud, upright army-sergeant bearing and a booming voice that was pure military. I'm not sure why Thommo invited him, but I reckon it was a conscious attempt to shake us up. Whatever his motives, it was a smart move. Despite the drinking culture of the team, our fitness levels were solid and we used to train hard. But our fitness wasn't up to the demands of Giles, who seemed to have a mandate to rough us up.

On this day we were doing a drill where players had to hold hands and run backwards and forwards, so your line became only as strong as your weakest link . . . which was Greg 'Fat Cat' Ritchie. At one point Giles ran backwards in front of Ritchie, who couldn't catch him even while running forwards, and started yelling at him to pick up the pace. But Fat Cat was gone. And angry. He blew up. 'This is an absolute joke – I'm not doing it. How many hundreds have you made?' he fumed at Giles, dropping the line that top players often use to pull rank. Totally unrepentant, Giles shot back, 'Mate, how many hundreds *could* you have scored if you'd been fit!' Fat Cat stormed off the ground and watched us complete our session from the sidelines. It was a pivotal moment, because the heavies – Border, Healy and McDermott – were in town. Crucially, *they* finished the session, which made a major impression on me and the rest of the squad. I remember thinking, *If seasoned internationals can train like that, then so can I.* In that one afternoon we saw a total shift in the team culture.

The drinking culture of the Queensland team was why we had so-called great teams that couldn't go the distance away from home, where the temptation to drink was at its strongest.

My attitude to drinking is somewhere between the old and the new eras. Jason Gillespie coined a line that summed up how things have changed: 'In the old days they used to put the beers on ice . . . now they put us on ice.' I've never been a big drinker, but I was always a fan of a quiet social beer. Apart from anything else, the socialising just helps you learn so much about the game. I can fully understand why Doug Walters would say, 'You often learn more about a bloke in five minutes over a dressing-room beer than in five days in the field.'

But there had to be a cut-off point with alcohol, and the Maroons of the pre-Giles session didn't know where it was. Queensland cricketers weren't the only culprits. Australian cricketers in general had too much to drink until the late 1990s. But now I think it's gone too far the other way – the game needs to chill out a bit. Current Queensland coach Trevor Barsby – my former opening partner at Queensland – has tried to reintroduce the culture of the quiet dressing-room ale to enhance the education and bonding of his young side. Good on him. I can't stand the 'get in, get out' mentality of English cricket, where you don't have time to celebrate a win. I'm not saying you have to drink much – it's more about enjoying the company of your mates. (This may surprise some people, but one bloke who managed his drink as well as anyone was Shane Warne. He was a master at having one or two beers, a few cigarettes, and letting everything go for another day.)

Despite the shortcomings in team culture, there were some great professionals in the Queensland team of the early 1990s. I still rate Craig 'Billy' McDermott as the fittest player ever to have played the game. He was way ahead of his time in that regard, and his efforts were all the more impressive because his contemporaries in Australia's bowling unit – Tim May and Merv

Hughes – were never going to get a podium finish in the local triathlon. McDermott challenged the contemporary belief that fitness was a side issue in cricket rather than a central ingredient for success. Despite his fitness, he could at times be troubled by confidence issues, which was a surprise given his immense talent for bowling – pace, swing, height, bounce and a great action. He did some of the best work of his career for Queensland in Sheffield Shield games, slaughtering the opposition by bowling with 150 kph outswing.

McDermott was also one of the first cricketers to embrace the corporate world and seek private sponsorships, which he generally flaunted in the dressing-room. Private sponsorships were considered a bit indulgent in those days, whereas now they're a fact of life. It was once said of English cricketer Phil Edmonds that he talked cricket in the board room and business in the dressing-room, and you could probably say the same of Billy. 'Bartercard Bill', we called him, after his best-known sponsor. But I admired his professionalism and the structured, disciplined way he went about his cricket. In fact, he was so disciplined that his meticulously prepared gear 'coffin' – the interior as beautifully organised as one of those pristine shelves in a top menswear store – was ripe for dressing-room pranksters. Fat Cat Ritchie was without peer as a 'gee-up' man, constantly super-stretching some of Billy's socks, or matching up odd ones and generally making the order into chaos.

My first Shield innings not only introduced me to mainstream cricket, but also to some new friends. As I was walking from the ground that first day I heard a little fellow scream out, 'Matty! Matty! Matty!' and though I couldn't talk to him then, I went back to speak to him afterwards because he looked like a nice kid. He told me his name was Bart Wilson and he was ten years old and came from Coolum, on the Sunshine Coast. When he asked me whether I would please sign his bat, I was impressed by his manners. Bart had heard that I liked surfing and asked me whether I'd like to come surfing with his family. To widespread laughter, he wrote out his address and gave it to me. But something inside me just knew he and his family were special people and worth meeting again. A few weeks later I was up their way, made contact and dropped in. Bart and his parents, Nola and Mick, soon became close friends. Years later, Bart was pageboy at my wedding, and I included Nola's famous chicken pie recipe in my first cookbook. When I met Nola and Mick they had a new baby boy, Julian, who has become one of the world's best young surfers and has made a surfing film.

That first-up century in the match against South Australia gave me hope that I could make a mark at interstate level and perhaps beyond. The South Australian attack included off-spinner Tim May and, significantly, tearaway Denis Hickey, whom Allan Border once called 'the fastest white guy around'. He certainly felt quick – but not unplayable, and that meant a lot to me. I felt if I could handle Hickey, pace-wise at least, I should be able to handle pretty much anything thrown at me.

Word leaked out that earlier in the week I'd asked whether anyone had made 200 on debut for Queensland. It was a throwaway question I'd asked at a function at the Queensland Cricketers' Club. By no means was I suggesting that this was my target. But it was picked up by the media and it became a bit of an urban myth that I had set my sights on a double century on debut. I was thereafter portrayed as an ambitious and run-hungry young man, but I couldn't complain too much. That's what I was.

7

Tanks for the Memories

Subtle diplomacy has never been my strong suit. For better or worse I tend to speak my mind and, as best I can recall, it has always been that way. This directness has brought me my share of awkward moments, but I've realised I like people who call it as they see it.

That's certainly one reason I so admire my first Queensland coach, Jeff Thomson. His methods may have been simple, but they were honest and effective. He knew how to handle me – he simply let me do my own thing – and I respected that. Thommo wasn't big on team meetings, but he was big on simple advice like, 'Watch the ball,' or, to bowlers, 'Just try to hit the top of off stump.' His coaching term ended the year before Queensland broke its seven-decade Sheffield Shield curse, and I really felt for him because he'd contributed so much to our cause during the barren years – 349 wickets as one of our greatest ever bowlers and five years as our coach.

Just after I retired, Thommo approached me at a function,

wished me well and said he hoped I had no hard feelings about some things he'd said recently. I don't even know what he'd said, but I suspect they were something along the lines of it being about time I retired. I certainly had no hard feelings. How could I? I agreed with him. I would never have criticised him for being honest.

As a boy ploughing the fields of our farm on Dad's tractor, I used to listen to the ABC's broadcast of the cricket, and one name always drew my attention: Trevor 'Tank' Barsby. I loved the cavalier way the Queensland opener played. When the commentators described a starburst of Barsby drives and pulls, their excitement seemed to flow through my headphones. Barsby inspired me to play attacking cricket. But it always irked me that the commentators who lauded Barsby's attacking instincts as breathtaking would turn upon him when he got out playing the same types of shots.

In 1991, at Queensland's preseason camp in the Gold Coast hinterland, I formed an enduring bond with my soon-to-be opening partner in an unexpected way. We were doing a high rope course and Tank, who was scared of heights, completely froze. I was with him at the time and took on the responsibility for getting him down. We didn't talk much about the incident, but it did establish an inherent trust between us. From that moment, I watched Tank's back and he watched mine. If he was struggling against a particular bowler, such as Paul Reiffel, I'd offer to 'take' him. If I was going through a difficult period, he'd do the same for me.

I never felt Tank was a rival. We were a team, and we came together at a crucial time in his cricketing life. The free-wheeling, devil-may-care performer I used to listen to on the tractor had been through a bleak period. Certain people had told him to curb his aggression, so he tried to tone it down and completely lost form and confidence, almost driving himself crazy through anguished self-denial, letting balls go that he once would have spanked over mid-off, and edging balls he was sparring at with less than total conviction. Just before we joined forces he scored a quickfire half-century in a trial match under coach Thommo's eye. Thommo asked Tank afterwards why he didn't bat like that all the time. When Tank replied that he'd been told not to, Thommo hit the roof and demanded that he return to his natural way. Tank reckoned it was the best advice he ever got, and he was a dream to bat with from then on.

In one of our early games together, he was on 42 and I was on 1. Greg Matthews, playing for NSW, even told me to get a move on. But I wasn't worried. In fact, I was enjoying the show from the best seat in the house. In another of our early games together, against South Australia, I remember being none for 153 – at lunch.

I always let Tank walk out first. He used to have a smoke before he batted, and even though I wasn't a smoker – my lungs couldn't handle it – I loved smelling the final deep drag of his cigarette as he walked on. It took me back to my country cricket days, when I was a boy playing against men, and just as I was about to face up for the first ball the umpire would call play and the old crinkle-faced wicketkeeper would have one last puff and throw away his durry.

Tank and I gelled so well that we'd unwittingly get under the skin of rival teams. We'd open the batting at the Gabba on a raging seamer and be scrambling like mad to keep our castles intact, yet we would regularly have a good laugh during mid-wicket catch-ups over anything from fishing to the absurdity of how severely the conditions were against us. Opposing teams hated watching us share a laugh. Our frivolity was never designed to be a weapon, but it inadvertently became one. The Sheffield Shield competition in those days was pretty dour and the opposition would think we should have been in crisis mode. Instead we were having fun.

Such was Queensland Cricket's desperation to win the Shield that in my first season, the chief executive, Barry Richards, had introduced a cash bonus incentive scheme. When Richards, a former South African batting great, played for South Australia in the early 1970s, he was on a 'dollar per run' bonus, and his stunning 1145-run summer probably convinced him that lesser mortals would also respond in this way. The sponsorship he organised meant that the team would receive a $1000 bonus if they scored 300 runs in a day. Now such a target seems almost routine, but back then it was swift progress. The scheme certainly provided some colourful moments. In my first season I scored 1028 runs at 54, and after I had reached 500, each boundary was worth $60. By today's standards $60 is a round of drinks, but when you're a battling semi-professional trying to earn a living from the game and looking for an excuse to bypass uni, it's like striking oil. Tank still laughs at the memory of me miming pulling a cash register handle and singing 'Ker-ching!' when I nicked one through slips for four, or playfully raising the bat to salute another $60 boundary.

Those early Shield seasons brought some new challenges, like facing the fastest bowler I'd ever confronted – Dave Gilbert, from Tasmania. We met in a Sheffield Shield game in Hobart in my first season, and he bowled like greased lightning. The season before, he'd produced a stunning spell to take four wickets in six balls, setting up Tasmania's first Sheffield Shield win at the Gabba. Gilbert had played the last of his nine Tests for Australia five years before he bowled to me, but there's no doubt he was a better bowler when I faced him than when he was rushed into the Australian side after the South African rebel tours of the mid-1980s. I wasn't the only one who was impressed by him. In one of my last seasons at Queensland, Trevor Hohns, who played first-class cricket for almost two decades, was asked to name his 'best of the best' and he hailed Gilbert as the most underrated bowler he'd ever faced. Gilbert modestly claims my high rating of him is due to circumstances rather than talent. As evidence, he told me that at the start of his Shield career he'd faced Rodney Hogg and was so rocked by his pace that he always felt Hoggy was the quickest he faced, even though Gilbert later confronted the great West Indian quicks of the mid-1980s. There could be something in this theory, but I'm not entirely convinced.

The problem with big dreams is big let-downs. Towards the end of my first season with Queensland I felt I might have a chance of gaining a Test cap. Geoff Marsh's Test career ended in early 1992 when he was dropped for the last Test against India in Perth. I felt right up to the challenge. Maybe I shouldn't have got my hopes up, but they were being pumped up all around me. The *Courier-Mail* in Brisbane printed stats comparing me favourably against Victorian Wayne Phillips, the other main contender. Even the then boss of Victorian cricket, Bill Lawry, broke ranks to support me – somewhat bravely, considering his position – asking the selectors, 'Why would you go for an old grafter like Phillips?' Bristling with ambition, confidence and the uncompromising impatience of youth, I felt ready for Test cricket.

On 29 January 1992 the news came through that Phillips would indeed go to Perth, not me, and it hurt more deeply than it probably should've, given I'd played just a handful of first-class matches. Maybe I would have stumbled and failed. Part of me has wondered over the years whether I could have developed like Michael Clarke – learning the game at the top level from a young age – if I'd been given the chance. But instead, I learnt my cricket at the time-honoured school of hard knocks, and it was a decent education. Gaz gave an interview soon after Phillips got the nod, saying the setback had jolted both of us but that we had learnt from it and would never again fall victim to the high-expectations syndrome. As it turned out, Phillips played only that one Test: there would be other chances for me.

I may have been out in the cold at national level, but I was still in a very warm place in a Queensland dressing-room brimming with personalities I admire to this day. Carl Rackemann was the first big-name cricketer I ever saw in the flesh. We lived in the same town and both went to Kingaroy High School, though a decade apart. I remember the commotion when he came to the nets at little Tabinga Primary School. I was too shy to go up and speak to him or get his autograph, but I remember thinking his mere presence proved there was a pathway to the top, from my life to his. It could be done. At that stage Gaz was my one and only cricketing hero. But just setting eyes on Carl was inspiring.

Carl's colourful ways will never be forgotten by those who played with him, and I always liked his personalised pain scale for injuries, from 'thumb tacks' to 'knives' with all sorts of rankings in between. He was genuine character with a sense of humour as dry as a bush highway. One of his most characteristic lines came during a rock-climbing exercise at training, when he ruefully looked up and down the wall before asking, 'I'm not sure about this . . . Do you think Sir Edmund Hillary had a hit in the nets before he climbed Mt Everest?' And I shared his passion for the land and the region. When precious rain fell on his Kingaroy property he'd just sit on his verandah and watch it in blissful silence. Only a rain-starved farmer could truly understand that feeling. Carl was once asked before a crucial Sheffield Shield game at the Gabba what he would prefer – rain for drought-stricken farmers or a dry weekend for the cricket. He looked at the reporter as if they were stupid. The farmers' plight was always going to be far more important to him than a game of cricket.

There was one area where Carl was well ahead of the game. Long before television introduced the grey zone to line up lbw decisions and help decide whether balls hit or pitched on the stumps, he was banging on about how bowlers got a raw deal. Because he bowled from wide of the crease with an action that cut across his body, many umpires were very reluctant to give him lbw decisions because they reckoned his natural angle would take any ball hitting pads in front of the stumps down the leg side. One day at training, Carl produced a long piece of string, stood in his own footmarks and traced a line with the string from his raised hand to where the ball pitched and then on to the leg stump, proving that he could pitch a ball on the stumps and hit leg – and that he should be getting more lbws. He even invited one of Brisbane's top umpires to watch the exercise.

Carl's other pet frustration was that batsmen got the benefit of the doubt whenever there was a suggestion that the ball was going near leg stump rather than middle. He reckoned no one ever took into account the fact that the ball didn't have to hit the stumps flush on. It only had to clip it enough to remove the bail. Whenever I watch the modern game and see a batsman given out lbw because the ball clipped one coat of varnish, I picture Carl looking on from his Kingaroy property, thinking, *Justice at last!*

Opposition players gravitated towards Carl in the dressing-room. Warnie only did one tour with Carl – the West Indies in 1995 – but said at the time his biggest regret in cricket was not touring more with him. Carl never announced his retirement, which was very rare for a big-time player, but just phased himself out of the game. When asked why, he said simply, 'I didn't announce my arrival – why should I announce my departure?'

My life gathered pace in many ways after my Shield debut, and in January 1993 I met the future love of my life, Kellie Culey, then a 17-year-old schoolgirl. Years before on the farm, Dad, Gaz and I used to follow the progress of Uncle Pat's greyhounds by listening to the races from the Gabba on the radio. The only place we could get reception was on the tractor, so Dad would drive to the top of a hill, put the aerial up as high as he could and we'd gather around to listen to the fortunes of Uncle Pat's most famous dog, Stationmaster, who won 21 races in a row. When I subsequently started training at the Gabba on Thursday afternoons, I was always interested as the greyhound people arrived for the races that night. The team was also often encouraged by Tank, a mad punter, to stay and watch the first few races. One night, when Uncle Pat was in town, he suggested Gary and I come to the dogs and meet some friends of his, Bernie and Maureen Culey. He knew they had their pretty young daughter with them and I think he was quietly trying to play matchmaker.

It worked. I was instantly taken with Kell. One of the first things she said to me was that she disliked cricket. It was the perfect line! If she had been a cricket tragic, I'm not sure we'd have been meant for each other. I always wanted a strong woman and Kell, though young, was definitely that. One element of that strength, sadly, came from a family tragedy. Losing her older brother when she was only sixteen meant Kell had to grow up very quickly and gave her a clear perspective on what was truly important. In the car on the way home that night, I told Gary how gorgeous I thought she was.

At first we were just mates. I was conscious of the fact that she was still at school and didn't want to push things, so we waited a while before we got serious. I knew all along that the wait would be worth it.

8

Greenhorns at Greenmount – English League Cricket

There are many ways you can tour England, and I'm yet to find a bad way. I have been there as a county player, a Test player, a commentator and a league cricketer and enjoyed every trip.

In 1992, my long-time friend and Queensland squad mate, Chris Holding, and I were approached by the Greenmount club in the Bolton League to play for them, and we headed off on a great adventure. That trip was only my second visit abroad, and my first to England, and I just loved it. The excellent batting wickets, the company of our league cricket mates, and all the people I met in everyday life – I was charmed and impressed by everything. Chris and I were ambitious young men who played cricket on Saturday and Sunday and spent a lot of time training midweek.

League cricket has some quaint and endearing traditions. If you take five wickets or score 50 runs, they take a hat or a bucket around the ground for a collection for you, which you're subsequently supposed to put on the bar. Sometimes they carry out this ritual while you're still batting and – try as you might – you simply can't take your eyes off that bucket. On one occasion a collection was going around for me and a gentleman who initially declined to contribute saw me looking on, changed his mind and coughed up a few quid. Chris used to joke that the blanket tradition said a lot about English cricket. He'd say, 'When you get a collection for scoring 50 runs, you know your country's in trouble.'

In subsequent years, one of the joys of an Ashes tour would occur when the cricketing caravan passed through the northern counties of Yorkshire and Lancashire. The bar would fill up with old friends from league cricket, where an Australian player might earn around $20 000 a season to play weekend cricket and carry a bunch of enthusiastic amateurs. Over the years famous names such as Garry Sobers, Dennis Lillee and Viv Richards have been guest players in the leagues. Even Warnie spent a season in league cricket playing for the Bristol Imperials – he later joked it was terrible for his self-esteem because he 'kept being hit out of the park by 50-year-olds who wouldn't play fourth grade at home'. Allan Border took league wickets bowling for East Lancashire with a Jeff Thomson-style action in 1978, and Viv Richards' recruitment to Rishton became part of league legend after one of the club's officials kept phoning him until he finally ran out of reasons to say no. Viv grandly arrived by helicopter for one of his first games.

You meet all sorts of quirky characters in the league scene. I remember playing one match against a former West Indian Test bowler, then watching him drink an entire bottle of Mount Gay rum in the dressing-room after the game. My northern summer with Greenmount was also significant for another reason – it marked my first sighting of the Ashes urn. Chris and I went to London to visit Lord's and its famous museum, where the even more famous little urn is kept. I felt all sorts of contrasting emotions at the sight of it. There was the humbling feeling of being the unknown novice in cricket's sacred church. Then there was the slightly rebellious feeling of wanting to take the mickey out of a stuffy English institution – to look at the ground and think, *Hey, at the end of the day, it's only a piece of grass . . . and guess what? It's sloped!* To look at the Ashes urn and think, *How small is it? It's sure no FA Cup!*

But beneath it all there was a respect for the game's history. Cricket has centuries of soul, and Lord's embodies that. I could not have known that within a year of my pilgrimage to worship at the Ashes altar, I'd be visiting again – and that time I'd be touring for my country.

When it comes to playing soccer I've got hands for feet. I've always known it, but my inadequacies have never been more brutally exposed than during my time at Greenmount when Chris and I spent time with two young bucks, Gary and Phil Neville. The duo were sons of club stalwart Neville Neville – I still love that name – and Gary played with us for Greenmount. The Nevilles just toyed with us on the soccer pitch. Our embarrassment has receded over the years as those two little powerhouses came to embarrass many other players – including the world's finest – during their celebrated careers at Manchester United and Everton. In fact, Gary and Phil became two of the finest English footballers of their generation. Gary captained England and Man U, and is England's most capped right back, while Phil moved on to captain Everton after a decorated career at Man U. To know them as teenagers and then follow their careers has been a great thrill. Even at age 17 and 15 respectively, it was obvious that Gary and Phil were exceptional. They had already been inducted into Manchester United's development squad.

One day Gary Neville and I made centuries in a winning 50-over Cup semi-final side against Astley Bridge (featuring former Australian all-rounder Ian Harvey). The next day I picked up the local paper and was surprised to read a story declaring Gary's cricket career was over – Man U had decided they didn't want to risk him getting injured.

The Neville boys were great kids. Phil was a little bookworm and an outstanding cricketer, and Gaz was fiercely determined to get the best out of himself. They remain the same today. Very much at the centre of the Neville family was the great man himself, Neville Neville, who became something of cult figure in English soccer. When the boys started to do well, Man U fans invented a popular, long-lasting chant to the tune of David Bowie's 'Rebel Rebel':

Neville, Neville, they're in defence,
Neville, Neville, their talent's immense,
Neville, Neville, they ain't half bad,
Neville, Neville . . . the name of their dad!

Of course, big Nev loved it. He had all the big-man mannerisms, like a hearty laugh and a big appetite. He was also big-hearted. Neville was formerly director of English Football League club Bury, and was widely lauded for his efforts to spearhead a campaign to generate financial assistance for the club after it went into administration. Chris and I used to go around to the Nevilles' every Sunday and have lunch cooked by Neville's wife, Jill. The family is so talented – as if two cricket- and soccer-playing sons weren't enough, daughter Tracey played netball for England.

Playing league cricket was lots of fun. It's obviously rungs beneath county cricket in standard – at that stage of my career I hadn't done enough to snare a county deal – but there was still pressure, and an expectation for me to perform. I had a bountiful summer, topping the league averages with more than 1200 runs at 80. Mark Taylor had been at the club before me, and when we were both chosen to tour England in 1993, the club's newsletter trumpeted, 'If you want to open for Australia, come to Greenmount!'

INSIDE THE GAME

Superstitions

If I could take you into the mind of a Test cricketer, you'd be surprised by what you'd discover. Men who look and play as if they're bulletproof have the quirkiest fears. Take Jason Gillespie, for example. As a fast bowler, Dizzy was all poise, calculation and control. Only his teammates knew he held it together with the help of a host of superstitions. He'd never stay on the 13th floor of a hotel. He would count the steps down from the pavilion and skip from the 12th to the 14th, deliberately missing the 13th. And if his seat was in the 13th row on a plane, he'd change it.

Dizzy says his problems started when he made his one-day international debut and was given the dreaded number 13. He had a run of injuries and promptly asked for a new number – four, which he wore for the rest of his career. Dizzy was coy about his superstitions, which, of course, made me keener to figure them out. Sometimes when I'd go back from gully to meet him and take his hat before an over, I could see him silently counting his steps from the boundary. He was desperate not to hand me the hat on the 13th step, so I started counting his steps to make sure he did. I'd say, 'Gotcha!' and he would playfully blow up.

Yet superstitions are no indication of a fragile mind. Just look at Steve Waugh. Cricket's man of steel for more than a decade wouldn't have felt the same playing without his little red rag in his pocket. He even loved looking down at the crease and seeing where strands of the red cloth had fallen around his feet. He'd think, *Good, I've marked my turf.* If Steve saw a ladybird flying around while he was at the crease, he'd catch it, put it on his clothing and give it a free ride for the rest of his innings. I've done the same. I've lost count of the number of ladybirds I've put on Ricky Ponting's clothes when he was standing near me in the slips cordon.

Little things can make you superstitious. It's said to be good luck to have a bird cast its droppings on you, and once in Adelaide Ian Healy had a seagull poop on his gloves. He took a catch several overs later, convincing us all of the merit of this theory.

Superstitions are definitely not a sign of softness. There was no tougher competitor than Allan Border, yet even he felt a bit funny about being photographed with the Sheffield Shield just before one of Queensland's ill-fated finals against NSW in the mid-1980s. AB swore he'd never get photographed with the Shield again until Queensland won it, and he kept his word, even though the Bulls' famous drought-breaking win at the Gabba didn't occur for another decade.

During the second season of the IPL, I played a part in spreading superstitions among my Chennai Super Kings teammates. The tournament was held in South Africa that year, and I loved visiting places like Durban and Port Elizabeth because I was able to hook up with my surfing buddies and tackle some of the greatest surfing breaks in the world. Initially I saw the occasional raised eyebrow when my teammates headed off to voluntary training sessions and I headed off to the beach. But as the tournament progressed, my form remained solid and my teammates became quite happy for me to do as much surfing as I needed to. My performance seemed mysteriously linked to my surfing, and of course I went along with it – you've got to do your bit for the team! The bewildered 'Surfing again?' looks at the start of the tournament slowly turned to expressions of, 'Haydos, you *will* be surfing today, won't you?' I milked it for all it was worth. The team knew I'd found the perfect routine and wanted me to keep it going.

Good or bad form can enhance existing superstitions. Pigeon, Dizzy and Gilly were having a swim in a hotel pool in Brisbane in 2004 when, much to their horror, a couple of stray ducks flew in and joined them. The boys were mortified and sensed the worst, but then a strange thing happened – in the next innings Gilly made 126, Gillespie made 54 and Pigeon a career-best of 61. After initially being spooked by the ducks, they were sorry they never saw them again.

Ducks play with batsmen's minds. Once, in Sydney, Kell and I had a beautiful dinner at the renowned Aria restaurant and chef Matt Moran came out with a special treat between courses – duck consommé. It was the restaurant's signature dish so I simply had to eat it – and it was delicious. But it was tempting fate and, sure enough, the next day I failed in a Test. I can understand how 100-metre sprinters may not be as troubled by superstitions because they haven't got time. They just get out and go. But cricket is the longest game and your thoughts have time to drift to quirky corners of your mind. My mother-in-law used to serve me coffee in a lovely mug with an ornate duck on it, but it was just too much. It had to go. Similarly, while most children like playing with rubber ducks in the bath, I always denied mine this pleasure. I didn't make a big fuss about it, but there are plenty of other inflatable animals that fare just as well in the bath. Sorry, kids – no ducks.

Perhaps the most superstitious cricketer of my era was South African batsman Neil McKenzie, who had a long list of quirks that included taping his bats to the ceiling of the dressing-room, making sure all the toilet seats in the dressing-room were down when he batted and making sure he never stepped on the crease line when he batted. The last thing he always did before facing up was turn and look over his left shoulder behind square leg. In his 58-Test career he made 16 fifties but just five centuries, and I subscribe to the widely held view that his energy-sapping superstitions made him run out of mental energy. Everyone's limit is different but you've only got so much fuel each day. It got to the stage where McKenzie couldn't go to bed if the sheets had a crease in them. Everything had to be perfect. It probably says a lot about the true worth of superstitions that towards the end of his career McKenzie gave them all up, feeling that they were too much of a burden.

Was I superstitious? Not really, but I was a man of routine, and if these routines were disrupted it could affect me without leaving me feeling totally cursed or vulnerable. For example, on a changeover between innings, if the opposition was nine wickets down, I'd promise myself not to think about batting. The message to my brain was, *Not now.* I'd try to have a joke with the boys and stay light and bright. But when the last wicket fell, my adrenalin would spike. Funnily enough, I'd start to feel quite flat mentally, even though my heart would be racing, and I'd want to go to the toilet. I'd rush off the field without even bothering to congratulate the bowler, because that could be done at the end of the day.

Once off the field, I'd wet my face then submerge myself in an ice bath before having a hot shower. I'd repeat the process twice more to make the blood flow, feeling fresher as I did it. Then I'd pad up and find a place where I could be by myself. At the back of the rooms you could sometimes hear the fast bowlers carrying on about what they were about to eat, where they were going for dinner. But all I wanted were the three pieces of Wrigley's P.K. – no other brand would do, and I took boxes around the world because the overseas stuff doesn't taste the same – that I had set aside in advance. (In my kit at home I still have unopened boxes of the gum.) During the 10-minute break between innings, I kept my conversations with teammates to a minimum. If I was asked a question I'd answer it, but I was almost uncomfortable doing so because this was my precious time. Justin

Langer was different. He loved talking, and enjoyed the music and the crackling vibe of the changeover.

My only words when I left the dressing-room were always a short, sharp message of encouragement – something like 'Good luck, boys' or 'C'mon, Australia'. When I crossed the boundary rope I always did so right foot first, and I'd say 'On!' as soon as I touched down, a little mental switch to ensure I was fully activated for the challenge. I'd yell it out and then take off across the field, for no other reason than because I hated the television camera in my face. Once I was past the camera I'd stop and wait for Justin, because I didn't want to walk out to bat by myself. I always felt a bit uncomfortable about rushing off – it certainly wasn't for show. Alfie would catch up to me and he'd drop a little line like 'What a beautiful day' or 'You wouldn't be dead for quids!' Alfie would always face up first.

So I suppose you could accuse me of being superstitious, but I think of myself more as a structured player who liked routine. In fact, I loved opening precisely because I always knew my job when I went to the crease – to tackle the new ball.

Ricky Ponting is also a man of strong routine. When he comes to the wicket, he'll walk straight past his batting partner and stay in his own little world. Most batsmen like to touch base with their partner for a few words, but Punter, with that firm confident stride of his, walks alone. Just before he faces his first ball, however, he'll come down the wicket with one simple message, the same one every time: 'Good loud calls, mate.'

9

Baggy Green

There are some beautiful moments in cricket, and I don't mean raising your bat after a century, taking a spectacular catch or chanting the team war cry after a win. Sometimes just opening a cardboard box can be the stuff of dreams, especially when it carries Australian sport's most cherished piece of headgear – the baggy green cap. Some of the centuries I've scored are just a blur to me now, yet the memory of unpacking my first baggy green is strikingly clear. I can still see the plain brown box it came in.

It was just before my first Australian tour – the 1993 Ashes tour – and a large box arrived at the house Gaz and I shared in Gordon Park, Brisbane. To imagine how I felt opening that box, you only have to recall your own emotions as a youngster on Christmas Day. Paper flew everywhere. That box never stood a chance. I dived in and threw stuff around wildly until I found, right at the bottom, the treasure I was chasing.

The hairs on the back of my neck still prickle when I remember putting on the baggy green for the first time. I knew it was only the start of the journey and I wasn't guaranteed to ever wear it in a Test match. But that didn't matter. That afternoon I luxuriated in my new piece of headgear, a time made even more special because Gaz, Mum and Dad were there to share the moment.

The press had been saying for a few weeks that I was certain to tour, and on the morning of the day the team was to be announced, the *Courier-Mail* categorically declared me a starter. The selectors apparently chatted for hours about the top three spots before deciding to leave Justin Langer, who had played most of the summer at number three, out of the squad, drop David Boon from opener to three and promote me and Michael Slater to duel for the right to partner Mark Taylor at the top of the order. Nonetheless, I refused to believe it until my name was read out at an afternoon press conference. I was overjoyed. Earlier, Gaz had claimed I was close to national selection, and his intuition was not based on reading the press but on our mailbox. When you get close to national selection you seem to get more correspondence from the Australian Cricket Board. Unbeknown to me, Gaz would open letters from the board and run his fingers across the embossed gold of the national emblem, thinking, *We're so close I can almost touch it*. I didn't believe him until the official announcement. The near-misses had left their mark. And for Gaz, it took even longer to sink in. Only when we got the tour itinerary from the ACB did he flash the grin of a man receiving a letter that says, 'Yes, you have won the lotto.'

I wore my cap to bed the night it arrived, and I slept soundly. It had been one of the most satisfying days of my life. Despite my abiding preference for a helmet, I promised myself I'd wear the cap in my first match of the Ashes tour, and so I did. Someone took a photo of me that day, when I made 151 against an English Amateur XI at Radlett, and put it on a players' card.

My biggest challenge on my first day as an Australian batsman came not from the English attack, but from the charging rhino who confronted me in the bus on the way home. The trip back to our hotel in London saw a full-on wrestling bout between a man who may have been a sumo wrestler in another life – David Boon – and someone who wasn't really spoiling for a rumble but was happy to oblige – me.

It started not long after we left the ground. In the true style of those times there were beers on offer on the bus, and after a first-up century, I'd enjoyed a few and was feeling like the king of the world. I was down the back with Merv and AB when Boonie challenged me. As young and naïve as I was, I knew there was one certainty about the contest. If I beat Boonie, no one would challenge me for the rest of the trip. He was as strong as an ox and he came at me hard. We began relatively calmly, but it all changed when he pushed me head-first into the side of the bus. There was an almighty crack, which I think was the bus and not, mercifully, Boonie or me. How we didn't go straight through the window and end up rolling down the highway is still beyond me.

By this stage the boys were egging us on. It became a battle of egos as well as bodies, a full-on World Wrestling Federation bout between Hitman Hayden and Bad to the Bone Boon. Despite this, there was no malice involved. It started out as a bit of fun, but then it became a little more serious. It was the old bull versus the young bull. Pride was on the line, and there are few prouder characters than Boonie. I grabbed him in a headlock and powered him down to the back of the bus, jamming his head between two seats. 'Do you give up? Do you give up?' I roared. 'No!' came a muffled reply.

When Boonie started making gurgling sounds I let him go for fear I was choking him, but he's one of those blokes who never gives up – on the cricket field or in the back of a bus, even when he's in danger of finishing with a giraffe-sized neck on his rhino-sized body. He got back up and we kept at it, and I forced him back into the same spot twice more. Each time I asked him whether he would give up, and he was defiant. He was unbelievably tough. Finally, through sheer exhaustion, we stopped and limped our separate ways, but I felt confident that he wouldn't challenge me again on tour.

In fact, the two of us became good friends over the next four months. I liked him then and I like him now. Neither of us could have foreseen that, 15 years later, we'd sit down for the heart-to-heart – me as player, Boonie as selector – that was the prelude to my retirement from the game.

I didn't play a Test on that tour but I had some wonderful cricket tutorials along the way, the memories of which I treasure. Many of them happened in bars. Because of my Queensland and Valleys links with AB, I felt comfortable drinking with him, and Boonie was never far from his side. I looked forward to those bar nights as much as – and sometimes even more than – any game I played on tour. Damien Martyn and I had sneaky bets on how many beers Boonie would have. Boonie was a creature of habit. He'd have six or so beers, go up to his room, ring his wife Pip, have a smoke, then go to bed. It was Boonie who created the idea of the first three batsmen being what he called the 'engine room' of the side. I loved that. It was his way of putting his hand in the air and taking responsibility for the hard yakka of the early overs. That concept stayed with me throughout my career and was one of the reasons I developed such special bonds with Justin Langer and Ricky Ponting. At press conferences I'd often say, 'It's been a good day for the engine room.'

I started the tour well and made my Australian debut opening with Mark Taylor in the three-match one-day series, but didn't really get going, managing scores of only 29, 14 and 4. There were no excuses – I just didn't fire. It hurt my tour because it immediately made me less likely to win Test selection, which brought Uncle Gary's sage words back to me: 'Give them reasons to pick you, not reasons to leave you out.' I made seven successive scores under 39 at a time when Michael Slater was gaining enormous momentum, and he slipped past me into the First Test team.

Slats and I started the tour on level terms but the truth was that his game was more advanced than mine. He was more expansive, more dominant and a freer player. Neither of us had played a Test and it was down to one of us to win the spot as Mark Taylor's opening partner.

It came down to a man-on-man showdown in a county game against Leicester on a modest pitch. Everyone knew the stakes. The media had built it up as a shootout for a Test place, and for once they were on the money. In Steve Waugh's autobiography, he notes that he looked at both of us leaving the dressing-room and clearly sensed our careers were going to be defined – at least in the short term – that day. He was right. Slats won the battle. He made 91 and 50 not out, while I scored 2 and 15. I knew my fate instantly. I picked a bad month to have a bad month, and I just didn't have the brightness of Michael Slater in top gear.

The competition between Slats and I never stopped us from

getting along. Slats is always great company, and on that tour he and Stephanie, whom he subsequently married, were full of fun. We got along so well there never seemed to be a life-or-death edge to our rivalry. At that stage we were all kids just living the dream.

I'm proud of my career record, but there is one big weakness I must acknowledge, which plagued me until the second half of my career: I underperformed when on trial. It happened in representative carnivals as a junior, in World Cups as a senior, and when I went head-to-head with someone, like with Slats in 1993 and with Matthew Elliott in 1996. I know why now: I was concentrating on everything except the only thing that mattered – the ball. I was distracted by the 'What ifs?', and in England I just wasn't mature enough to handle the battle with Slats at that time. Luckily, this didn't remain a problem forever. When I returned to Test cricket in New Zealand in 2000 – when it was Greg Blewett or me for a Test spot – I was ice-cold about the whole thing and just *played*. I won back my place in the side and went on to play 86 Tests in a row.

In 1993 I didn't have the game to repel these sorts of challenges. It's one thing to back yourself when you've played 80 Tests and have the mental reassurance of knowing that even if you bomb out, you'll still be regarded as a decent player. It's quite another when you haven't played a single Test. At the time of my first England tour, I'd had a few big Shield seasons but didn't have the necessary experience to help me stay calm and true to the methods that had got me there.

When we assembled for the announcement of the First Test team in London, Slats sat beside AB and noticed his name on a team sheet (which AB hurriedly tried to cover up) before the team was announced. Until that point Slats was unsure of his destiny, but I could have saved him the anguish. I just knew he was in. The force wasn't with me. In addition to his form, Slats would provide the team with a right- and left-handed combination with Tubby, which was considered more fashionable than two lefties (Tubby and me). Plus Tubby and Slats were both from NSW – even hailing from the same country town – Wagga Wagga – and there was no question of whom Tubby would be more comfortable with. I had no problem with knowing that Tubby preferred Slats. Team dynamics should always be an important part of selection.

Slats' fabulous tour was topped off with a stunning century at Lord's, when he famously kissed his helmet after reaching three figures. He was the new wunderkind, and his Lord's century was, for me, the highlight of the tour, which we won 4–1, with England snatching a consolation win in the last Test at the Oval. Slats' century was pure inspiration for me. I wanted to do what he'd done. I found myself left with two choices – accept my fate and work hard, or sit around and whinge, and there was no way I was going to do the latter. I became the hungry young buck, scrambling to get whatever I could out of the tour. Damien Martyn and I finished with more than 1000 first-class runs each, despite not playing a Test, which were little ticks, if not quite the gold stars we were chasing. (And the scoreline of 4–1 meant there were no vacancies in the Australian Test side.) I notched the 1000-run milestone in the match against Kent, and the press took me down to be photographed under the famous lime tree that grew inside the boundary (if you hit it during your innings, it was automatically four).

That tour also marked the last time in my memory that Australia saw world-class off spin being delivered by one of its own. Tim May was bowling so well in England that he made the ball drift away through the air towards slips then snap back across all the right-handed batsmen. It was pretty to watch and it was a perfect foil for Warnie, who was doing exactly the same thing in the other direction. When Maysie was bowling like that, your footwork was stuffed and you just couldn't play him. You'd get into position to play one ball, then suddenly, through drift and turn, you'd be playing another. No coaching manual can really tell you what to do in those situations.

There were other high points of the 1993 tour for me – like rooming with Merv Hughes. He was terrific. It didn't matter how he or the team was going, he was the class clown right to the end and the boys loved him for it – players like Tubby, Steve Waugh and Heals all named him as one of their favourite teammates when they retired. Merv was great for me because he kept me loose on a tour that didn't always go swimmingly. One day we had a shaving-cream fight, during which I ducked my head away quickly and cut my eye on a mirror in the vanity cupboard in the bathroom. He raised his arms and claimed a cheap victory on the grounds that he'd drawn first blood. Merv was one of those blokes who always had the courage to be himself, even when he became a national selector. When he flew to Lord's for the Second Test of our 2005 Ashes tour, having been recently elected to the selection panel, I said, 'Ah, I've finally met the prick who's going to drop me.' Quick as a flash he responded, 'Mate, I'm not going to drop ya. I'm going to select you until you're 60. That will hurt you even more!'

My baggy green cap stayed with me from that first day in 1993 until January 2008, when someone stole it as I was returning from the Adelaide Test against India. I was shattered.

I remember the euphoria I'd felt when I first received that cap. I'd sweated in it, celebrated in it. It wasn't so much a part of my gear as a part of me. I opened my gear coffin in Brisbane after returning from the Adelaide and it just wasn't there. Initially I thought I must have misplaced it, and Dad said he thought he'd seen it at home and put it in a bag. I said to him, 'Did you or didn't you? This is my baggy green!' That triggered a frantic search under the house, where I have about 30 bags of gear. It proved fruitless. I reckon someone just flipped the lid of my coffin and took it.

When you first wear the baggy green it tends to be quite uncomfortable. I recall sitting near Alfie Langer in the dressing-room after I'd played about 40 Tests and saying, 'This hat is finally starting to feel part of me now.' The way it sat on my head, how dirty it was getting – it all helped me to feel like a battle-hardened performer. But I paid the price for not carrying my baggy green in my hand luggage like players such as Adam Gilchrist did. Gilly was so organised he even had a 'drinking' baggy green – his match cap was falling apart so he wore another one for celebrations.

I averaged 53 in my first cap, which was with me for the first 15 years of my international career, and only 24 in the replacement I wore for my final year. That new baggy green just never felt quite right.

10

Bob Simpson

The first Australian coach I played under was Bob Simpson, and in my early years he picked apart my game like a judge on Batting Idol. When I scored my 151 against the English Amateur XI in the opening match of the 1993 Ashes tour, Simmo's mental notes were, *Poor strike rotation, can't play spin, too wooden . . . Needs heaps of work*. And work I did. In fact, I worked as hard as Simmo wanted me to, and he later told me that was why he enjoyed trying to make me the best player I could be. At a time when I saw rosy opportunities ahead of me, Simmo saw a flawed product that needed correction, a work in progress that was far from finished. And, of course, he was right.

Simmo was so brutally direct that I always felt a little off-balance in my dealings with him. Many people did. I still remember an encounter at the MCG one day early in my career, when I was playing for Australia A. I walked into the lunch room after being dismissed early, and Simmo asked how the pitch was playing. I replied, 'Slow. Bounce is a bit up and down.'

Forget the floaties, where's my board? Dad gives me an early introduction to the water, which I clearly enjoyed.

Gaz and I were never far apart when we were growing up. Here we are mucking around in a sorghum patch on the farm.

Pick the athlete. Gaz, on the right, looks very much the model young cricketer he was, while I look like I have a bit of work to do.

Ready to tackle the world. Decked out in my suit of armour, I was up for any challenge on our backyard deck.

Country cricket was always fun. That's me in the middle surrounded by a few local lads.

I started to make progress as a cricketer in my mid-teens. I'm second from the left in the second row, and you can see by my smile how excited I was about making one of my first Queensland junior representative teams.

Long before Michael Kasprowicz and I played together for Australia, we were Queensland Under-17 teammates. He's the big guy in the middle of the back row while I'm second from the left in the same row.

After my teens I shed my baby fat and enjoyed the challenge of staying in shape. Gaz and I often trained together as my career started to develop.

Top: Celebrating my 20th birthday with Bill Brown, a distinguished opening batsman of the Bradman era. He was a great person and gave me plenty of encouragement throughout my career.
Bottom: My first-class debut just after my 20th birthday.

Left: Here's to England and my first tour. After a tense few months I was picked to join the Australian team for the 1993 Ashes tour, reason enough to raise a glass in celebration.

Below: It's green and gold and it's mine. Gaz looks infatuated with my first green and gold cap and I don't blame him. I was too. The night before I left for my first tour, I slept with it on.

Left: I didn't play a Test on the 1993 Ashes tour but there was plenty of fun to be had in the warm-up games, such as this one against Hampshire at Southhampton, England.

Below: During the 1993 Ashes tour, the great Ian Botham decided to retire from first-class cricket. Here he seemed determined to make me one of his final first-class wickets, but the appeal was rejected.

Playing cricket at Lord's was always memorable. Here the members give me a nice ovation after a century against Middlesex in the 1993 Ashes tour.

Left and above: My second tour, the 1994 tour of South Africa, was a real eye-opener and there were relatively few moments of comfort. As I nursed a broken finger in the dressing-room I was feeling pretty down about my prospects in the short-term future.

There are not many more breathtaking views in the world than from the top of Table Mountain in Cape Town, South Africa. Steve Waugh and I soaked it up in 1994 on the South African tour.

Meeting Nelson Mandela was a highlight for the whole team. Just the mention of the great man's name took the heat out of every tense conversation.

Plenty of smiles after, but there were screams of sheer terror when a South African army helicoptor pilot playfully cut the engine during a joy flight. And I thought facing Allan Donald was scary!

Pressing the flesh with a South African dancer during the 1994 tour. I didn't experience many on-field delights but off the field I enjoyed myself.

Ours at last! Queensland had to wait almost seven decades to win the Sheffield Shield. When we finally did in 1994–95 we made the most of it with a street parade (*above*), a big celebration straight after the match (*above right*) and a country tour with the Shield, where I met up with Gaz and his daughter, Ellie (*right*).

XXXX

I married my best friend, Kellie, in May 1996. I thought I knew happiness then, but now I know there was much more to come. We have laughed, cried, celebrated the birth of our three children and shared 17 wonderful years together.

Just at that moment, Damien Martyn smashed a straight six. 'Bounce doesn't seem to be bothering him too much,' Simmo said, immediately turning away and heading off without waiting for my reply.

That was Simmo. 'Burr Under the Saddle Bob', you might call him, because that's what he tried to be, not just with me but with all the boys. I'm not going to tell you I adored him, but I can tell you that I respected him, which was probably more important. Maybe he could have been better at 'man management' but he certainly knew his cricket.

I only made two tours with Simmo – England in '93 and South Africa a year later – but I got along well with him. I was very much a junior member of the squad and all I wanted to do was learn – I had no intention of trying to change Simmo or the system. The one thing I was certain of was that for all his chastening directness – or maybe because of it – Simmo was going to do me much more good than harm. If he'd mollycoddled me I'm not sure I would've made the changes I needed to make. Once, after a net session during the South African tour, he said to me, 'I was a much more talented player than you are.' I wasn't sure how to react. Maybe he simply was better? Maybe he was stirring me up and sending a message not to get ahead of myself? Maybe he was trying to see what was inside me? I felt like saying, 'Give it a rest, you old bastard,' but something stopped me. I tried hard to be seriously annoyed with him but just couldn't get worked up. I had to acknowledge that not only had he achieved a lot, but he was improving my game, and I decided to fight the fights that mattered.

But Simmo definitely had his detractors. I played a round of golf with the great Norman Von Nida before the 1993 tour of England, and he made a point of telling me, 'Just make sure you ignore every word Bob Simpson says to you!' They had played together in a sponsored golf day. Simmo made one observation that was 100 per cent correct – I needed to improve against spin. In Australia, top-class spinners like Tim May would render me almost shotless. I never felt as if Maysie was going to get me out, but I just couldn't score off him. I needed an extra weapon, and that was the sweep shot. It's the shot spin bowlers hate having played against them, and I made it my mission in life to get not one but three versions of it. During the rest of that tour and the subsequent South African one, I worked ad nauseum on it, and picked the brains of both Simmo and AB, since AB was one of the great exponents of the stroke. They taught me about getting my pad in line with the ball and swinging around my body, and also showed me that the higher you lift your bat before you play the shot, the finer it went.

Simmo's mind was a fascinating thing. At times it seemed to work like a steel trap; at others like a flapping tent. As house detective he used his senses brilliantly, almost too well for the players' peace of mind. The boys always reckoned that if someone had had a few too many beers, Simmo found out about it before most. Sometimes he'd simply smell them on the bus, or observe their slightly sheepish body language. Knowing we all had big mouths, he'd keep a keen ear out for back-of-the-bus banter. Invariably, a word or two would slip out about someone who'd had too much to drink the night before. Being that person at training was like being on a personal boot camp. Simmo would work you into oblivion. He didn't have a problem if you completed your training, but if you faltered, in Simmo's eyes it meant you were getting sloppy.

For all his alertness, the boys also reckoned Simmo suffered from memory loss, which became evident during some comical exchanges in our fielding sessions. When Simmo was hitting high balls and looking for a target, Merv or someone would shout out, 'Swampy's been on the piss, Simmo.' Simmo would reply, 'Has he now?' before hitting a high ball and roaring 'SWAMPEEEEE,' nominating Geoff Marsh to catch it. As the ball thudded to earth, someone else would yell, 'Swampy was dropped last year, Simmo – he's missed the last two tours and is back in Perth!' and another voice would chime in with, 'Yeah, but he still wants it.' We'd all crack up, which would only sentence us to another 100 balls. As benchies, Marto and I were slaughtered at those training sessions in England in '93, yet we both finished the tour feeling as if we were never going to drop another catch.

Simmo coached Australia before computer analysis came into vogue, although it didn't matter a jot. He had the best computer of all – a brain that could process the relevant information and spit out the right answer. There were always muffled suggestions that he was manipulative in the selection room, but his head was on the block too, so you could understand why he had strong views. He had a great eye for technical problems, a shrewd understanding of players' personalities and could see when they were drifting off the rails.

Few people loved the game more than Simmo. A Lord's Test match was special for all of us, but for Simmo it was akin to a personal invitation to the Vatican for a parish priest. When we played there in 1993, it was 32 years since Simmo had played his first Test at Lord's, but the passing years had in no way diminished the experience for him. He spoke with genuine reverence on the team bus en route to Lord's in a way we wouldn't witness elsewhere on the tour.

England was Simmo's spiritual home. There never seemed to be enough room on the team bus, but you could always get a seat next to Simmo as the boys grew a tad weary of his tour-guide monologues. They went along the lines of, 'That three-storey building used to be set of horse stables, and the cooks used to live out the back!' Surprisingly, we were quite a way into the tour before I worked out why I was always the one sitting next to Simmo. I enjoyed his stories and his wisdom, and I became a bit of a hero with the boys for sitting through it so often. Still, there are only so many *wow*s a person can offer at the sight of a renovated horse stable.

I owe Bob Simpson a great deal. It was no coincidence that my form went through the roof immediately after that Ashes tour. When I met him, I was a solid cricketer who knew my game within fairly narrow parameters. Simmo improved and broadened my skills. He had a philosophy of continuous improvement, with perfection as the objective, and he used every opportunity to reinforce it. On that first tour, Simmo even got stuck into the team about our attitude at the breakfast table. He noted how demanding we were with waiting staff, complaining if our tea wasn't hot or our eggs weren't done properly. Why, he asked, did we not bring this attitude to training? 'You're expecting perfection from everyone except yourselves,' he contended.

If you were prepared to challenge that expectation, Simmo was right behind you.

11

Matt the Bat

Support can be a fickle thing in cricket. I had years when I felt I didn't get enough, but in the summer of 1993–94 a strange thing happened: I may have got too much for my own good. Queensland fans – God love them – are probably the second most parochial supporters in Australia, behind West Australians. I was always proud of the support they gave me, right up to my final lap of the Gabba on the day I retired. It inspired me in the rough times and made the good times even better. But the push from my home state for me to make my Test debut became so strong it may have been counter-productive.

In 1993 I returned from the Ashes tour without having played a Test, but bursting with enthusiasm, having topped 1000 first-class runs for the tour. Sure, with Slats' performance I had a bolted door in front of me for Test selection, but I was full of ambition and could almost feel myself improving by the innings. I had new methods against spin and I'd observed some of the best batsmen in the world from close range. I was ready to explode out of the blocks like one of those greyhounds that used to race at our beloved home ground, the Gabba.

I'd rarely hit the ball better than at the start of the 1993–94 season, and by December had made 708 first-class runs at an average of 118. I was so pumped about my prospects I shared my thoughts with a journalist after a Sheffield Shield match at the Gabba. Asked about my form and whether I felt it was putting pressure on Tubby and Slats, I said I was totally happy with the way I was playing and that 'they have to be feeling the pressure – neither has come close to a big score'. I wasn't wrong, because both had relatively slow starts to the summer after great tours of England, but I'd also broken an unwritten code: you can talk up your own form as much as you like, but commenting on the form of others is distinctly inadvisable. You can imagine how that line went down in the Australian dressing-room, and it got back to me that Tubby was not impressed. I'd still employ the defence that feeling the pressure from beneath you is what makes Australian cricket so strong.

It wasn't just me putting pressure on Tubby and Slats. In November 1993, Brisbane's *Sunday Mail* started a campaign to get me into the Test side, claiming I'd have a 'long flowing beard' before I'd be chosen for Australia. The paper certainly did its best to give me a full Hollywood makeover and obviously wasn't aware of all those gags about my false teeth. They invited readers to tell them in 50 words or less why they thought the 'tall young hunk with the film-star looks should gain his rightful place in the Australian team', promising to send the responses to the national selectors. The paper even named its 'Cane Toad All Stars', in which I was part of a team of Queenslanders the *Sunday Mail* considered had been unfairly snubbed at national level, such as rugby union winger Paul Carozza and the former long-serving Shield batsman Sam Trimble.

The paper received a bagful of letters, including one from an eight-year-old boy and another from my aunty Lorna. One said my biggest chance for selection was to move the NSW border north, a suggestion which had many Queensland fans nodding in agreement. I may even have nodded myself. I must admit that the old saying, 'When NSW is strong, Australia is strong,' left me slightly bewildered. Did that mean when Queensland or Western Australia was strong Australia was in serious trouble? Or that when Tassie was strong Australia would be beaten by Bangladesh? Were good players from NSW better than good ones from other states? One southerner who did give me support – bless his soul – was the late David Hookes, who, in typically colourful fashion, said, 'If they don't pick Hayden they will tear down the Clem Jones Stand which, come to think of it, wouldn't be such a bad thing!'

The 'Matt the Bat' campaign was all very flattering and delivered good-naturedly, which took any caustic edge off it. But I always felt – and isn't this often the case with public protests? – that the more people demanded my promotion, the less likely it was to happen. The selectors were in an unwinnable position. If they left me out, they were bagged for being too conservative. If they put me in, they were seen to be bowing to public pressure, and if I excelled, then they faced the obvious question: why wasn't I there in the first place? Sentiment even flowed into the outer at the Gabba during the Test against New Zealand in 1993–94, when someone held up a banner saying, 'The only thing bigger than Taylor's backside is Hayden's average.'

Not everyone was backing my cause. Plenty of people had

reservations about my technique, which I conceded was different to the norm. Ever since Don Bradman had suggested that moving back and across was the best way to handle fast bowling, this method had been deemed the definitive option – but it just didn't feel right to me, so I moved forward. I was also aware that most of the game's greatest batsmen – Bradman, Border, Miandad and Gavaskar among them – had one thing in common: they were small. While many observers seemed to have reservations about my big build, batting great and former Queensland Cricket chief executive Barry Richards was one of my greatest supporters. For a while he was the only big-time name who seemed to see my size as a potential bonus. He likened me to a young Graeme Pollock, and there could be no higher praise – Barry rated Pollock second only to Bradman. It was a wonderful compliment that gave me great heart at a sensitive time in my development.

Nonetheless, Barry was a worldly character who'd lived through some of cricket's most sensitive political issues, and he knew you could only push a good cause so far. He realised the passionate campaign for my promotion had reached a level that was potentially damaging to my career, and said as much at the time: 'When I came to Queensland I could see from an outsider's point of view that Queenslanders were too desperate about what they wanted to achieve in cricket. They were desperate to win the Sheffield Shield, desperate for Matthew to play for Australia, desperate for new Test stars. It was all a bit much. It was not so much the campaign in the paper as the mentality of the state in general. I always felt Matthew would get there in his own good time and to push him would have been counterproductive to his learning curve.'

I know the campaign really got under the skin of the ACB,

which I suppose was partially what it was meant to do. I found that out a few years later, when at my instigation I flew to meet ACB boss Malcolm Speed. I was still struggling to get Australian selection and had a gnawing feeling that it might have been hindered by the fact that I'd upset someone or even several people in power.

Looking back on it, I'm reminded of the value of face-to-face contact. We now live in an age where people can hide behind emails and text messages, and I'll always be grateful that meeting was in person. Speed said later, 'I was new in the job – Matthew didn't know me and I didn't know him, so I suppose he was taking a bit of a risk. But I respected him for doing it. The only other player who approached me for a similar conversation while I was in the job was Justin Langer.'

Speed didn't say much at the time, but he did mention the 'Matt the Bat' campaign. 'Hang on a minute,' I said. 'It wasn't my campaign. It was done by News Limited, who I understand you have a good relationship with.' The visit cleared the air. Speed let me know he had no problem with me, nor was there a hidden reason for me being passed over for selection. My time would come.

I don't know whether the 'Matt the Bat' campaign had an effect or not, but I did make the Australian squad in the summer of 1993–94, shoehorned into a outfit with a strange look about it. It had five opening batsmen – Boon, Tubby, Slats, Mark Waugh and me. Dad, Mum and Gaz considered my first game on Australian soil in Australian colours to be such a big occasion that they drove from Brisbane to Adelaide to see me make an unbeaten 50 against New Zealand.

At that point in my career some people claimed I was

wooden, and I took no offence for a good reason – I *was* wooden. As much as I felt ready for big-time cricket and desperate for any opportunity that came my way, I also knew I was far from the finished product. I was risk-averse. My bat swung like a pendulum. The issue was my home ground, the Gabba. I'd developed what I thought was a water-tight technique to survive, based on my knowledge of that ground. My footwork was set up so I could let go the many baited hooks dangled outside the batsman's off stump on Australia's most demanding seaming wicket. Really, I wanted to play the role of enforcer, and deep down felt I had the potential to do so, but at the Gabba the first thing you have to do is not get out. To achieve what I wanted in cricket, I had to have a solid defensive game. Before you can do the fancy interior decorating you must slap down the bricks and mortar. If that meant being slightly wooden and mechanical for the time being, so be it. To me, the far greater crime would have been to be too loose.

Over the next few years, I broadened my game. A slight change of grip enabled me to get more power on the ball. I started to hit the ball around corners, and suddenly leg-side play, once a weakness, became a strength. I was proud of the fact that my proficiency against spin bowling – a clear weakness early in my career – became one of my greatest strengths later on. People have often said to me it must have killed me to play just seven Tests in the six years after I was first chosen for Australia, but it didn't. I was so dedicated to improving myself that I actually found those years rewarding.

12

First Test – Fire in the Bullring

'You're playing and you're opening!'

These five simple words rocked my world when captain Allan Border delivered them in his firm, forthright tone at the Wanderers Stadium, Johannesburg, before play on day one of the First Test against South Africa. It was 4 March 1994.

Players dream about their first Test appearance. It's usually the culmination of a week that starts with the uplifting announcement of the team and peaks in the grand moment when you walk out for the first time wearing your newly presented Test cap. Any last-minute issues tend to revolve around bowlers, so debutant batsmen usually get a few days to prepare themselves mentally. Not in my case. After so much waiting and hoping, I wasn't ready for the moment when it suddenly came.

When you're in a touring squad, all players are technically on standby to play until the first ball is bowled. I was officially covering for Mark Waugh, who had an injured thumb. It was my elevation, Dean Jones later said, that prompted him to retire mid-tour. He said that if an opening batsman was placed on standby ahead of a middle-order player, he felt he knew which way the wind was blowing. But I'd had dinner with Junior the night before and he'd told me, 'Don't get all keen, because I'm going to play. It's sore but I can bat with it.' I mentally consigned myself to the bench. Junior was always as straight as a railway sleeper – if he said he would play, he would play. And he did.

What I didn't know until match morning was that Tubby Taylor had been sick overnight with a virus. I'd watched him during the warm-up and still thought he would play. The first sign that he wouldn't came about 10 minutes before the toss, when he went into the dressing-room. AB emerged a few minutes later and delivered his news abruptly. He was under pressure, having just lost his vice-captain for one of his most important Tests as captain. There were none of the customary pleasantries such as, 'Well done, mate, you really deserve this.' There was no time. The mood was one of grim intensity rather than celebration. While AB was in full battle mode I was in full bench mode, and he surely must have noticed my jaw drop to somewhere near my waist.

I was so unprepared to play I didn't even have a thigh pad. I had ordered one from the cricket shop at the Wanderers earlier and said to them, 'There's no rush, it doesn't have to be today, I'm not going to play.' My mind just wasn't where it needed to be. I felt rushed. I *was* rushed. So rushed, in fact, that there wasn't even time for a phone call home – and there was certainly no tweeting in those days. (Fortunately, tour manager Dr Cam Battersby rang Kell, who phoned Mum and Dad on the farm to tell them the news.) I felt a bit like a student going into that crucial final exam without having done the required study.

I always prided myself on being prepared for any challenge, yet on the biggest day of my career to date, I wasn't.

Apart from the thigh pad drama, I hadn't done any homework on the venue. I'd never played there before and it's a very hard place to prepare for: it doesn't quite have the pace and bounce of Perth, but it's not far from it. And it wasn't just the venue that was a mystery to me, but the entire country. South Africa itself, now so familiar and close to my heart, was then a very foreign land. That day, to my great relief, we lost the toss and were fielding first, so I had a day extra to prepare.

I was stoked to be playing but because of my mild shock the game remains something of a blur. One indelible memory is of my first ball in Test cricket, delivered by Allan Donald. We'd done strong work in the field to bowl South Africa out for 251 and Donald was revved up to make sure my welcome to Test cricket was as inhospitable as possible. His first ball to me was one of the finest bouncers I faced in Test cricket, an Adam's-apple-seeking missile that my defensive scramble somehow managed to fend off. He followed up with the mandatory, 'Welcome to Test cricket, son,' and I replied, 'Well bowled,' hardly a line to have him recoiling in fear, but the best I could squeeze out at the time.

Slats was shooting bullets like a Wild West gunfighter at the other end, making 26 off 32 balls, but he left before I did. I made just 15 in 15 overs before sparring at a wide ball from Donald and edging behind. I felt starved of scoring opportunities – and it was a measure of the size of the step up from first-class cricket. That innings we managed 248 to South Africa's 251, but lost our foothold in the match in their second innings, when they were bowled out for 450.

For me, disaster struck on the second ball of the second

innings, when Donald arrowed another short ball at my heart. I got rid of it but it cracked my left thumb and I knew instantly I was in serious trouble. It left me in a quandary. I was badly injured but I didn't want to call out for help – that'd be like washing your cut hand in the water when there's a great white shark in the area. Donald, who was already far too fired up for my liking, would target me even more.

Glumly, I reasoned that this would be the last Test I'd play on tour – maybe my last, full stop. But I'd worked so hard for this chance that I simply couldn't walk away from it. I batted on, hoping the pain would subside, but had no control at all with my lower hand and finally dragged a ball from Fanie de Villiers onto my stumps. My two innings had netted just 15 and 5, and as I walked up the infamously long, open-aired players' race to the dressing-room, surrounded by the boisterous crowd, I was consumed by one dismal thought: *What a poor Test.*

Someone wrote that one consoling feature of my debut was that I made one more run than Don Bradman on his Test debut in Brisbane in 1928–29, when he scored 18 and 1 against England on a sticky track and was subsequently dropped. But I was beyond any consolation, particularly after I was taken to hospital for X-rays that revealed a double break of my left thumb. All the momentum of a storming domestic summer, which had realised 1136 first-class runs from six matches, vanished into Johannesburg's thin air. Had the injury happened in today's team I would have been sent home. But I stayed, unable to practise or do much at all. Boonie had a saying that there was no such thing as a hero in Test cricket, which basically means if you're injured, get off the ground. Later in my career I'd have followed his advice and simply retired hurt.

Fifteen years after my debut, I watched young Phil Hughes get a duck in his first Test, also at the Wanderers, flashing at a short ball. The memories flooded back, so I sent him a text saying something like, 'Stress less, mate. I know how you feel. It happened to me as well.'

In that series Australia lost the First Test, won the Second and drew the Third – which turned out to be AB's farewell match, though we didn't know it at the time. My main memory of the days after the First Test are not of my own mood but of AB's – he was livid we'd lost. I felt like a choirboy who'd been roused on by the master, and I trod very warily when the captain was around.

AB felt we were getting caught up in our own importance on a tour during which we were treated like rock stars, and there was an element of truth to that. I can't recall any other tour I've been part of where the visiting side was so warmly embraced by the locals. We were the first Australian team to visit South Africa post-apartheid, and the South African people almost killed us with enthusiasm. They were hungry for international cricket and their appetite had been whetted by the rugged one-all series the two sides had just played in Australia. This ramped up the pressure on us to perform, and even Warnie, who was well on his way to superstardom, admitted he was feeling it, saying during an interview, 'I feel as if I'm burning up inside.'

South Africans may have been keen for cricket, but they could also prove hostile in some respects. Merv Hughes was fined for bashing his bat on the side of the players' race at the Wanderers Stadium, protesting against abuse from local fans. I couldn't condone his behaviour, but I could genuinely relate to his frustration. There were plenty of interesting places to visit in South Africa, but that race was not one of them. For any Australian player it was the ugliest 40-metre walk of your cricketing life. You'd be spat on, have drinks poured on you or South African flags waved in your face. And there was nowhere to hide. After frequent player protests, the race was eventually covered, but it was too late for Merv. When Australia won a Test at the Wanderers a few years later, we made a point of going down to the race after dark to sing our victory song, 'Beneath the Southern Cross'. We felt like a group of soldiers who'd kicked down the door of the enemy bunker and were parading the Australian flag inside.

That South African tour was also a fascinating – and at times shocking – cultural experience. Soon after arriving, some of the boys checked in at a hotel where people were asked to leave their handguns at the door. Although apartheid was over, there were still stark reminders everywhere you went. When our team visited the Afrikaner stronghold of Bloemfontein, I watched from the bus in bewilderment as 'coloured' people and 'white' people walked on opposite sides of the street. I clearly remember thinking, *I'm on a different planet here*. But in contrast to this, the enormous charisma and presence of Nelson Mandela was felt throughout the entire country during that tour. We could sense it, even in simple conversations with South African people. Whenever any type of discussion about race took place, you felt a sense of calm as soon as his name was mentioned. It was as if everyone felt at ease at the thought of Mandela – such was his power.

It was during that tour that I was contacted by Pierre Tostee, a photographer and former professional surfer, who asked to have a surf with me and do a story on it. I couldn't have been happier to oblige. We established an instant connection and have been mates ever since. In 1986 'Toast' had endured one of most bizarre experiences any sportsman – or anyone – could imagine. He was surfing at a tournament in Newcastle, Australia, when he took a break before the next heat and stood on a rock ledge beside 14-year-old Matthew Cougle, who was minding Toast's board. It was a clear day, barring one small, black cloud that was floating harmlessly by, when, to everyone's amazement, a bolt of lightning shot out of it and struck Toast and Matthew. Toast was knocked unconscious but recovered quickly and gave Matthew, who was in a worse state, mouth-to-mouth. He feared his young friend had died. Although Matthew stayed in a coma for three days, he made a full recovery. As Toast and I surfed together at Durban late in the tour, we both shaped up to catch the same wave but I hesitated for a moment as he took off. 'You snooze, you lose,' he quipped as he surged away towards the shore. The comment stayed with me and I couldn't help relating it back to my first Test preparation. I had snoozed and I lost.

A small consolation came later in the tour when I replaced Dean Jones in the one-day squad. Given how disappointing my South African tour had been, I gained some confidence by performing well in the one-day series, held in Sharjah in the United Arab Emirates. I managed 67 against New Zealand then a free-swinging 48 off 46 balls against India in my two innings – progress at last.

At least, it seemed that way. I didn't play another one-day game for Australia for six years.

13

Mozzie Bites – Secrets of a Bulls' Stampede

I can still hear the giggles and see the smirks when the news came through – the Queensland cricket team were henceforth to be known as the Bulls. I was on the 1993 Ashes tour in London when the announcement was made. For a few days the Queenslanders in the squad – Healy, Hayden, Border and McDermott – weren't so much the Bulls as the Sitting Ducks or the Clay Pigeons. We were under fire from all directions. 'The Bullshitters . . . certainly got a ring to it,' was the kind of comment coming from the likes of Steve Waugh, who devoted a substantial portion of his cricketing life to playfully tormenting Queenslanders.

The Bulls were early adopters. These days every team has an emblem, but back then no one did. It just wasn't cricket. It was like someone walking out to bat in a Test wearing short pants. But I loved it. As much as the old maroon caps with big Q on the front of them had a noble look and a good feel, I remember really identifying with the new cap with the stern-faced bull the first time I saw it. Our only awkward moment with the new emblem came courtesy of a 1035 kg Santa Gertrudis bull that was paraded at the season launch the following summer and provided an unofficial christening when it dropped a giant, steaming cow pat during the parade. One southern cynic said the only difference was that Queensland teams normally did that at the end rather than the start of the season!

Being a country boy, I liked the strength and character of the bull emblem, and I say with pride that the ultimate vindication of the name change came as everyone else followed our lead: other states, English counties, South African provinces, IPL teams. They all jumped on the emblem bandwagon. In fact, cricket's got to the stage where you wouldn't dream of starting a team without a emblem, even though less than two decades ago you wouldn't think of having one. The move was the brainchild of forward-thinking Queensland marketing man Andrew Blucher. When I retired from Australian cricket, I mentioned Andrew among the many officials who had helped me in the game. He's barely been recognised for his groundbreaking initiative, so I felt he deserved a pat on the back.

The large NSW contingent in our '93 Ashes squad – is it ever *not* a large contingent? – always felt they had the upper hand in interstate banter because of one indisputable fact: Queensland had never won the Shield. But in the 1994–95 season final at the Gabba, we finally broke the 68-year drought by thumping South Australia by an innings and 101 runs. The tone of the match was set early when South Australia was dismissed for 214. Tank and I put on 144 for the first wicket, and the innings just sailed away to 664, allowing fans a boisterous five-day party to blissfully sweep away those sorrowful demons accrued over seven painful decades.

The six hours or so in the Queensland dressing-room after we won the Shield were among the most enjoyable of my career, right up there with World Cup and Ashes wins. The sense of euphoria, mateship and devotion to a common cause in the face of adversity was overwhelming. The outpouring of emotion from former players entering the dressing-room was wonderful, too. Bill Brown, Sam Trimble and Peter Burge came in, and there were even three cheers for Chilla Christ, the Queensland Shield paceman of the 1930s, who, then in his eighties, was helped into the rooms by former players Mike Lucas and Peter Allan. Premier Wayne Goss got sprayed with a can of beer and said he planned to get his shirt framed – unwashed – in recognition of the celebration.

Being in the rooms after the Shield win was as good as singing the Australian team song in the Lord's dressing-room after an Ashes Test win, and you can't get much better than that. I'm not one for having cricket memorabilia in my house, but if there's one photo I really cherish, it's the one of Carl Rackemann taking the final catch of the match to dismiss Jason Gillespie. Another picture that's part of the same set was taken a few seconds later, when thousands of people stormed onto the Gabba. Every Queensland cricket fan probably knows someone in that photo. We all remembered the heartbreaking scenes of Rackemann leaving the SCG in tears after Queensland's one-wicket loss in the final against NSW a decade before. He was just about to join the South African rebels and feared he might never play for Queensland again. When teams like South Australia came to the Gabba, Rackemann terrorised them with his extra bounce. Even outstanding players like Jamie Siddons just had no answer to him.

When we won the Shield, Carl's only regret was missing the celebrations – he was whisked off to the West Indies as a late replacement for Craig McDermott, who hurt his ankle jumping off an ocean wall in Guyana. Wearing state gear on national duty is something you generally don't do, but Carl turned up for his first Caribbean breakfast proudly wearing his 'Year of the Bulls . . . Shield Champions' shirt.

The entire culture of Queensland cricket was changing and I loved it. We confronted all sorts of historical hurdles – playing spin, playing away from home, winning after Christmas – and one by one they were swept away. New coach John 'Buck' Buchanan recruited psychologist Phil Jauncey to the team staff, in a move that took us to another level. We were suddenly ahead of our time. I enjoyed Jauncey's talks so much I made notes and took them on tour. I'm not a big team-meeting man, but I revelled in Jauncey's talks because they were relevant and stimulating, with fascinating insights into how you could get inside a teammate's head, and undermine a rival by doing the same. For once that tortured sporting cliché 'mind games' had genuine meaning.

Jauncey was very close to Broncos' coach Wayne Bennett, and had first applied his psychological theories in sport when Bennett wanted to understand more about individual personalities in his team. Bennett was rotating two of his team's hookers – Greg Conescu and Kerrod Walters – and found that their vastly different personalities made the players around them play differently. Phil explained to us that personalities could basically be split into four types: the 'feelers', the sensitive types among us who worry about what people think of them; the 'enforcers', who like to dominate; the 'thinkers', who sit there and methodically work something out; and the 'mozzies', who are the instinct players, buzzing around like mosquitoes, going on gut feeling. It helped us understand each other and, just as significantly, understand rival teams, not by the customary method of assessing their techniques, but by analysing what was going on inside their helmets.

I was a classic enforcer who liked to dominate. Andrew Symonds and Jimmy Maher were mozzies, the boys who just went out and played and didn't think too much about it. Martin Love was a thinker, and Adam Dale was a feeler. People used to stir him because they knew he felt everything, and once our profiling confirmed this, he copped even more – but he seemed to handle it okay. There's also a part of the feelers that loves being the centre of attention. In later profile assessments, 'Chippin' Dale deliberately tried to manipulate his answers so he didn't come across as a feeler – which, of course, only confirmed what a true feeler he was.

The system gave us a fabulous insight into human nature and we felt like amateur psychologists. It drew us together and we hatched all sorts of novel plans to undermine our opponents. We knew Mike Hussey was a thinker-feeler, which meant he was fairly sensitive. So our plan was to hit him with full-blown harassment. Symo would get in his ear and count his dot balls to remind him how defensively he was playing, or just start talking to him and wearing him down. It seemed to work every time. In fact, Huss's first eight scores against Queensland in the Sheffield Shield were 7, 5, 4, 31, 15, 2, 12 and 1. This from a batsman who would dominate international cricket a decade later. We derailed his confidence badly. Even though he never chirped you back – or perhaps because of it – you just knew every word was getting in and staying in.

Dean Jones was an enforcer, but he also liked to be liked, and we all knew he loved AB. Thus AB would make a point of not talking to him and, soon enough, Deano would become a bit concerned. He'd ask our fieldsmen, 'What's the matter with AB?' When they'd say, 'He's fine . . . just talk to him,' Deano would say, 'No, no, I know what he's like in these moods,' and this very conversation would prove he was getting distracted.

Mark Waugh was a classic mozzie who played purely on instinct. We'd bowl wide outside the off stump to him, knowing that he just loved feeling bat on ball, and he would eventually succumb to temptation.

Steve Waugh was an enforcer and a thinker, a structured player. To counteract this, we'd be totally unstructured and bowl over the wicket to him, then around the wicket, then over the wicket, changing for no apparent reason – anything to challenge his routine and make him wonder, *What's going on here?* Being the sharp-eyed observer he was, Steve figured it out. A few years later, when Buck applied for the national coaching job, Steve was apparently a supporting voice, telling senior officials that they should look for a forward-thinking coach like Buchanan and 'not a seventies-style coach'.

When discussing players at our team meetings we'd say things like, 'Let's take a punt on him being an enforcer,' and drag out our enforcer profiles. Enforcers like me would be asked, 'So, what would you like least?' and I would say, 'Bowling wide to stop me from controlling things and dominating play . . . and maybe random fielders who don't do anything but are just there.'

Darren Lehmann was an enforcer who loved challenges. So we'd stack the off side behind point for his beloved cut shot and drop provocative lines like, 'Even you couldn't find a gap through there, Boof.' He would relish the challenge of doing so. Sometimes he was simply too good. Sometimes we got him. But it was always worth a try. Even my mate Justin Langer was a target. We chirped him because we always felt he would lose control and get emotional and punchy. Alfie is at his best when he is happy and smiling – even though that isn't necessarily what he might be feeling inside. He could be inwardly churning, but if he's smiling it means he's telling himself, *Everything is okay*, and that's when he's at his most dangerous. We used to stir him up in the hope his blood would boil and he'd start fighting not only us, but his own emotions.

It was during this 1994–95 season that my brother Gary moved from Brisbane to North Queensland with his wife Alex. Without even realising it, I suddenly found that my preparation for games wasn't what it had been and my form dropped accordingly. My season bottomed out in Adelaide, where I made a pair against South Australia, twice falling to airy drives in a match Queensland lost by an innings. It hurt, because I always considered Adelaide a heavenly place to bat. The season before I'd made 165 and 116 there.

The occasion of my first and only first-class pair did not pass without official recognition from my teammates. A gift wrapped in brown paper was delivered to my hotel room, containing three ornamental ducks and a message, penned by Jimmy Maher and Allan Border. 'Welcome to our exclusive duck club. Bring a partner. Come as a pair. On the menu we have Peking duck, double duck burger . . . You'll find us at the corner of Zero St and Duck Terrace.' Jimmy had even contemplated buying two live ducks and letting them loose in my hotel room before deciding it probably wouldn't thrill the hotel staff.

I had to laugh – what else could you do? – but when we arrived in Hobart for our next game on tour I taped the ducks to the lid of my coffin as a sort of voodoo symbol that I was ready to pass on to whoever made the next duck. Of course it had to be Mahbo, and I made an official presentation to him in the dressing-room after play. He sombrely put the ducks in his coffin.

Buck struck gold in his first year of big-time coaching with our first Shield win. Despite impressing as coach of University in Brisbane grade cricket, he had still been a surprise appointment for the job, which was his first major step towards the Australian role he later filled for eight years. I felt instantly comfortable with his style. Where Thommo gave me freedom, Buck gave me something even more important – structure. He looked at what a player like me needed to fire – a ball machine, video analysis of rival players and perhaps a psychologist to help me cope with the strain of being on the periphery of national selection – and put all of them at my disposal.

Thommo was a 'play hard, train hard, celebrate hard' sort of coach. Players like Stuey Law worked well with that style, but someone like spin bowler Paul Jackson found he'd needed more. Under Thommo, Jacko was a 70 per cent player. Buck elevated him to 90 per cent of what he could be by giving him a clearly defined role in the team and the confidence to pull it off. This ability to lift fringe players to a higher level was one of Buck's biggest triumphs at state level. Jacko came from Victoria, where he had been simply judged on runs and wickets, and he was low on confidence when he landed in Queensland in 1992. Buck changed Jacko's view of himself by redefining the terms on which he was assessed.

Buck noted that Carl Rackemann and Jacko had the best strike rate of any bowling partnership for Queensland in 1994–95, and pointed that out to Jacko in post-game assessments, particularly when Jacko was feeling down on his own figures. Buck also called Jacko his 'partnership batsman', and in noting the amount of profitable partnerships he had shared, encouraged him to work out ways to get off strike. He enhanced Jacko's self-esteem by consistently referring to him as the 'glue' of the team, making him boss of a new 'strategy group'. Not all of the strategy group's ideas came off – like one experiment where a net session was over if you got out twice – but for the first time players were given a sense of ownership of the team. And a team we truly were. Under Buck, our payment system changed from individual to team incentives.

Buck came along at the perfect time for me. I'd just lost Gaz, and Buck and his staff helped to fill that void. One of Buck's valued assistants, Jimmy Hunter, fed me thousands of balls and I consider him an unsung hero of my career.

As we celebrated our Shield win I was particularly pleased for Stuey Law, who I'd grown up and played with from my Valleys days. He was an exceptional cricketer, and I include him in a bunch of players such as Brad Hodge, Martin Love, Jamie Siddons and Darren Lehmann who all should have played much more international cricket than they did. We had some great moments taking the Sheffield Shield around Queensland. I remember visiting Ingham and displaying the Shield at the Ingham festival where Tina Arena sang. One of her big numbers was 'I'm In Chains' – the Queensland side was mightily relieved that ours had finally been broken.

14

A Spy Called Deano

There have been many stories written about John 'Buck' Buchanan's leaked and stolen game plans. But there's one story that has never been printed. Until now.

It happened in October 1995, when the Victorian Sheffield Shield team visited Brisbane. Dean Jones noticed a library of Queensland's video research at the back of the indoor nets at the Gabba. Overwhelmed by curiosity, Deano swiped the tape with 'Victoria' marked on it and watched it soon after, fast-forwarding to the part where we clinically dissected his cavalier game. Deano was at once affronted and highly motivated. The first thing he saw on the tape was himself playing a series of airy drives outside off stump and edging behind or to slips. He instantly realised our game plan was to bait him outside off stump and try to get him playing the shot he never felt comfortable with – the cover drive.

Deano was always his own man. He was one of the first players to wear sunglasses and it seemed the entire world branded him a lair as he sported his new Oakleys. Six months later, everyone was wearing them. That was Deano: a convention challenger. This day he challenged our notion of him.

'I thought, Stuff them, I'm just not going there,' he told me more than a decade later. 'I was really shocked by what I saw on that tape. These days every batsman is analysed and even Don Bradman would have his game picked apart. But back then it was pretty new and it challenged your ego, particularly when it was right. I couldn't cover drive and they knew it. They wanted me to cover drive, so I decided to bore them to death and just not play the shot. I bored everyone, even my own team, but I proved a point.'

He did, too, with an innings so tough it had a pigskin hide. It was a bonus for me that he swiped that tape, because it spurred him to produce a lesson in self-denial that left an indelible impression on my batting psyche. Despite receiving over after over, hour after hour, session after session of balls wide of off stump, Deano refused to bite. He made 145, and for me it was a priceless tutorial. I thought back to it many, many times, including just before my career-saving century at the Oval on the 2005 Ashes tour.

Sometimes, quite contemptuously, Deano wouldn't even bother shouldering arms or moving his feet as the ball went past. He'd just keep tapping the crease and act as if the ball hadn't been bowled, effectively saying, 'Bowl your crap wide line if you like – I'm not even going to look at it and I'm going to bat until you can't breathe.' Occasionally, when a ball passed unchallenged, he'd look over at me at gully and say, 'Mate, I'm not playing that game.'

Years later, he said that those of us – me included – who kept saying, 'You're going to get bored,' actually made him concentrate more. He said if we hadn't chirped him he probably *would* have got bored and got out. I got off on his contrariness that day, even as I rued his progress from my team's point of view.

They say pioneers always finish with spears in their backs, and Deano could certainly relate to that. But he was exactly the sort of player I wanted to be. I didn't want a foundation in my game like everyone else's. I didn't want to be a poor man's someone-else or a batsman who played a certain way just because people always played that way – that was part of the reason I played forward to almost every ball I faced. If I'd followed the leader, I wouldn't have been picked anyway.

Dean has always been very good to me. We have a connection through the Macquarie Bank Sports Foundation and our relationship is strong enough for him to be able to ring out of the blue and offer advice, without any fear that I'll be offended. During my last international season, for instance, he rang and said, 'Mate, you don't look as if you're having fun. Just go out and smash it, and once you do that, you'll inspire yourself and be the player you can be.'

When asked whether he felt any sense of shame over swiping the Bulls' tape, Dean didn't raise an eyebrow. 'Nah,' he said, laughing. 'Espionage is fun.'

15

A is for Acrimony

In the summer of 1994–95, Australian cricket's marketing men had a problem. England and Zimbabwe had been invited to join the Australian World Series Cup 50-over competition, but Zimbabwe were thought of as the competition easybeats and made the contenders for the finals too predictable. Australian cricket was so strong at the time it had become known that Australia could, if need be, field a second XI that would be instantly competitive on the world stage.

And so it proved. An Australia A side, captained by Damien Martyn and including the likes of Greg Blewett, Ricky Ponting, Merv Hughes, Paul Reiffel and me, performed strongly and knocked both Zimbabwe and England out of the competition, making the finals against an Australian side containing Slats, Boonie, Michael Bevan and my Queensland teammate Stuart Law. For the marketers it was the dream result – Australia A had beaten an England side containing Mike Atherton, Graham Gooch and Alec Stewart, and everyone enjoyed watching the men-in-waiting tackling the players blocking their path to the top.

In sport, civil wars and family feuds can be choice viewing if you're a spectator with no vested interest. But if you're a participant, it can be unnerving. As much as the A-team concept advanced the causes of several fringe players (particularly Greg Blewett, who was in exceptional form), it became an awkward series for all involved. The Australian team felt they had everything to lose, and rightly so. Winning earned them no plaudits, because they were supposed to win. Yet if they lost, their reputations would be tarnished and, in some cases, their futures on the line. Those of us in the A team had a lot to gain by winning, but there was also that uncomfortable feeling that we were alienating those in the team we really wanted to play for. There were some high-spirited clashes – some off the field, some on it. We played Australia four times – including two clashes in the finals – and lost all four. But they were bare-knuckle affairs, much closer than the final margins indicated.

Because I knew the top team so well, I also knew how to press their buttons, and the temptation was too great to refuse against someone like my Queensland teammate Craig McDermott. I knew how structured he was, from the way he arranged his socks in the dressing-room to the routines and rhythms of his bowling. His routine was both his strength and a potential soft spot.

When Billy was ready to bowl, he wanted you to be ready too. So I made sure I wasn't. He'd be back at his mark ready to charge in as I dawdled and fidgeted and did everything but bring out a deckchair – stretching, checking the field, taking block, anything I could think of to slow him down. I'd look up, see him becoming progressively angrier at the top of his mark, and offer an innocent 'What's your problem?' shrug of the shoulders.

Australian captain Mark Taylor was never at ease with the A-team concept and said so publicly on several occasions, feeling it just wasn't right to have local crowds not supporting the main Australian team. Australians being Australians, the crowds rallied behind the underdog and took sneaky pleasure in seeing the top side stretched. Steve Waugh captained Australia during one match in Sydney and afterwards said, 'I felt we had at least three or four supporters tonight.'

Our first contest in Adelaide was a thriller. Australia won by six runs and it was a hard slog all the way on a difficult pitch that yielded just 15 fours for the match. The crowd gave us raucous support, which Tubby took objection to. He spoke out strongly against the concept. 'I didn't enjoy the game,' he said. 'I don't like playing against my own players. I don't like it when the crowd doesn't support us when we play at home. I can't blame the crowd. I don't think they should have been made to choose whether to back Australia or the other Australian team. They [Australia A] are probably more jovial in their rooms than we are in ours, and we're the winners. I'd be surprised if the Australia A thing happens again.' It didn't.

During that tournament, the tension boiled over between Tubby Taylor and me. My Queensland and Australia A teammate Greg Rowell bowled like the wind that series, and even though his figures didn't show it, he was really testing Australia. Tubby flexed his muscles as captain and said something to Rowell in one match, to which I replied, 'What are you talking about? You've got one crap shot, a little pull over mid wicket, and you're putting the crowd to sleep. Shut up and bat.' After the game I went into the Australian dressing-room, where coach Geoff Marsh and Tubby were talking. I half-interrupted them because I thought

I heard something said about me. Tubby erupted, saying, 'As for you, you're the ringleader in all this trouble.' I said, 'I don't give a stuff, mate. You are an embarrassment.' We parted on that frosty note and I returned to the Australia A dressing-room. Stephen Waugh came into our room soon after and said to me, 'Take it easy. Don't worry. Tubby will get over it.'

Stephen looks back at the incident with a smile. 'I remember feeling at the time that a player had a right to declare he wanted your spot. It's competition, and that's what I was trying to get across to Haydos that night. I didn't feel he had to apologise for his attitude. That's the way it should be. If you're good enough, come and get it. I have never had a problem with that and I know what it's like to be in both positions.'

I never quite restored my relations with Tubby, and never thought I enjoyed his confidence. Now we are both directors on the Cricket Australia board, and I believe we'll work really well together, offering positive things for the development of Australian cricket. During our playing days, however, I felt Tubby did everything in his power not to let me into that Australian side. I don't blame him for that – he was Australian captain, a good one at that, and had a lot to fight for. There were sheep stations on the line in those years, or at least that's how it felt to me. But I don't regret throwing down the challenge.

I played in a competitive era when our greatest opponents were often other Australians, rather than the rest of the world. Stuart Law's biggest rivals were the Waugh brothers. Darren Lehmann and Jamie Siddons could tell a similar tale and Brad Hodge could easily nominate Ricky Ponting as the man who stood between him and a long Test career. The hardest part of international cricket for players like these was getting the chance to play at all.

I've lost count of the number of times I've heard the statement – said of many other players as well as me – 'Bad luck, mate . . . you'd make any other side on earth.' I was unashamedly competitive. Whether it was Mark Taylor or even my great mate Justin Langer in front of me, I wanted to win the battle, even though I learnt in time that these man-on-man contests brought out the absolute worst in my game. For most of my time in the wings, Mark was the man blocking my path. Between the years 1994 and 1999, the year Tubby retired, I played seven Tests. After he retired, I played 86 in a row.

During the Australia A series, I also had an infamous blue with Glenn McGrath in Sydney. The incident said everything about the tension in the air as our team – the young guns – tried to blast the top guns off their pedestal. I cut McGrath to the fence, and when I crossed after my first run, he shouldered me, which made me say something like, 'Mate, if you ever do that again I'm going to punch your head in.' He responded by telling me where to go. That was it. I'm told people watching the game through binoculars noticed Stephen Waugh smiling broadly at gully, and I can imagine him enjoying the theatre of it all, but it was no joke to us. I was batting with Marto, and he could sense both McGrath and I were bristling with anger. He tried to rescue me by saying, 'Mate, just let it go.'

Fifteen years after the incident, McGrath and his children, Holly and James, visited our family in Brisbane. We had the television on in the background that day, and the cricket had been washed out. Guess what they played instead? At the same time we both realised what was coming up and said, 'Oh . . . this isn't the one where . . .?' Sure enough, it was. We dropped what we were doing and watched it. The sniping started immediately – 'You're a wanker', 'You definitely did that' – and we laughed our way through it. Even after 15 years there was no resolution, and I'm sure there won't be after another 15 either.

When I watch the replay now I shake my head – try that sort of thing on today and you could write your own ticket for how long you'd be banned, or how much you'd get fined. We copped nothing, owing to a quirk in the system. The match referee, New Zealand's John Reid, learnt that because it wasn't officially an international game (games in that series with Australia A weren't considered official internationals), he had no jurisdiction – much to his frustration and our relief. He could scold us until paint flaked off the walls, but he could go no further. The hearing into the incident was held an hour after the game and I was on my second beer at the time, so I took it in with me. I still remember Reid's disgust at my apparent disrespect. 'You're not here for a bloody holiday – put that down, son,' he said, nodding towards my stubby.

Beneath the aggro of the stoush, there was a method in my apparent madness. I felt the best way to handle McGrath was to unsettle him, rather than yield to him and let him dictate terms, as teams so often seemed to. The yielding tactic was always a huge mistake. You could say the same about the way teams tackled Warne. Warne and McGrath were masters of their craft and, generally, masters of their own destiny. They had beautiful control, which in turn gave them control of the people they bowled to. But if someone wrested control back for a while, it took them out of their comfort zone and they could get a bit frazzled – they were only human, after all. Sit back and let them run the show – as most did – and you might as well put your head on the chopping block and hand them an axe.

Jason Gillespie was a different type of bowler. He just did what he did. If it happened, then all well and good. If not, he'd keep thumping away. He loved hard rock, but rocking the man himself was no easy task. Trying to take him down with blatant aggression at the prime of his career wouldn't have rattled him in the way that it might've got you a bit of leverage against McGrath and Warne. Brett Lee was different as well. He was quick, but batsmen felt they could wear him down and that he might not be as effective as the other three through the back parts of the game. When McGrath and Warne and Gillespie were together, there was simply no respite for batsmen. It was like having three hands on your neck and the choker hold applied.

At his absolute best, McGrath was a cool killer, so if he got angry or down on himself, it was a significant victory for the batsman. I certainly hadn't planned the physical contact that day, but I was mindful of how important it was to hold my own. It wasn't my style to lie there and become 'Door Matt' Hayden.

INSIDE THE GAME

Getting Out

I'm the first to admit that I wasn't a man to be trifled with when I got out. The boys knew I was not up for small talk after arriving back in the rooms. Even now that my first-class career is over, I'm still filthy when I get out.

Sometimes I could control myself. Sometimes not. There was a notorious incident in Sydney, when I came into the dressing-room and unleashed a mighty right-foot kick that left my foot wedged in an oval-shaped hole I'd blasted in the back of a chair. I raged around the room like a man hopping on hot coals, but the harder I tried to shed the chair, the more firmly it seemed attached. In my peripheral vision, I could see blokes trying not to laugh at the sight of my new footwear. Eventually I surrendered to the hopelessness of my predicament, lay on the ground and burst out laughing, prompting everyone to do the same. Stephen Waugh came to my rescue and pulled the chair off my foot, mumbling something like, 'You nuffy,' with that crooked-mouthed grin of his. Even after this experience, I didn't lose my habit of kicking things in disgruntlement until I finally broke my toe kicking my gear coffin.

Huge amounts of adrenalin can run through your body when you get out, giving you a false sense of bravado and making the risk of injury very real. Greg Ritchie once needed stitches in his face when splinters flew from the bat he'd broken against a concrete post in the old Gabba dressing-room, and many a cricketer has done serious damage to an inanimate object in venting their frustrations. My philosophy was 'better out than in', for better or worse. If I didn't let my frustrations out, they'd force themselves out later. Usually my dressing-room explosions saw my innermost feelings vented – ones I hadn't let into my conscious thoughts pre-innings for fear of distraction. Reviewing what I'd said later – almost as if I was a detached observer – often helped me understand who or what was bothering me.

I wasn't the only man to avoid in the dressing-room after getting out. Michael Bevan was in a league of his own. I can still see him walking off after a one-day game, not even getting changed, grabbing a chair and sitting under a shower, yelling, 'WHAT ARE YOU PLAYING FOR?' Glenn McGrath was an interesting case study. There were times when Pigeon would still be shattered from getting out when he was bowling with the new ball 10 minutes later. Given Pigeon's limited batting abilities, I reckon just getting out alive would be reason to celebrate. Maybe his feelings were tied in with the bowlers' need to use whatever he could to fire himself up.

The funniest incident I ever saw involving a player getting out was in a county game in England during the 1993 Ashes tour. Bob Simpson had given the team a lecture about how bat throwing was a bad habit that too many of us were getting into. 'It's just not how you go about it,' Simmo said. 'If you're *that* disappointed then go to the nets.' Warnie must have been out of the room when the lecture was delivered, because after being dismissed that day, he threw his bat with great force into his coffin – which in those days had a hard cover on it. That was bad news for Simmo, because the bat rebounded off the coffin and sped like one of William Tell's arrows straight into the coach's shin. It was a bit like a schoolmaster warning children in the playground to stop throwing water bombs then copping one in the head as soon as his back was turned.

Simmo may have been one of cricket's hardest men (at fielding training, when Merv Hughes was catching returns, he'd sometimes mischievously let one go and it would hit Simmo on the body or the head; the old fella never flinched), but the day Warnie's bat flew into his shin, his Scottish blood boiled. He erupted, grabbed the bat and started belting Warnie's coffin.

I wasn't playing in the game so I had the worst seat in the dressing-room, near the door – and because the room was so small, you couldn't escape Simmo's fury. Tim May, Steve Waugh and I sat there with faces as white as the sightboard as we watched him in full flight. Champion axemen at the Brisbane Exhibition would have been outmuscled by Simmo that day. While he was thrashing away, no one dared laugh, but once he left the room we all exploded. Warnie, inevitably, got away with it. In fact, given that that was his breakthrough tour featuring his famous 'ball of the century', I reckon he could have stolen the crown jewels and been forgiven, such was his status as the game's new golden boy.

The coolest players I ever saw after they got out were Paul Reiffel and Mark Waugh. Pistol would return to the room much like a public servant returning from lunch. One minute his seat would be empty, the next there he was, quiet and undemonstrative. Junior Waugh was a classic when he got out because he always believed it was never his fault, which apparently prevented him brooding: if he never made a mistake, how could he be out of form? After reverse-sweeping Phil Tufnell onto his stumps when on 99 during the 1993 Lord's Test, Junior returned to the dressing-room, watched the replay, and complained incredulously, 'I just can't believe that ball hit the stumps!' A couple of the boys started laughing and one said, 'Have you ever played that shot before?' and when Junior said, 'No . . . never,' they laughed ever more. 'Practised it in the nets maybe?' 'Not really.'

Adam Gilchrist was an interesting post-dismissal study. A very emotional cricketer, Gilly could be either genuinely spewing or not too bad at all, but rarely in between. He was generally unflappable, but wicketkeeping setbacks affected him deeply. He would brood on them and get horribly down on himself. I had a feeling that a bad missed catch cost him hours of sleep in the middle of the night. He was a very proud keeper. So proud, in fact, that a dropped catch in his final Test at the Adelaide Oval prompted him to leave the game. He had high standards.

16

Lamb to the Slaughter

As a cricketer, I was often accused of being too arrogant. Once, though, I was accused of being too timid, and by someone I really respected – Allan Border. AB took me to task in a column he wrote just before the 1996 Boxing Day Test, when Matthew Elliott had been ruled out by injury. I'd been making plenty of runs for Queensland but was still being downbeat about my selection prospects, saying, 'I've learnt not to expect anything.' AB wrote, 'I would like to see him say, "Pick me, I have been ready for years!"' Fair enough. That was how I felt too, although I'd reached a point where I hardly dared to say it.

Earlier in the summer, Australia made the bold move to drop Michael Slater, despite him averaging over 47 for his first 34 Tests, deciding it was time to replace him with an ambitious young left-hander – sadly, not yours truly, but my Victorian rival Matthew Elliott, who joined Mark Taylor at the top of the order for the domestic Test series against the West Indies. I'd given it my best shot in an Australian XI game against the West Indies in

Hobart, where I made 224 and Elliott made 158. Despite this, the media seemed to find his innings much better than mine. Admittedly, he was a fine player with a very good record, and perhaps he seemed the fresher, brighter choice because I'd been in contention for the Test side a while longer than him. I felt as if I'd given everything and had a right to believe, at the very least, I was on level terms with Elliott, but he got the nod ahead of me. Experiences like this made me tentative in public statements, and even after I became a fixture in the Australian team, I always used expressions like 'If I make the Ashes tour . . .' or 'If I go to South Africa . . .' – even if my last start was a century or I was in the form of my life.

The Queensland press was not so restrained. On 8 December 1996, Brisbane's *Sunday Mail* printed a letter that people were encouraged to send to the ACB. It started with the line, 'Dear Australian selectors, I believe Matt Hayden deserves to open the batting in the Third Test against the West Indies because . . .' ACB staff were less than impressed to see hundreds of these flooding their office when they arrived at work the next morning.

When Elliott was ruled out following a knee injury sustained in the Second Test when he had collided with Mark Waugh while running between wickets, Kell and I knew that I was a chance to get the nod in the Boxing Day Test. While I was trying not to get my hopes up, Kell ploughed through the mothballs to get my blazer from the 1994 South African tour and hung it in the hallway while I was out doing an errand. When I returned and saw it, I felt a dull ache in the pit of my stomach. It was a bit like admiring the suit you'd bought for the graduation ball, then remembering you weren't going to graduate. But 15 minutes later the phone rang, and chairman of selectors Trevor Hohns was on the line saying, 'I have some good news for you . . .' Cracker Hohns later told people, 'I'd delivered [Hayden] a lot of bad news over the years so it was a nice feeling to give him some good news.' I was graduating after all! I kept my baggy green cap in a presentation cabinet in our house, but the cabinet had a latch on it, which said a lot. In my mind I wasn't finished. I just knew my time would come again.

The recall topped a great year in which Kell and I got married. On the day I planned to propose, I decided to cook a seafood extravaganza. Like all men in that situation, I was nervous, but finally asked the question and got the answer I was hoping for. After calling our parents, our next call was to Uncle Pat, because he'd been the one who introduced us at the greyhound races three years earlier.

We were married on 4 May 1996 at Kellie's childhood church, St John Vianney's, in the bayside suburb of Manly in Brisbane. I was 24 and Kell was just 21. We were young, but I wouldn't have had it any other way. We are blessed to have had our children young, but we also had several years together before they arrived. Kell was a few minutes late for the wedding after a last-minute visit to her great-aunt Teresa, a sister with the Order of Carmelites, who, along with her order, had petitioned for a papal blessing for us. I thought the odds were strongly in favour of us getting a fine day for the wedding, given that it was in early winter. How wrong I was. It rained so much I half-expected to have to get to the church via my fishing tinnie.

After my Test recall was announced, I presented the confident face of a young man ready to take on the world as I joined a team that was 2–0 up in the series and included big-name performers such as Shane Warne, Glenn McGrath, Mark Taylor, the Waughs and a young Jason Gillespie playing only his second Test. I was brimming with desire and self-belief. At least, that's how I played it. Deep down, I was so nervous that my gloomy fate was sealed long before I took the crease.

We stayed at the Hilton Hotel in Melbourne, which is only a few hundred metres from the MCG, and I just couldn't relax. I was totally overwhelmed by the enormity of the Boxing Day Test and all the fanfare that surrounds it. It was my first Test on Australian soil, my second overall and my first in three years. The traditional team Christmas lunch, when all the families assembled, would be a time of relative relaxation later in my career, but not this time. I just didn't feel a part of it. And I simply hated the MCG nets. The punters seemed to be all around and all over you, and the wickets were generally modest, to the point that it felt like the ball was coming through as if it was shot out of a cannon. I felt underprepared, and I was also carrying the scars of my first unsuccessful Test a few years before in South Africa.

Big moments in your life become frozen in your mind. Subtle smells or sounds can stay with you forever. I swear I can still hear the hollow thud of leather on wood when the great West Indian Curtly Ambrose uprooted my unprotected off stump during the Boxing Day Test of 1996. It was the fifth ball I faced in the second innings.

The walk from the centre wicket block at the MCG to the dressing-rooms can be a stairway to heaven or hell, depending on how you've fared. You walk 80 metres or so off the field to open the massive gates on the fence, then you get sledged ('Go back to

Queensland – you're useless!') or cheered for another 20 metres as you trudge through the crowd. And then you have to walk down two flights of stairs and along a corridor before you finally get to the dressing-room. It's the longest walk to a dressing-room on earth, and twice during the Melbourne Test it felt even longer. In the first innings I made just 5 before edging Ambrose to Carl Hooper in the slips. In the second, I made a duck after I banked on the ball clearing the stumps, which I'm sure it would've done in the first innings had it pitched in the same spot. Unfortunately, my radar was out – the wicket was deteriorating, and so were my prospects of a long-lasting Test career.

There wasn't any bad luck about my dismissal. I was a lamb to the slaughter, and I knew it. The West Indies knew it. Curtly Ambrose certainly knew it. If Curtly hadn't got me out that over then it would have happened in his next, or the one after that. I might as well not have bothered padding up because I was out before I got in. Every sportsman will tell you that there are times when you feel way out of your depth and you categorically know you're going to fail. That was me in that Test. A few years later I had matches where I felt I was never going to get out. This match was the antithesis of those.

Curtly was irresistible in that Test. The big fellow was famously media-shy, but to everyone's surprise he gave a rare interview after bagging five wickets in the first innings. He said, 'When I saw the wicket I said at the team meeting, "I'll take 10 wickets here and we will win easily." ' Mark Waugh took to parroting that killer line – 'I'll take 10 and we'll win easily' – out of awe rather than mockery. Curtly's 10-wicket prophecy wasn't quite right, but that gave us precious little joy – he took nine wickets and they won by six! Australia took the series 3–2 but it was quite a battle between a West Indian side in slight decline – although still very competitive – and an Australian side that had recently become the world's number-one team, but was still working towards complete world domination.

Curtly was the best opposition bowler I ever faced – by far. You were always under pressure with him. Mark Waugh once said after a one-day innings, 'Does he ever bowl a bad first over?' but I can extend the compliment a little further. I would ask, Did he bowl a bad over . . . ever? A bad ball? A full toss? I'm sure he did, but it never seemed that way when you were facing him.

I rated Curtly significantly ahead of his bowling partner Courtney Walsh because Walsh was often a guaranteed 'leave'. You could almost bet most balls he bowled would pass over or outside off stump, and that gave you a 'sighter' for the more dangerous ones. But not big Curtly. Every ball seemed a threat. From ball one at 11 a.m. to ball 120 delivered some seven hours later, he'd be boring into the top of off stump. You couldn't pull his short balls because they weren't short enough. You couldn't drive his full ones because they weren't full enough. You couldn't cut him because he gave you no width. I never felt comfortable on the front foot against him and I couldn't get back far enough. Strangely enough, the deck on which I felt most comfortable against Curtly was the one on which he once took seven wickets for one run – Perth – because his deliveries rose just enough to give you a chance at pulling them. But you'd hardly call them gift runs.

Of the nine bowlers to have taken more than 400 Test wickets, Curtly, in the hottest field of all time, was the most economical. He bowled 1001 maiden overs (that's about two in seven). Like Warnie, he was a champion blessed with the rare gift of attacking and defending at the same time. He could go through teams like a knife, or just slowly choke them until they turned blue in the face. He was the ultimate fast-bowling package.

The only bowler who came anywhere near Ambrose was the great Pakistani Wasim Akram, whom I faced only in one-day cricket, and towards the end of his illustrious career. He was amazing – almost too good for his own good. His swing bowling was so technically pristine that the seam was always in perfect position – so clear, in fact, that you could get a good look at it and see what he was trying to do with the ball. If it was an outswinger you'd see the seam pointing like an arrow to first or second slip; if it was an inswinger the seam would be pointing towards fine leg. Facing him was brilliant, because I knew every part of my game had to be in the groove to cope with his genius. You had to admire what was being dished up to you, and in this way it was a bit like watching Brian Lara bat – you'd find yourself drooling and despairing at the same time.

I felt I never saw the best of Wasim's exceptional opening partner Waqar Younis, but I admired him for the sheer artistry of his bowling – the textbook wrist and seam positions – even though I never found him as threatening as Wasim.

Nonetheless, Curtly Ambrose was the top of the pile. He remained an enigma throughout his career, dismissing requests for most media interviews with a line only a champion or a king could feel comfortable with: 'Curtly talks to no man.' Nor would he fraternise with the opposition. 'Mornin', Skipper,' was all we'd get out of him, and that would be to AB. The rest of us went unacknowledged. He was such a private person that apparently when he picked his daughter up from school he'd park well away from the front gate to avoid attention. (Although I understand his mother would go out on the balcony of her tiny house in Swetes village, Antigua, and ring a cow bell whenever her famous son took a Test wicket. She must have caused quite a racket over the years – he took 405 of them!)

I think I spoke more to Curtly in one night during the 2008 West Indian tour than I did in a decade playing against him. I was being sent home injured and he was retired, and I told him he was the best I'd faced. He laughed and said something like, 'Maybe it would be different now.' He was just being modest, I reckon. Deep down he probably thought he'd still have my measure – and I wouldn't argue with that.

He may not have been talkative when playing, but his gestures spoke for him. His signature piece of body language was the dreaded 'double clap'. It was a little pre-emptive celebration when he thought a wicket was coming, say after the ball had just hit you on the pads or was edged and on its way to gully. A lot of times he wouldn't even bother appealing. He'd just produce his little double clap. If you saw or heard it you knew you were in serious trouble because, more often than not, it signalled goodbye.

When I learned about Curtly's contribution in team meetings, it reinforced my own opinion that they were generally time-wasting, hot-air-blowing competitions. Ambrose would simply remind his team, 'Curtly bowls one line, one length!' There was no bravado, no theorising. It echoed my view that a bowling game plan aiming to hit the top of off stump beats any of the alternatives proposed – and there have been a million of them. And it also reminded me that for the best of the best (McGrath's view was almost identical to Curtly's) the game really can be disarmingly simple.

Even in retirement, Curtly never lost that bulletproof aura. In 2003, an Australian press photographer saw him in the crowd on the last morning of a Test match in Antigua. The big fella actually agreed to answer one – just one – question. He was asked, 'How would you bowl today if you were still playing?' Curtly replied, 'If I was still playing today, the game would have been over yesterday.' Enough said.

17

A Ton of Anguish

There is a strange paradox about human emotions that decrees the more you try to relax and chill out, the more unsettled you become. I know that from painful experience. In January 1997, I scored my first Test century, but don't ask me how. Just breathing seemed a big enough challenge that week, never mind making runs. I was an emotional mess and reaching out in all directions for salvation.

After my poor showing at the Melbourne Test, I felt surprisingly okay. I had no idea whether I'd be picked for the next Test, but the sensation that things couldn't get worse was strangely liberating. When I visited the Queensland Cricket offices, people seemed surprised by how upbeat I was, but I was strangely at peace. I always found scores under 10 easy to reconcile because they were essentially no result.

For me, the scores that niggled most weren't the outright failures but the half-results. If you went back and look at every first-class innings I played, you'd occasionally notice periods of trouble on 30–35 and 60–65. When I reached these scores I used to put my foot on the clutch, but was often a bit uncertain about changing gears. They were tricky stages for me because, like any opener, I felt I'd confronted and overcome my greatest dangers and it was now time to switch on the afterburners. If I was 30 the side was 50, and we were away. If I was 60, we were 100 or more and starting to own the game, so I was more prepared to take risks.

I entered a Sheffield Shield game against South Australia in Adelaide soon after the Boxing Day Test knowing that failure there could cost me a Test berth at the same venue in just a few weeks. Somehow I squeezed out 38 and 69. I wasn't sure whether these innings sealed the deal, but I got a good indication on selection day when I was batting in a club game for Valleys at St Lucia against University and a news crew arrived. I'd just made a grade century, but I suspected the ton wasn't the reason for their visit. I don't think I've ever been happier to see television cameras. I was in.

As the Test approached I started to seriously stress out. And my worrying only made me worry more, because the Adelaide Oval was one place I never worried – it was my cricketing nirvana. I'd always done well there, inspired by the venue's ambience and history – it had been the venue for three of my first 15 Shield centuries – and I felt I owned the place. I loved it so much that often after I got out, I'd go down to the nets for throwdowns, not because I particularly needed them but because I loved the atmosphere. Just walking past the boisterous corporate tents on the way to the nets was uplifting – you felt you were in the middle of a city genuinely celebrating its Test match.

Yet not even the atmosphere could ease my mind this time.

I tried to convince myself that everything was okay, and did everything I could in an attempt to relax. I phoned Gaz, but the more I talked to him the more intense I became. I had a massage at the team hotel and went to another hotel that was offering guided meditation classes. During my sole visit to this class I drifted into a trance-like state and actually fell asleep. For a while it seemed my problems had been solved but then, halfway through the class, I woke up in a nervous sweat. It was as if I'd dreamt about edging Curtly's first ball to second slip! I had always been an ordinary sleeper on tour and had used ocean and rainforest music to settle me, much to the amusement of Jimmy Maher and Symo, who used to stir me by making bird calls.

My nerves were shot. Nothing worked. I was sweating badly in my sleep and couldn't get modes of dismissals out of my head at night. I remember one recurring dream in which I was batting in the nets when a wicket fell and I rushed to the dressing-room to get a protector. Unable to find one, I hurried to the boundary only to learn I'd been timed out for being late. Then I would wake up in fright, sit bolt upright and declare, 'This is absolutely ridiculous!' and curse myself for being too intense. For a while I'd relax, but the cycle of gloom would start again. I'd be consumed by anguish then get angry at myself for being that way. I'm not the first player to be haunted by life on the edge of selection, and I won't be the last, but I can tell you this – it's a miserable part of cricketing life.

Later in my career I still had these sorts of thoughts but was able to short-circuit the anxiety by comforting myself with the belief that as long as I stayed within the flags of my game, everything would work out fine. Before that Adelaide Test I visited a sports psychologist, who told me that instead of eliminating the anxiety, I should try to go with it, embrace it, and see if it could elevate me. It felt like a big shift in my thinking – I should embrace the pressure instead of fight it? The theory was that if you did go down with the ship, at least you did it your way rather than trying to kid yourself that there was no pressure at all.

Of course there *was* pressure, due to the huge discrepancy between my first-class and international results. When I finally walked out to bat with Mark Taylor that day at Adelaide Oval, my Sheffield Shield average (just over 60) was the best since champion opener Arthur Morris; my Test average (6) was just one run better than that of Jim Higgs.

An article had just been published in Brisbane about the customs of committed local fans. Apparently, regardless of whether I batted for Queensland or Australia, while I was at the crease my home fans would go out and do the mowing. When I was in a maroon cap they did it because they knew I'd be on for four or more hours and they'd catch up with the scores later. When I was in a green cap they did it because they were so nervous for me, they couldn't watch.

My own family also felt that way. Poor old Gaz, in Ingham, saw the pre-day pitch report and took his catamaran out to sea as soon as I went into bat. It was the first time he couldn't watch my innings. Instead, he organised a colour-coded system with his wife, Alex, where a green flag hanging from their deck meant I was in, a red was out, and a yellow nappy meant I was nearing my century.

I had to fight hard for that first big score. I was dropped a few times and caught off a no-ball on 66, but I felt I deserved some good luck. For all my pre-match stress, the venue did ultimately inspire and reassure me. These days the Adelaide dressing-room has been modernised and moved to the opposite side of the ground, but back then it was ancient but quaintly attractive. It had comfortable rooms at the side, open-air so you could feel the pulse of the members' stand. When you took the walk down to the field through the members' area, history just washed over you: Bradman, Chappell and many other greats had walked those steps before you. Adelaide always felt welcoming.

While I was playing, Gaz was living on his nerves out on the water. Several times when he looked towards the deck he saw something red flashing, but it was a red plastic swing seat used by their children, Ellen and Billy. A little later Alex saw a wicket fall and reached for the red rag only to realise it was Justin Langer who'd been dismissed.

As I raced through the nineties with four fours in five balls from Cameron Cuffy, Alex frantically waved a yellow nappy. Gaz quickly turned the catamaran around, sprinted up the beach and stood in front of the TV dripping wet. He arrived in time to see my first Test century, raised after four and a half hours at the crease. Over in Adelaide, I stood there drowning in relief, removed my helmet, crossed myself and shook hands with Mark Waugh, who said, 'First of many, young fella . . . good boy.' The 'good boy' line stuck in my head and I later used it myself when I was at the crease and other young colleagues bagged major milestones.

Watching the highlights of my innings, Gaz was happy for me, but not as joyous as could have been expected. Something was niggling him. He knew I had something extra that international fans had yet to see, that the real me remained hidden beneath several thick layers of anxiety. He was right. I was hoping to play well. Hoping to be selected. Hoping to fit in. I was on trial every innings, and extremely nervous. Who wouldn't be? And I was in awe of some of the players I was playing with, like the Waugh twins.

Throughout my career my greatest challenge was never proving myself to the opposition. My biggest battles were internal. I had to prove myself to me, then my teammates and the selectors. At that time I knew there were plenty of teammates who didn't especially rate me. Mark Waugh would have been one of these. The game came so easily to Junior that he didn't rate many people. I could just imagine him saying of me, 'Works hard, good player but you wouldn't call him a champion.' The thought doesn't offend me – Junior was Junior and I loved the way he said precisely what he thought. But it was also why, despite my affection for him, I gravitated more towards Stephen, because he knew how hard the game could be. Stephen and I could relate to each other's struggles. In fact, I don't think I ever banished them for good. After scoring a Test century, I still doubted myself and had plenty of doubters, but that doubt became a close friend and a precious spur to my own motivation.

Though many people questioned the worth of my century, there were a few kind words written about it also. *The Australian*'s Malcolm Conn, a journalist I'd always respected, gave me generous praise: 'In a match which raised so many questions about character and courage, it was fitting that Hayden was the Australian standard-bearer.' News Limited's Ron Reed also saw the bright side: 'You could say he was lucky but so what? In his two previous, widely separated Test opportunities, he had none of that precious commodity and as all cricketers know, this is one game where luck will eventually even itself out – especially if you throw a few counter punches yourself.'

Worthy or not, I luxuriated in my breakthrough innings. I couldn't hide my joy. I'd always appreciated the achievements of others, particularly Michael Slater, whose first Ashes series in 1993 had been a major inspiration for me. For once, I was able to appreciate my own achievements, and I felt justified in feeling very good about myself that day. It was my turn to bask quietly in the glory. I remember thinking, 'I'm going to be humble – but I'm going to enjoy every bit of this.'

A good thing I did, because further potholes were just around the corner.

18

Life on the Edge

My New Year's resolution for 1997 was to get to England. I achieved it, and made lots of runs, but not the way I'd planned. Australia's Ashes tour set off without me; I had to settle for the experience of county cricket with Hampshire.

The fact I didn't make the Ashes squad hurt at first. I'd scored my first Test century the previous summer against the West Indies in Adelaide, top-scored with 47 on a nightmare wicket in Perth in the final Test, then managed a sound 40 in the first innings of the First Test of the South African tour (a tour we won 2–1, following exceptional victories in the first two Tests). I probably only had to slap down one half-century in the closing two Tests in South Africa to make the Ashes squad, but with scores of 0, 14, 10 and 0, I missed out.

My state of mind throughout that South African tour was not improved when Matthew Elliott relayed a conversation he'd had with chairman of selectors Trevor Hohns. Apparently, Cracker had told Elliott he was Ashes-bound, and to 'just relax and play'. It jolted me. Cracker hadn't given me the same guarantee, which meant I was still on trial. Mark Taylor, despite a form drought, was a certainty for England, and with Elliott pencilled in I was left to jostle with the likes of Michael Slater, who had been dropped at the start of the home summer, for the final batting berth.

There was so much competition between Matthew Elliott and me that we never really got along. One night in Sydney in 1997, when he was in his prime, we went out with a group to a restaurant and he dropped a line about getting a $100 000 contract. It really riled me, because I had just been left off the 22-man contract list and given a $10 000 development players' grant. I felt he was rubbing my nose in it a bit, which says a lot about how I was feeling at the time. Elliott and I both had our dreams but there was room for only one of us. It was hard yakka and mate against mate. If he remembers that incident and thinks I was a bit too sensitive, I'd understand. Life on the periphery can draw the worst from people, and I was no exception.

Elliott and I also had a big falling-out when we were playing for our respective state teams in a Sheffield Shield game at the MCG. The Queensland boys were always on Elliott's case when he batted, but this day he really bit back. As we broke for lunch, he followed me towards the dressing-room. 'I couldn't give a stuff about you or your team,' he said. I retorted, 'It's quite obvious you only care about one person – Matthew Elliott!' And I followed up with a few spicy expletives.

I think he was shocked. We parted ways at that point, having reached the end of the players' race, and went into our separate dressing-rooms. Whenever we played Victoria there was always a fair bit of feeling in our matches, and we loved trying to smash the southerners. One of the driving forces of my career was the desire to lift Queensland from mediocrity and to play with great purpose and poise at big venues like the MCG and the SCG. I sensed an unspoken assumption of superiority from the Victorian and NSW teams. For all of the harmony built up at national level, when the Test players went back to their states, the boundaries were clearly marked and strongly defended.

So in South Africa I was back in the place I liked least in cricket – on trial for my future. Auditioning drew the absolute worst from my game – again. Two of my dismissals were heartbreakers. One came during the second innings of the Second Test at Port Elizabeth, when Elliott and I ended up sprinting to the same end in a calling mix-up as Hansie Cronje took the bails off at the other end. Second man home, I was run out for 14. Before my last innings of the Test series, at Centurion, things were so tight I'm told that when Trevor Hohns sat down behind the bowler's arm, he said quietly, 'I wouldn't mind seeing Matthew [Hayden] nail this.' When someone said, 'What – the Ashes tour?', Cracker nodded. It was that close. I didn't need much, but I needed something. A sixth-ball duck was never going to suffice.

I fell to lively left-armed quick Brett Schultz, a gifted fast bowler whose career was cruelly cut short by a succession of major injuries. He was an animated, high-spirited character who played every Test as if it was his last, and he certainly had the force with him during that game. Schultz got me lbw playing forward and not offering a shot. It felt like a 50/50 call, but I remember thinking the instant the ball hit the pads, *He's going to give this . . . I'm gone.* And so I was – for almost three years.

Cracker told me on the plane home from South Africa that

I had missed the Ashes tour. Slats hadn't played a Test for six months after failing twice in a one-off Test against India in New Delhi and being subsequently overlooked for the entire home summer and the South African tour, but he was given the reserve opening spot for England behind Mark Taylor and Matthew Elliott. Though Slats had not been in great form, the panel decided his experience and the strength of his overall Test record warranted another chance. Cracker later revealed he was worried about my future, saying, 'That was probably the one time when I feared Matthew might not make it. He didn't bat well in South Africa and I wondered whether he would end up really cracking it. I told him early about his Ashes omission because I knew him and I didn't want to leave him hanging. But the thing we really respected about him was that he just kept coming back harder each time. He worked harder and harder and made sure we had reason to select him again.'

I felt like I was walking a tightrope every innings. I was full of doubts about the present and the future. And looking back, I can see there was another problem: I wasn't good enough. I was close, but not the full package – I lacked the mental stamina to thrive in Test cricket. The nuts and bolts of my game were up to Test standard, but crucial self-belief was missing. I had it a few years later, when I was able to absorb some setbacks in the comfort of knowing I'd made 20-plus Test tons. But I didn't have it in 1997. Only by embracing this truth could I move forward.

After missing the 1997 Ashes squad I joined the Hampshire County Cricket Club. I had agreed to play for the team many months before and my contract had been reported in the press as 'the contract I signed but didn't want to deliver'. I wanted to be in England playing for Australia rather than Hampshire, but it was a nice fall-back position.

During my Hampshire stint we played the Australian team and I was desperate to do well – probably too desperate. Dizzy Gillespie uprooted my off stump second ball with a pearler that did something I rarely saw from him – it seamed in to me. His stock ball almost always went away, so this one caught me unawares. I didn't play a shot and was absolutely filthy – with myself, with the world and even with the umpire who had given me my guard. Unlike Australian umpires, who mark centre through the middle of your bat, English umpires mark centre through the edge, which can put you a centimetre or two away from where you think you are. This was the way my mind was working at the time, looking for excuses, when in fact I'd made a bad error of judgement and got out.

I didn't know it then, but as I left the field a shattered man at least one other player felt his heart sink – Stephen Waugh. He said as much in his tour diary, but tipped that my day in the sun would come eventually because I had a 'hunger and desire few other players possess'. It was crucial support at a time when there were plenty of spare seats on the Hayden bandwagon.

My career journey was taking the scenic route, but there was still much to enjoy. I made lots of runs for Hampshire, and piled up lots of memories. I struck up a great friendship with Robin Smith, the county's high-profile Test batsman, who was wonderful company and a terrific bloke.

Kell came with me, and it was thanks to her that I had the chance to bat as much as I did. We'd put in hours at the nets, Kell feeding a ball machine I had set, and though it mightn't seem the most romantic way to spend our mornings, in a way it was. We were together, overseas, and it was fantastic. Kell was working in promotions with the Gandel Group, the owners of the Myer

Centre, and took four months off so we could travel together – I cherished her presence. Those months together gave us time for our relationship to blossom. We didn't have children until six years after we married, and after 2001, when I became a permanent Test player, I spent up to 10 months of the year on the road. That time away made me appreciate even more the time we spent together in the early years. These days the whole WAG (wives and girlfriends) culture has turned tinsel, but it was anything but for us back then, and we were just a happy young couple abroad. When we went on a holiday to Europe, teammates joked that the 'three' of us would have a great time, asking, 'Who's sleeping with the ball machine?'

For a while, the ball machine, Kell and me were the happiest of trios, but things changed back in Brisbane soon after when we were having a session and I miscued a ball that then struck Kell on the body. She went straight down, and though she escaped without major injury, I felt absolutely terrible and declared it would never happen again. That was pretty much the end of our net sessions together.

Hampshire's bowling coach, Malcolm Marshall, 39 and six years out of Test cricket, was still a scheming nightmare to face in the nets. He remains the only bowler I ever met with a more forensic approach to his craft than Glenn McGrath. That's saying something, for McGrath is cricket's Mr Memory. Ask him who his 245th Test wicket was and he'll spit out a name, venue and mode of dismissal.

But Malcolm was something else. We spent a lot of time together because he was the overseas coach and I was the overseas pro. He not only worked me over in the nets, but would tell me why he was working me over and even nominate how he was going to get me out. And when he did, he'd reveal what he had learnt previously that had helped him to do so. He would playfully add my name to his 'total' of Test wickets – not that his self-esteem needed much reinforcement after a Test career that netted 376 victims at an astonishing average of 20.94!

I remember well the theme of several net dismissals to him – inswinger, inswinger, inswinger, inswinger, outswinger . . . snick! Malcolm remembered everything, and because he'd played in such a triumphant era for West Indian cricket, he was full of great stories. Allan Border always said that Malcolm was the toughest bowler he ever faced, a swinging, skidding nightmare. Interestingly, Malcolm told me he loathed bowling to AB and found him the most difficult opponent he confronted. He said that when he bowled to Australia it was a case of 'AB out, everyone out'. It just confirmed to me that Marshall vs. Border must have been *the* heavyweight contest of world cricket in the 1980s.

Malcolm had a special bond with Kell, calling her 'my little cherry', in reference to the white cherries he'd bring over to our place whenever he visited. He loved laughing, brandy and life. I cherish these memories all the more because within two years of our time together he died of colon cancer: a tremendous loss to cricket, and to life.

19

County Capers

Two years later, in 1999, I joined Northamptonshire as captain and learnt a big lesson – you can't turn England into Australia. I tried to introduce an Australian work ethic into a system not set up for it, and it was a huge mistake. Almost immediately I ran into the brick wall that was the institutionalised nature of county cricket, where you did things in a certain way at a certain time just because that's how they'd always been done.

After being dropped from the Test team in 1997 I had played well for Queensland, but it was a difficult time to be a fringe player. Between 1996, when Matthew Elliott played his first Test, and 2001, there were 17 Australian debutants but only one specialist batsman – Darren Lehmann. That's how tough it was to be in the green and gold waiting room. You couldn't say the door was bolted but at times it felt that way. Australia cemented its reputation as the game's number-one cricketing nation, and with success came stability of selection. So off I went to England, only to find a set-up that had a real staleness about it.

It seemed strange to me that I could average around 60 in county cricket while a lot of my teammates had averages of around 35. Was I twice as good as them? No. Was I hungrier? It seemed that way. I wanted desperately to instil some strong team values into the culture and find a more open way of communicating. The Northants boys clearly hadn't enjoyed their cricket for some time. But they had made me captain, and a captain I was going to be. Inspired by what I'd experienced when Queensland became the Bulls, I suggested we give our club a nickname and we adopted 'the Steelbacks' – after the famous group of Northamptonshire-based infantry in the British Armed Forces, a proud and fierce group of men. It was a start.

I enjoyed the role but it never sparked ambitions to captain Australia. In any case, my international career didn't sprout wings until I was approaching my 30th birthday, and that was too late for captaincy. Maybe it wasn't a bad thing. In psychological profiles done at state level by the Bulls' Phil Jauncey, you could see that the longer I played, the more of an 'enforcer' I became. I was definitely a 'lead from the front' person. If you profiled Ricky Ponting, he'd be part-enforcer but you'd also find other aspects to his personality that make him better suited to dealing with the different needs of individuals within a team, especially when a 'rally the troops from behind' approach is needed.

At Northamptonshire, I decided I wasn't going to shy away from tough decisions. I made up my mind quite early that former England fast bowler Devon Malcolm had to go. Devon in his prime was a proud and beautiful athlete. He had an unpredictable Test career studded with magical moments, such as the day at the Oval in 1994 when he produced the stunning returns of 9/54 against South Africa after being riled by a hit in the helmet from

Fanie de Villiers. Devon furiously and famously declared, 'You guys are history,' and produced an effort the BBC rated number 91 in the top 100 sporting performances of all time by British athletes.

But at 37, Devon's best days were clearly behind him. He was finished at the top level and had come back to county cricket to support his family. As honourable as that intention was, Northants needed more from him. County cricket should be an incubator for players on the rise, not a retreat for those on the way down. You need the drive and energy to contribute in whatever way you're required, and when you fall beneath these standards, you miss out. As it turned out, Devon found another home at Leicester and went on to play three more seasons, and although I felt there was no future for him at Northants, I certainly didn't begrudge him a start elsewhere.

Former England batsman Rob Bailey was another I felt had to go. He was a very distinguished cricketer who played 374 first-class matches, including four Tests, in a first-class career that spanned 20 years. But five minutes after play had started he'd be asking, 'What's for lunch?' I felt cricket had ceased to inspire him and I couldn't see how the team was going to move forward with his type of attitude. Northamptonshire did not renew his contract at the end of the 1999 season, but fortunately he was a given a soft landing at Derbyshire and then went on to be a respected first-class umpire.

A lot of English cricketers play on too long. Graeme Hick had a great county record, but was it enough to warrant him playing on to age 42, retiring in 2008? The English system didn't help. Good county players didn't earn great money – say $70 000 to $90 000 per season in the late 1990s – but there was the lure of staying on for the so-called 'benefit year', which came after lengthy service. The benefit year was minimally taxed, and a potential income of, say, $250 000 after tax is a carrot hard to resist.

One Northants player I particularly struggled to play with was Mal Loye. He seemed unable to accept the team ethos I was trying to instil. To put it mildly, Mal didn't have the highest opinion of me. And you wouldn't say he treated me like a long-lost brother when we crossed paths at the SCG in 2006–07. He was touring with England's one-day side, having made his international debut at age 34. As we crossed between overs while he was batting, he gave me a short, sharp kick with his right boot. I said, shocked, 'What do you think you're doing? This isn't county cricket. You know there are 16 cameras covering this game?' Mal, a man of few words, didn't respond. I turned to Gilly and said, 'Did you see that?' and he said, 'I can't believe he just did that!' I replied, 'It says a bit about the relationship.' Amazingly, no one picked it up.

I always felt the difference between Australian and English teams at all levels of the game came down to team support. Someone had your back in Australia, but in England every man seemed to be for himself. Because of this attitude and all the changes I'd made, my first year at Northants was a bit shaky, but there were enough good people around to give me a shot the second year. We played beautifully and progressed to first division, after which Mike Hussey replaced me as captain and enjoyed the ethos our coach, New Zealander Bob Carter, and I had helped to create.

During my time with Northants, Kell and I made great friends off the field, such as former England batsman Allan Lamb and his wife Lindsay, and children Richard and Katie. Lamby is one of the most lovable humans on the planet. He was amazing to me the whole time I was in England, and was just the sort of person I needed in my life at that time. We'd often go fishing together, and he not only provided me with an escape from the pressure of continuous cricket but also broadened my outlook on life. I still cherish the friendship between our families.

I also became great friends with club chief executive Lynn Wilson. Lynn had two sons – Nick and Giles – and they were wonderful to me. Because the Wilsons were within the club yet outside it at the same time, I could get away to their property when I needed to find some balance. Lynn reckoned I made him £50 000 by catching a salmon there. Salmon were pretty scarce, and he said that the place skyrocketed in value as soon as it became known I'd landed one. On my last Ashes tour in 2005, I again visited his property, where he had his own majestic, quintessentially English cricket ground. I used to think the Hayden family were doing pretty well to have a net in our backyard, but the Wilsons had their own ground and a pavilion to go with it! I was devastated to learn of Lynn's death in a car accident in Scotland in July 2008. He is buried in a plot overlooking his cricket ground, and in 2009, during my stint commentating for the Ashes, I sat with Giles and his wife Polly in the pavilion there on a sublime English afternoon and drank a toast to their father.

What I learnt about county culture during my time as Northants captain was that you had the best chance of gaining acceptance if you simply went with the flow. But I've always struggled to be a conformist. In my view, if there's an opportunity to be different and get an edge on the pack, you have to take it.

Still, there is much to like about the traditions of English cricket. There's only one Lord's. There's only one Long Room, where you walk out to bat and hear lines like, 'Good luck, but not too much luck,' or, 'See you soon.'

Strangely, being in England that year made me feel all the more Australian – something that intensified when out of the blue I received a call from Stephen Waugh in late 1999 urging me not to give up. He asked how things were going and I joked that my captaincy career was taking off to the point where I was after his stripes. He pointed out that we were still in second division so I shouldn't get too carried away. We chatted away about nothing much and then he dropped a line like, 'Keep going – you're not far away.' It was just the sort of encouragement I needed. And it meant even more because a few months earlier Stephen had taken over the Australian Test captaincy from Mark Taylor, who had retired after leading Australia to a home Ashes triumph.

A month or two after Stephen's phone call, I was named in the Australian squad for a 10-week tour of Sri Lanka and Zimbabwe. Matthew Elliott had been dropped after a modest series in the West Indies, and I was chosen as the reserve opener to Slats and Greg Blewett. I didn't play a Test on that tour, but I was edging ever closer to where I wanted to be.

20

Tough Love – AB

Through the countless ups and down I experienced in international cricket there was one reassuring constant – Allan Border thought I could play. I've got no idea what was said behind closed doors in national selection meetings, but I always knew AB was a robust supporter of mine and that he would have me in his team if he could.

Sometimes I wondered if AB sensed what road my cricket journey would take even before I did. During my first Australian tour, to England in 1993, I asked him to sign a sketch of himself that stills hangs in the living room at the family farm in Kingaroy. He wrote, 'To Matthew . . . Nothing worthwhile comes easily.' I hadn't played one Test when he signed it, yet in four words he summed up the next 16 years of my sporting life.

AB and I first met during a club fixture at Valleys, and he says he can still see me walking in with my gear. He thought I was a fast bowler and, because he didn't know me, that I must be from the opposition. His first thoughts were along the lines of, *That's great . . . just what I need – some young punk trying to knock my head off!*

The gloomy mid-1980s had taken their toll on AB – he was a hard man shaped by hard times. You only had to watch a game of cricket with him to see that. He could never relax. He was a big fingernail chewer and had an ever-present worry ball, tossing it from one hand to the other as he poured out his litany of concerns over what was happening in the middle: 'Arrgggh! What's he doing? Why would he play that shot?' He could barely watch the game. His experience had conditioned him to expect trouble at every turn; with all he'd been through, how could you blame him? In AB's mind, no match was ever in the bag until the fat lady had not only sung, but delivered three encores, showered and waddled off to her next gig.

He could be intimidating. On the 1993 Ashes tour, for reasons that still elude me, the team had two different-coloured tracksuits for training, and each day team management would nominate which one we had to wear the following day. This particular day at Lord's, after finishing my 12th man duties, I left the rooms straightaway for the nets and missed the critical moment of the 'tracksuit decision'. Of course, I arrived at training the next morning wearing the wrong one. AB sailed into me: 'Any danger of you wearing the right bloody tracksuit?' he asked. 'Look, I'll solve the problem for you – just carry both tracksuits with you all the time.'

I must admit this shook me. And I also must admit I haven't totally learnt my lesson. When it comes to preparing for a game, I'm an absolute stickler for getting the big-picture things in place, but concede I'm pretty hopeless at the smaller stuff. Ian Healy always did it well, which is why I used to call him 'the Stickler'.

Long before diaries became fashionable for modern sportsmen, Heals kept them with the meticulousness of the school teacher he once was. He'd make notes on the foot movement, thought processes and mood swings of himself and his teammates, looking for patterns that could help his performance. Even now when he does guest-speaking gigs nothing is left to chance with his carefully assembled notes. Where the game's most minute details were concerned, Heals was a great role model. I was not.

AB's temper was legendary. I remember him giving the Bulls a rousing address late on day one in a match against NSW at the Gabba in 1993, just after we'd been bowled out. Those early-season full-strength games against the Blues always had a special edge. AB was stoking us up for a red-hot effort with the ball because he thought we still had five overs to play before stumps. But when he disappeared for a moment, the umpires came in to advise that stumps had been drawn.

Back came AB with a cry of, 'Let's get into 'em!' There was a long pause. 'AB,' I finally said, 'we'll have to get into 'em tomorrow because they've drawn stumps.'

He just exploded. 'So you're happy with your performance today, are you?' he raged. I had made 9. This set me off. 'We've known each other for a long time,' I retorted. 'Do you think I'm happy with my performance? It's all right for you to hide down at number five or six – why don't you come up to the top of the order and see how happy you are?'

When I took it a step further and stormed across the dressing-room towards him, Ian Healy stepped in and deftly manoeuvred me outside. I was steaming as Heals and I walked across the dog track. He hit some catches to me at a deliberately frantic pace, designed to wear me out, and we didn't speak for about

30 minutes. Later Heals said, 'If it's any consolation, one great thing about AB is that he'll wake up in the morning and it will be as if it never happened. Just drop it and we'll rock up tomorrow and all will be good.'

But the next morning life wasn't quite as rosy as Heals suggested. When AB and I batted together in the match we didn't exchange a word, and we got into a bizarre – and, looking back, pretty comical – routine of walking down the wicket, eyeballing each other and then returning to our respective ends. We batted together for an hour without exchanging a word.

Strangely enough, the players who got away with the most with AB were Andrew Symonds and his great mate Matthew Mott. They were just big kids when they played with AB in the early 1990s. They roomed with him a couple of times (AB got the master bedroom, of course) and became so friendly that they'd refer to him as 'Grandpa Smurf'. Somehow I couldn't imagine AB reacting with the same little grin if Mike Atherton had tossed up that nickname in the middle of an Ashes series.

During one road trip to Adelaide when AB was rooming with Jimmy Maher, some of the young guys were bold enough to call them 'Maher and Pa'. And when AB was out of form, Mott and Symonds even suggested he do the drills first used by former Test batsman John Inverarity – practising driving a ball rolled along the ground – to help him time the ball better, thus becoming the only youngsters bold enough to offer a batting tutorial to a man who'd played over 150 Tests. But instead of getting riled up, AB took it on board, and he later conceded the Inver drills helped him find form. Sometimes, when Motty and Symo needled AB, Stuey Law and I would look at each other with raised eyebrows, thinking, *This is going to blow*, but it never did.

I loved the flint-hard way AB played the game. Has anyone ever played it tougher? I certainly didn't think so after we had another fiery exchange during a match against Tasmania at the Gabba in AB's last season, 1995–96. I was on 60 and played a sweep shot when I felt a shooting pain in my back that instantly suggested bad news. I battled on to finally make 234, before being stumped after I felt my back go while advancing to Colin Miller. I wobbled off and collapsed in the dressing-room, telling AB I wouldn't be fielding. He reacted as if I'd said I was taking the afternoon off because I'd heard the surf was up. 'Mate, you've just scored 200, so you'll be fielding! Get up!' he barked. He then prodded me with his boot as I lay on the floor.

I was probably paying the penalty for my reputation as someone who hated fielding. When I was a kid, the boys would call me Malcolm Francke, after the Queensland leg-spinner who was so consumed by his specialist craft that he couldn't care much about the rest of the game. Later the nickname changed to Inzamam, after the Pakistani skipper who was very happy batting but seemed to think fielding beneath him. AB walked away muttering under his breath as I gingerly wobbled out to mid-off. Sure enough – doesn't fate always work this way? – early in the innings a ball flew in my direction. I launched myself at it and went down in a screaming heap. I couldn't move. Eventually I was unceremoniously carted off the ground.

In hospital, waiting for the results of the scans, I was thinking, *Please, oh please, let there be something major wrong with me!* I couldn't bear the thought of having to say to AB, 'The X-rays were all clear. You were right – I *am* the biggest sook in Australia.' How's that for a twisted frame of mind? When the news came that I had a stress fracture in my lower back,

I almost raised my hands to the heavens thinking, *Yes!* I would have done star jumps, only I couldn't move.

But misery and frustration quickly set in as I was ordered to wear something resembling a Batman suit around my torso, to protect my lower spine. I sweated and chafed badly in it, which was all the worse because I passed most of my several weeks' recovery time by going crabbing and fishing in North Queensland. I had to get away because I was never much good at being an injured hanger-on at training, being asked about my injury 10 times a day. But when the fish are biting or the crabs plentiful, it's amazing how good you can feel. In fact, it's almost impossible to pull up a pot with a giant Queensland muddie in it and feel any pain.

Then a strange thing happened. I was still wearing the suit when I returned to the batting crease, and I made a double century for a Queensland XI against New Zealand in a trial match. Apart from my 380, I reckon it was the best I've ever hit the ball, and it reinforced my sense that I actually played my best when there was something wrong with me. I'm not sure what AB made of my comeback double century, but I reckon he might have thought, *I just knew he was faking it!*

AB now looks back at our time together with a smile. 'One thing that used to get me really worked up was players just leaving the field. The Indians and Pakistanis used to do it all the time so I promised myself no one from my team would ever do it. Maybe I expected a bit much sometimes.'

AB was quite a paradox, but when it really mattered, he was with me. After he became a columnist for News Limited in the mid-1990s, he made a point of trying to lift my profile. He wrote a piece saying he was fed up with people questioning my technique and that the word 'orthodox' only meant the way 'most people' did something, not 'the way it had to be'. He used himself as an example, saying some English critics had pronounced that there would be no way he'd survive at Test level with such a homespun technique. An epic 17-year Test career had proved them wrong. And he didn't just support me in print. In casual visits to press boxes, he'd tell reporters, 'off the record', 'You can't tell me that if a bloke's good enough to open the innings and average 60 in first-class matches at the Gabba, he's not good enough for Test cricket. I just don't buy that.'

AB must also get credit for maintaining the chain of tradition in the hard years of the mid-1980s. Much has been written about how the defection of a large group of Australian players to the South African rebel tours, and the retirements of Dennis Lillee, Greg Chappell and Rod Marsh, threatened to break that chain completely. But that was only part of the story. Another busload of top players – such as Doug Walters, Kerry O'Keeffe, Jeff Thomson, Steve Rixon, Roger Woolley, Peter Toohey, Ray Phillips, Dav Whatmore, Kepler Wessels and many other top state players – also left the game around this time. The 1980s was a decade of incredible change for cricket, as a whole senior generation disappeared and Australia went three years without winning a series. Through it all, the one constant was AB, who was in the mid-stages of his run of 153 Tests in a row. One of the reasons I played on as long as I did after the departures of Warne, McGrath, Martyn, Langer and Gilchrist was to ensure that the chain linking one great era to the next wasn't completely broken.

AB handed out his share of tough love to me, but I have no complaints. We have a great mutual respect. I have wonderful memories not only of our times together for Queensland and Australia, but also at Valleys. At the end of each day's play at grade level he'd go to the bar and buy a round for the entire team. We'd sit and listen to his wise words and his anecdotes, which made us feel as if we were in the front row at a sportsmen's night. AB was always in a more relaxed state of mind at Valleys than when he was playing at the higher levels. He's as good a person as anyone I know to have a beer with, and he loves to laugh.

I reckon AB and I have similar personalities. We both have our insecurities, but have managed to overcome them through hard work and a love of competition. AB was always most comfortable in the heat of battle. Take him out of that and you will find a relatively introverted individual. He never wanted public adoration – it just happened.

Standing on stage with him after winning the Allan Border Medal in 2002 was a special moment, especially because I used to get so nervous ahead of awards nights. The Border Medal nights I enjoyed most were the ones where I had no chance of winning, because I could just relax and enjoy myself. But that night I felt no pain. When the announcement came and I joined AB on stage, I remember him saying simply, 'Well played.'

He didn't have to say anything else. That was enough.

21

Shipwrecked

Many fishermen dream of returning from a day in their boat with their catch making the nightly news. But you know you've had a bad day when you come back to shore without your boat and *you* are the news. That's what happened to me, Andrew Symonds and Trent Butler, a columnist for *Queensland Fishing Monthly*, about dawn on 2 January 2000, when we went fishing off North Stradbroke Island and the 16-foot Hayden family boat, a Haines Hunter called *Our Lady*, was swamped and sank.

Our biggest mistake was that we took the sea for granted, which is something I seldom do, whether I'm fishing or surfing. Our guard was probably low because it wasn't even a 'dangerous' day. If we'd been barrelled by a three-metre swell, it would have been bad enough, but the sea was pretty flat.

We set out in the darkness just before dawn. With Symo at the wheel, we'd been going on steadily when we climbed up the face of an unexpectedly steep wave at pace, became airborne and came crashing down on our stern. The motor cut and, as

I checked if the jolt had dislodged the battery, the next wave hit us. I asked Symo whether the kill switch on the back of the remote had snapped out of place. But just as the words got out – boof! – another wave hit us. As the stern of the boat was facing directly into the waves the only thing left was to utter those fateful words no fisherman wants to hear: 'Boys, we're swimming!' We didn't even have time to get the life jackets.

Within seconds, another big wave hit and soon only the boat's nose was showing. I knew the exact direction we had to take to get to North Stradbroke – we just had to swim quietly with the current to make the shore. Everything seemed fine. Symo and I were strong swimmers and Trent took off like Kieren Perkins. Unfortunately, after about 10 minutes, he looked up and said, 'I'm bloody rooted here.' I asked him what he meant. 'I'm gone!' he said.

I had a quiet word to Symo about our options, and as I was saying, 'Look, we might have to dust him up,' meaning that if Trent started panicking, we might have to knock him out and try to carry him to shore, I noticed the cause of the problem. Trent had on these massive Mambo boardshorts, which were a bit like dragging a parachute through the water. 'Mate,' I said, 'I don't care if you end up in your birthday suit . . . they have to go.' Even though they were a Christmas present from his girlfriend, they were immediately cast adrift. Thank goodness Trent did have his undies on. The last thing we needed was another lure in the water for the sinister creatures lurking below. I didn't alert the other two, but several times I was sure the cloudy masses below us were schools of pilchards, and as any angler will tell you, where pilchards go, sharks soon follow.

On the beach, about a kilometre away, there were signs that

some mates of mine had noticed the boat had gone down and were running search patterns. I presented two plans to the boys. Plan A – and I'm not sure why I even suggested this – was for me to swim back to the boat, which would soon be found by the rescuers, and then I'd tell them where to look for the others. Plan B was to teach Trent how to swim sidestroke, put him between me and Symo, and see if we could drag him in. I said to him, 'Mate, I need to know right now whether you're committed to getting in, because our lives are in danger.' He had a bit of a think about it and then said, 'I reckon I can do it.' So we scissor-kicked our way in, keeping our word to stay close to him.

By the time we reached the outer bank, Trent was exhausted, but we made it to shore. All I'd salvaged from the boat were my Oakley sunglasses, having slipped them down my Speedos just before jumping into the water. I took them out and put them on – very James Bond. Or at least Symo thought so. He kept saying, 'Have a go at this dingo, will ya?'

An old local picked us up in his jeep and took us back to his house. I was shivering as I called Kell, but burning with embarrassment too. Watching the Channel 7 chopper circling overhead, I knew that the pictures would be beamed around the world, back to my family and into the Queensland dressing-room, where Symo and I would just have to take our medicine. We were duly nicknamed the Skipper and Gilligan for a while, until Jimmy Maher pointed out that while I had a fair chance of resembling the skipper, Symo was never going to be a genuine Gilligan. We soon became Salt and Pepper.

The one redeeming aspect of the day was that I was subsequently asked to be part of an annual series of commercials for the National Maritime Safety Committee. I featured in their life-jacket campaign, which ran the basic message, 'If it's not on, it's not on,' stressing that you are putting yourself at risk if you cross the bar without wearing a life jacket. I still feel indebted to the Volunteer Marine Rescue Services. They were brilliant. They saved the boat – and would have saved our lives if they'd had to.

Things happen so quickly at sea and the weather has its own mind. Everyone makes mistakes on the water. I've made worse mistakes than we did that day and got away with them. The trouble with boating is that you only have one or two days a week to invest in it, so you make your plans around those days, sometimes going out when you probably shouldn't. If you live on the water, you know when the time is right. One thing's for sure: I will never take the sea for granted again.

22

Indian Uprising, 2001

When you're sitting on top of a sand dune at North Stradbroke Island, soaking up the splendour of a sunlit Moreton Bay, it's natural to feel everything is right in the world. Kell and I shared that blissful view together in early 2001. We'd bought a holiday house on the island and were really enjoying life there. Who wouldn't? The fishing, the surf, the privacy – you couldn't ask for more. But as I told Kell that afternoon, I needed to ask more myself. Things had to change. One thing that remained constant was that Kell never stopped believing in me. And as I became stronger, so did she.

But I was sick of scraping by. Of making excuses. I was then just hanging on to my third spell in the Test team, after replacing Greg Blewett for the final Test of the 2000 New Zealand tour. My first full home summer in the Australian team produced two half-centuries but no score better than 69 in five Tests against the West Indies. We won the series comfortably 5–0, with Stephen Waugh making 121 not out in the Fourth Test, but it wasn't thanks to me. I'd made starts, blown them, had some bad luck, made mistakes and been run out twice, including a heartbreaker at the Gabba when I was just starting to blossom.

My momentum and confidence was better than it looked on paper. But cricketers will always be judged by numbers, and mine weren't pretty – after 13 Tests spanning six years, I was averaging 24. So I made a promise right there on top of the sand dunes: it was time to deliver. It was crunch time. The selectors and I'm sure the fans knew it too.

And another thing happened. Early in my Test career I had been intimidated by that tortured feeling of extreme anxiety before I batted. Suddenly I was welcoming those stresses on board. I not only ceased to dread those stomach-churning emotions, I accepted that I needed them as well. In life after cricket I realise that I actually miss them and now search for them in other places. And I stopped getting ahead of myself as I had in the preceding Australian summer. Ball by ball, I just ground it out, living beautifully in the moment.

We went to India with high expectations, for we were a strong team in world-beating form – we'd won 15 matches in a row over 15 months. Many of our wins were landslides but there was also the occasional great escape such as the epic victory against Pakistan in Hobart in which Justin Langer and Adam Gilchrist shared a fabulous stand that enabled us to snatch a game that had seemed all but lost. We felt we could win from anywhere. With Warnie as our spinner, an outstanding pace attack of Glenn McGrath, Damien Fleming, Jason Gillespie and Michael Kasprowicz and a top order that featured the Waugh twins, we seemed to be a team without a weakness.

I'd felt good enough against the West Indies that summer

to be looking forward to the forthcoming tour of India. To prepare further, I asked Border Field curator Ross Harris to prepare a bone-dry spinners' deck for me to practise on. And so he did. Hour after hour I swept and scuffed and scrapped away there, so I felt more than ready when I looked down a pitch in Vadodara, where we were playing an India A team, and first saw the man who would become my nemesis, off spinner Harbhajan Singh.

Harbhajan's opening line was provocative: 'Surely Australia has something better than this . . . I hope you get picked [in the Test team] because I am going to play with you.' I snapped back, 'We'll see,' and there may have been a sharp-edged expletive between those two words. But Harbhajan had every right to sledge me that day. I played like a nuffy, just occupying the crease, dead-batting everything.

It was boring, uninspired batting from a player who must've looked too limited for his own good, but there was method in my mediocrity. I didn't want Harbhajan or anyone else to know I had not one but several types of sweep shot. What I tried to do in that game was work on a defensive strategy for simply occupying the crease, playing with soft hands and a dead, straight bat. Sometimes learning what doesn't work is as important as finding out what does.

I soon discovered that this style of play was a complete waste of time, as I made totally unspectacular scores of 49 and 37. It taught me that in India the bowler must be placed under pressure. If you hide in your trench and let the enemy get too close, someone will eventually roll a grenade in. I decided to focus on the sweep, practising endlessly, almost obsessively. At one of our final training sessions in Mumbai before the First Test,

I exhausted every slow bowler on offer in the nets practising my sweep shot – no mean feat in India. But still I wanted more.

I recruited our liaison officer, Darshak Mehta, a former Bombay club leg spinner of 35 years' experience. He was living in Sydney and had been hired by Cricket Australia to smooth the logistics of our journey through India. Although he was dressed in his smart civvies, I got 'Loveshack' to peg endless off breaks to me, and I tried to sweep every single one of them. Darshak reckons he almost put his shoulder out that day and still tells people, 'Matthew had an exhaustive preparation for that Test – he certainly exhausted me!' The fact that many of his offies were off target was almost a bonus, because I perfected the art of sweeping balls from anywhere. Loveshack swears I had the faraway, driven look of a man about to set out on a great journey as I trained that day.

The net pitch given to the Australians was far inferior to the one laid on for the Indians, so in my quest for practice I even left our net and went into our rivals' to use the edge of it before they got to training. The groundsman made two attempts to shoo me off, but each time I told him I wasn't shifting. Even our manager, Steve Bernard, pleaded with me to move on, but I rebutted Brute as well, claiming, 'Hey, I'm not hurting anyone . . . I'm trying to prepare for a Test.' Never had I been more focused or desperate to succeed. As a team we were feeling very confident after a winning run that stretched to 15 Tests, and we felt our side had all options covered with our pace attack of McGrath, Fleming and Gillespie, supported by Warnie.

By the time we played the First Test in Mumbai, we'd had three practice games, and I decided to figuratively hit Harbhajan between the eyes. In his first over, I came down the wicket and whacked him over cover for four, following through with, 'Who's under pressure now?' Game on! I gave him everything I had. There would've been bar-room cleaners who didn't sweep as much as I did that day. I played the shot so often I might as well have been playing with a broom.

Harbhajan didn't know how to react. He's such an attacking bowler that his Plan A was just to bowl at me and search for an edge, lbw, bowled or a bat-pad catch. But I just kept sweeping and sweeping. A good line-and-length ball – the spinner's stock ball – is ideal for sweeping, which is why slow bowlers hate the shot so much. There are few things as frustrating as seeing your best work literally swept away, and seeing an attacking ball become a boundary option.

The sweep shot is not for everybody. It is a cross bat shot and these types of strokes have their own risks. Michael Clarke and Ricky Ponting are not great fans of the sweep. Players with quick feet like Clarke often like to program their thinking simply to go forward or back. One of the reasons I liked the sweep is because I had such a large forward stride that I landed my front foot far enough down the wicket to take the threat of being lbw out of play.

Our right-handers were seriously threatened by the fact that Harbhajan was turning the ball square, but it made my life very comfortable because he couldn't get me lbw or bowled pitching on the stumps. If he pitched too full, I could sweep him. If he pitched too short, the ball screwed sharply away enough to cut. He did some wonderful work at the other end, but against me he seemed immobilised.

I absolutely loved it. Only a few weeks before that innings I'd been sitting with Kell atop the Straddie sand dunes, lamenting how average I had been. Suddenly I was a player on the rise.

We bowled India out for 176 in their first innings and were under heavy pressure at 5/99, with Harbhajan taking his third wicket, when Gilly walked out for one of the most destructive innings in Test history. He completely changed the match, with 122 off 112 balls as he and I put together a sixth-wicket stand of 197 in just 32.1 overs. I fell caught behind off Javagal Srinath for 119, but by then we were well on the way to winning the match, which we did by 10 wickets. There is a photo of me leaping about a metre in the air with my pads on and arms thrust skywards when we nailed the victory.

As my form surged, much was made of my dusty deck practice at Border Field, but the truth was this was a tour eight years in the making. Way back in 1993, Bob Simpson had taught me three different types of sweep shot with different bat heights for different balls and intentions. And for the last two years, I'd been playing on decks at Northants kept dry for our two young spinners, Graeme Swann and Jason Brown. Nor was this the first time I'd been to India. In 1998, Australia, sensing it had a good deal of cricket ahead of it on the subcontinent, sent a small group of young spin bowlers and batsmen to India for a special spin clinic. I managed to sneak in when Greg Blewett withdrew at the last moment, and the experience was pure gold. We began at Chennai's MA Chidambaram Stadium, later my home base for the Chennai Super Kings. I remember scanning the historic stands and – ironically – telling Matthew Elliott, 'This ground will be good to me . . . I'll score a Test century here one day.'

At the clinic we heard from former champion Indian spinners Bishan Bedi and Srinivas Venkataraghavan, who explained the way slow bowlers strategised, and how you could tell a man's intentions from his field placings. For instance, if Harbhajan is bowling to me with six men on the off side, what is he looking to achieve? Answer: he is probably trying to coax me to hit against the spin towards the leg side. Going to that spin clinic was one of the best opportunities I ever had. Now I was back in India, and I felt I could almost read the bowlers' thoughts.

During that first Test in 2001, I found plenty to smile about, even away from the ground. From my room in the Taj Mahal Palace & Tower, in Mumbai, I spotted a group of men assembling across the road beneath the magnificent Gateway of India. The men were conducting what appeared to be a group meeting but did nothing except laugh uproariously together. I found it was almost impossible not to giggle along with them.

At crucial stages of my life when I was looking for inspiration or guidance, signs like this would sometimes arrive out of the blue. This time the message was clear: stay positive, stay happy.

It was so captivating a sight I even urged Alfie Langer to rise early and watch the group. I'd never seen or heard of anything like it before, but I reckon those blokes had a fair handle on life. Scientists tell us that laughing releases endorphins, which make you happy, and it's certainly hard to be eaten up with worry when you're laughing like that. I might not have been laughing on the pitch but I was relaxed and positive, and that change in attitude was the key to my change in performance.

The Second Test, in Kolkata, was one of the most memorable matches of all time: India recovered from a follow-on to score a stunning victory, ending our 16-match winning streak. The turning point was the epic partnership of Rahul Dravid and V.V.S. Laxman, who came together late on the third day when India were 4/232, needing 20 to make us bat again. You couldn't have predicted it on form. Dravid hadn't scored a run all series, and Laxman had failed twice in the First Test, but they gave not a solitary chance in 90 overs and made 335 together on day four. Some of the shots Laxman played against Warnie, advancing down the wicket and smacking him over the infield, were simply outrageous. They were so good that the replays should have displayed a warning: *Young cricketers, don't try this at home.*

On that fourth morning, we'd been so confident of preserving our winning streak that Michael Slater had produced a box of cigars, provocatively sniffing one as if to say, 'This result is so close I can smell it.' We all saw the humour, as you do when you've won 16 in a row and fully expect to extend the margin. At that point Gilly had played 15 Tests in his career – and won the lot. But it just shows what can happen when you take success for granted. Chasing 384 to win, we collapsed on the last day and lost the match in front of a crowd yelling so loudly you felt as if you were at an AC/DC concert. We were stunned. The bottle of Southern Comfort Stephen Waugh had put under his chair for the celebrations was broken open to drown our sorrows. Gilly snapped one of Slats' cigars over his knee.

Just after we lost that Second Test, our coach, John Buchanan, made a tactical error in publicly questioning Warnie's fitness. Warnie was filthy, and I don't blame him. We didn't need to make further trouble for ourselves. I thought Warnie's problem in India was simply that he tried to spin the ball too much. Big turn never worried the Indians. They've played it almost from the cradle. Warnie would've been much better bowling a straighter line, keeping the pressure on with sliders and zooters and other more subtle tricks. He did this brilliantly in Sri Lanka in 2004, in his comeback series after a year-long drug ban. Warnie loved his big-turning leg break, and it was one of the best natural deliveries the game has seen. There was no question Warnie had the ability to test the Indians, and it was never a matter of them being too good for him. He just had the wrong strategy.

On we went to Chennai for the Third Test, and I took great joy in living out the prediction I'd made to Matthew Elliott three years before. I made 203 of our first innings of 391, and had the pleasure of dedicating my score to Kell for her 26th birthday. I was 147 not out overnight, and so excited that when I spoke to Kell on the phone, she thought I was never going to get to sleep. My sweep shot was in such good order that at one point India had four men prowling the fence, including two standing 10 metres apart. (Scorers later calculated that I compiled 60 per cent of my 549 runs for the series with the sweep. I scored as many runs in that one series as I had in my previous 13 Tests.)

My elation was cut short, however, when we lost the match on the final day. It's difficult to do justice to the sheer pandemonium that broke out in Chennai when Harbhajan Singh pushed Glenn McGrath square of the wicket to give India their victory total of 155 runs for the loss of eight wickets. It had been one of the greatest series ever. For almost a year it had been hyped as the last frontier – and suddenly it became our lost frontier. It was such a close thing. You never expect to win when you set a side only 155 for victory, but we scrapped and scrambled and almost got there. All seemed lost at 2/102, and even at 5/132 at tea we looked like we were gone. Three late wickets gave us a chance, but then it really was over.

Steve Waugh admitted at his final press conference that the pain of the loss was slightly lessened by the knowledge that the teams had given cricket something very special. The series revitalised Test cricket and attracted record ratings in both countries.

I was asked to stay on for the one-day series, and fitness coach Jock Campbell still taunts me about one comment I made. I was being rested, and when I looked at the team sheet I said innocently, 'Actually, it's still not a bad side.'

My confidence was sky-high, and much of that confidence came from my relationship with Steve Waugh. In a press conference on a hotel rooftop in Pune, I gave Stephen some well-deserved praise. I didn't want my words to reflect badly on Mark Taylor, who'd retired just before the 1999 West Indies tour when I was still on the outer, but there was no escaping the truth. Only by spotlighting, very briefly and without malice, my struggle in the Taylor years, could I fully convey how indebted I felt to Stephen for his support.

I said, 'Tugga has had a huge influence. I don't think I would be here now but for Stephen. Even when I wasn't on contract he had a big influence on me. With Mark, it was a very different relationship. The most important thing for him to be playing well and captaining well was for him to be in the side. There was obviously no room for me in that relationship. That's not criticism. It's the facts.'

23

Slats – the Best Day, the Worst Day

I had been picked. I had been dropped. I thought by now I understood the sensations involved. But neither experience prepared me for the way I felt on 22 August 2001, when I had a close-up view of how demotion and promotion impacted on two men I regarded as close mates: Michael Slater and Justin Langer.

Stephen and Gilly – our tour selectors – had decided Slats needed a break for the final Test of the 2001 Ashes series. They outvoted Trevor Hohns (who was back in Brisbane) two to one. Stephen noted that Slats was constantly on the move at the crease, causing poor footwork and bringing his head position out of line. Batting with him, I could tell he wasn't himself, though I wasn't fully aware of the depth of his personal issues. In fact, he was in the process of breaking up with his wife Stephanie.

Our team huddle at the Oval the day before the Test felt like that of a team under pressure, not one that already had the Ashes in the bag. We'd won the first three Tests by landslide margins, before England snatched a consolation win in the Fourth Test, when Mark Butcher's exceptional century enabled them to chase down 315 for victory.

When Stephen began announcing the team, with Justin Langer in and Slater out, Slats chipped in with, 'C'mon, Tugga, tell them the real story.' I'm still not sure what the real story was – or even if there was another story – but the fact that Alfie hadn't been making runs prompted suggestions that Slats was dropped for reasons other than his form. When Gilly told Slats he was out of line, Slats peeled away from the group.

I felt shaken and uncertain. On the one hand, I was feeling for Slats; on the other, I was thrilled Alfie had the chance to revive his career, after having been left out for Damien Martyn in the First Test. Alfie's the sort of character you can never write off. He had opened before in first-class cricket and was a tough, combative player mentally suited to the position. But the omens hadn't been good to that point, and it had crossed his mind that he might never play again.

I shared Alfie's joy – we were and remain the greatest of mates – so I didn't want him to see me hanging my head for Slats. And as I shared Slats' pain, I didn't want him to see me doing star jumps for Alfie, who was looking at me and thinking, *This is the best thing that's ever happened to us!* When the huddle broke up to do some laps, I cut away from the group and caught up with Slats on the way to the dressing-room. He had to be my first priority because he was the man with the heavy heart.

I said to him, 'Mate, I am just so disappointed for you. I want you to know that I love you.'

He replied, 'Haydos, I can't train today. I just can't do this.' Slats reckons now he could see the tears welling in my eyes;

I don't dispute it. Had I known then how circumstances would play out, I would've been even more emotional.

I went back onto the ground and Slats went into the dressing-room, where he was handed a cigarette from Warnie with a cautioning message: 'Be careful, Slats . . . don't do anything that's going to affect your career.' He would never play another Test for Australia.

This was the day I reached a new understanding of the unique bonds that are formed at the top of the order. No other person in the side could have felt the way I did then. I played 103 Tests, yet I never went out to bat alone. Slats had been my first opening partner in Test cricket, when we walked out together in Johannesburg in March 1994. We'd made two century partnerships in Australia, one in India and another of 98 in England, but we only played 14 Tests together. It was one of those 'could've, should've, would've' situations. It niggles at both of us that we never quite nailed it.

Slats says today, 'I know Haydos had a special bond with Justin, but there was certainly a lot of untapped potential with us as well. My heart is still a bit heavy over it. We were very different players but we just sort of clicked. We'd get in the middle and he would listen to my rubbish and somehow put up with it, and I would listen to his. It was rah-rah stuff. I always felt from the 1993 Ashes tour there'd be a time down the track when we opened for a long period. We were young. The potential was there.'

There was such a contrast between Slats' career and mine. In racing parlance, Slats was the slick colt that exploded out of the gates and shot to an early lead. I was the old plodder from Kingaroy, grinding away at my own pace around the outside fence. Where his career hit a wall, I just kept thumping away. Slats admits in his autobiography that he was swept away by his early success into a rockstar sort of lifestyle, and I sometimes wonder what would've happened had I been the one who made runs in that game at Leicester in 1993. It's quite possible I'd have lacked the personal skills to handle early success. When I did break through, both my cricket and my character were more fully formed.

Justin Langer, understandably, was euphoric at being picked. He'd been a lost soul for much of the tour. Stephen had so dreaded telling Alfie he'd been dropped for Marto for the First Test that he later admitted that after doing it he felt like throwing up. The little fella had been completely shattered. Midway through the tour Alfie went to Buck's room for advice, and Buck gave him a hug because he felt he needed one. It mightn't be a textbook remedy, but I think it was good coaching. There are times when you reach out for people and need to know they're there for you. Even though you're a part of the team, you can still feel lost and lonely and a bit jaded.

But now Alfie had a Test to prepare for. Before the match, he said, 'I have vowed, no matter what happens, to have the time of my life.' I'll never forget the sight of him bouncing down the steps of the Oval for the Fifth Test, with his trademark jaunty stride. He was smiling broadly. 'Wouldn't be dead for quids, me old mate – not for quids.' And we put on 158 runs, the first of 14 century opening partnerships, and perhaps the most emotional of them all, before Alfie was hit on the head by Andrew Caddick and retired hurt on 102.

Our century stand was the best moment of an ordinary tour for me. Looking back, I think I was a victim of my own impatience, too full of myself after my runs in India. It never really clicked for me in England, despite my county runs. If I had my three Ashes tours again, I'd be more patient, try to wear the ball down rather than take it apart from the start, or even slot in down the order, because in England, when the ball stops swinging and seaming and there's no real grip for the spinners, there are days when you feel like you'll never get out.

The tour had one long-term impact. When we returned home, Stephen asked Cricket Australia to change the rules to ensure no captain would ever have to vote on a call similar to the one involving Slats. None have since. These days, the team takes a selector on tour, who collaborates with the panel at home and they make a collective call. After the captain, the selectors are the most crucial appointments made by Cricket Australia and it irks me that they are not all full-time employees, fully accountable to CA. The captain has his say but has no official vote.

It's a system I would like to see change – I believe the captain *should* have a vote in selections. It's important the captain has full confidence in the players he's taking on the field, and for them to know he supports them. The coach is different. It makes sense for him to be one step removed from the selection process, so players with problems can approach him and feel he's 100 per cent on their side and not reporting back at selection meetings. There will always be challenging decisions, though – and certainly no tougher decision than the one made at the Oval that day, which shaped the careers of two outstanding players.

The unguarded moment – I will never forget the sound of that Curtly Ambrose delivery rattling my off stump in the 1996 Boxing Day Test at the MCG.

There seemed to be waves of pressure crashing down on me at Adelaide during the Fourth Test against the West Indies in 1997. I finally managed to raise my first Test ton (*far right*) and was relieved rather than ecstatic.

Above: Michael Slater and I are great mates. Here we are pictured preparing for an Australia A game at the Gabba in 1994–95.

Left: Being an outdoors boy I relished preseason boot camps such as this one for the Queensland cricket team. I'm wet and wild at the Enoggera army barracks in Brisbane.

Above: When I was still playing for Australia, I launched the Eddie Gilbert program, which nurtures the talents of Indigenous cricketers in outback Queensland. Reaching out to Indigenous Australia remains an important goal post-cricket.

Right: Unhappy campers. Symo and I inspect my refloated boat after our unfortunate swim to shore when it sank in Moreton Bay in 2000. I have never taken the sea for granted again.

Breakthrough. Slats and I celebrate Australia's 10-wicket win against India in the First Test at Mumbai in 2001.

I swept so much on the 2001 tour of India that the edge of the bat started to fall off. The sweep shot was my key to success that tour.

The sights, sounds and smells of India are compelling. Here I sample them from a hotel balcony in Pune during the 2001 tour.

Left: Although cricket is very much a team sport, it's nice to be recognised individually sometimes. I was chuffed to be awarded Man of the Match in the Second Test against South Africa in the 2001–02 series.

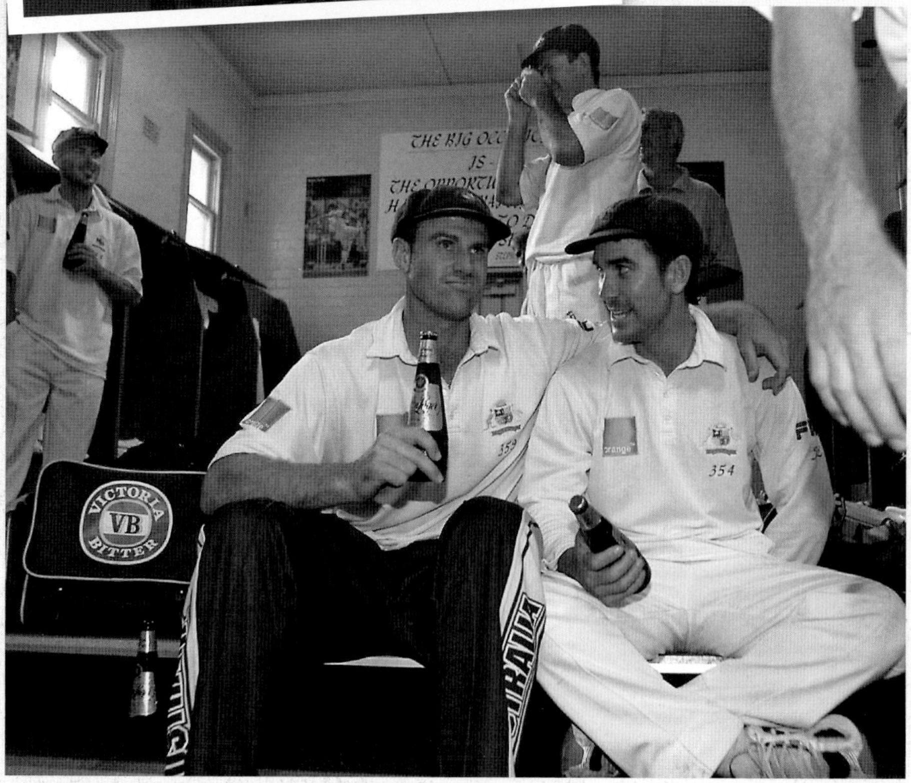

Below: Chilling out with my old mate Alfie at the SCG after a win against South Africa in the Third Test of the 2001–02 series. We were often together off the field.

Allan Border presenting me with the Allan Border Medal in 2002. AB has been a teammate, captain, mentor and inspiration of mine and to win the medal named in his honour was one of my proudest achievements.

Top: On my way to a century in the Second Test against Pakistan, October 2002, played in 50-degree heat in Sharjah.
Bottom: Is that the Sheikh of Sharjah or cricket's version of a well-cooked tandoori chicken? Damien Martyn and I cover our heads with wet blankets during our first innings in the Second Test.

Left: Happy days at the Gabba in 2002. An Ashes century against England in the First Test was reason to celebrate, particularly after a little verbal back-and-forth with Andy Caddick had got me fired up.

Below: Early in my career the Gabba used to fall silent when I batted because spectators were so nervous about my form. Eventually we all relaxed a bit, and it was always great to get out and meet the fans.

Top: Getting away from the game can be as important as playing it. Symo and I try our luck fly fishing in the Elgro River near Potchefstroom, South Africa, during the 2003 World Cup.
Bottom: Here I am surfing the Pier in Durban, home to the famous Gunston 500 pro surfing tournament. With its promise of mates, waves, runs and wins, Durban is one of my favourite tour destinations.

Playing Namibia in South Africa during the 2003 World Cup. We may have thrashed Namibia but their slow medium pacer Louis Burger did well to take three wickets against us, including mine.

During and after the 2003 World Cup victory in Johannesburg. The win was one of our greatest offshore triumphs.

Baggy green bliss in Antigua, 2003. The boys celebrate winning the Frank Worrell Trophy in the Test series against the West Indies by taking 'Frank' for a swim.

Hanging out with the locals on a visit to the Brazil–Guyana border during the 2003 West Indies tour.

Justin Langer and I were different dressing-room creatures before we batted. He liked to get into the buzz of the room, while I liked my own space. But once it was all over we often sat together and shared our thoughts.

INSIDE THE GAME

Umpires

Before my career-saving century against England at the Oval in 2005, New Zealand's Billy Bowden visited the nets and I approached him for advice. I told him my goal was to try to tighten up in the Test; I felt I'd been expanding my attacking game too quickly, and I asked him to speak up if he thought so too. During the match I'd say to him, 'What do you reckon?' and he'd say, 'Looking real good, just stay patient. Looking good, ay.' I'd sometimes ask, 'Is he swingin' that much?' and he'd say, 'Oh, it's just starting to reverse.' Billy was brilliant that week. He really helped me.

People might be surprised that I had conversations like this with umpires, but I never considered it insider trading. I used every resource I legally could to enhance my game, and umpires were part of that process. Sometimes they'd drop subtle lines that I considered important feedback. Bowden, in particular, was good this way. He might say, 'Gee, you're grumpy this week,' and suddenly you'd realise your mood had been dark, even though you hadn't been aware of it. Big Steve Bucknor, a genuine nice guy, solid decision-maker and probably my favourite umpire, would say, 'What's the hurry today? Plenty of time.' Then it would hit you he was right – you'd surged into fourth gear without any need to be so hasty. He got you thinking.

Most umpires were older men who really loved the game, and although I didn't always agree with them, I always enjoyed their company and their contribution. I found them interesting because they weren't often attracted to the traditional trappings of professional sport. Where cricketers might get off talking about bats or sponsorships,

Bucknor would much prefer to talk about his shoe fetish, which was no surprise given he had size 15 feet. He was always asking me for pairs of shoes and I gave him some for his daughter, but never had any large enough for the big fella.

I had great respect for the umpires of my generation. I had no reservations about being open with them, saying things like, 'I was really surprised you gave me out yesterday,' but I never attacked them. I tried to inquire rather than interrogate. I might have inherited this approach from my father, who always found great value in information-swapping with his neighbours – though Mum would probably say he just loved a chinwag. The lessons he learnt this way, whether they were about the right chemicals to use or some new technology, were invaluable to his farming life.

There were times when I was able to give the umpires feedback as well. Sometimes you'd be at the bowlers' end in the middle of a Test, and an umpire would tell you about a problem he had with a player or situation in the game.

Indian umpire Srinivas Venkataraghavan was a decorated former slow bowler who loved the game and knew it from all angles. He gave me invaluable tips about batting in India during the 1998 spin clinic I'd attended with him in Chennai. I had great respect for the man and his opinions, and would sometimes say to him, 'What about this field?' He'd say, 'They're obviously trying to make you hit across the line,' tutoring me at a vital stage of my career. I think he took pleasure in seeing me blossom in later years, in part due to the wisdom he passed on.

South Africa's Rudi Koertzen had a novel way of pulling me into line when I was in the midst of verbal combat. He'd take three or four big, slow and deliberately theatrical steps towards me, then pull an imaginary knife from his pocket and pretend to slit his own throat . . . then mime cutting his wrists. It was his way of saying, 'One more word and it will be off with your head.' It was a clever way of getting his point across – serious messages sprinkled with humour are more likely to be received and understood. I found him very disarming. Sometimes Rudi would simply walk slowly towards me with his hand cupped behind his ear. That would happen when someone had got to me and he knew I was about to return fire. When a wicket fell, I'd always join the players' huddle, but occasionally I'd also meander over to the umpires' huddle and Rudi would say things like, 'I know he just had a couple of cracks at you, and I am watching you veeeeee-ry closely.' He'd be ahead of my game.

I also had a good connection with Pakistani umpire Aleem Dar, a very genuine and generous man, who now gives a portion of his monthly wage to the family of the bus driver killed in Lahore in 2009, when terrorists attacked the bus carrying the Sri Lankan Test team. My friendship with him started around 2003, when it became known that his young daughter had died while he was in South Africa for the World Cup that year. Aware that the World Cup meant so much to him, his wife had kept the news from him until just before the final. I felt so sorry for him. His daughter's death was one of the reasons Aleem developed one of his signature habits: as he walked out to umpire, he'd raise his hand in the air, then touch his heart and then the ground. It was influenced by his Muslim faith, and was his way of saying thanks to the Almighty above, saying a prayer for himself and recognising the fact that from the earth he had come and to earth one day he would return. When Aleem umpired, I'd mark a line for him to stand on before he got there, then after he arrived he'd draw a line across it. Together, the two lines made the sign of the cross. It was always one of my favourite on-field moments.

Brisbane-based umpire Peter 'Porky' Parker was another great character and a terrific bloke. One of the long-running gags in the Queensland and Australian dressing-rooms was based on the august way Porky would give you guard. He'd say, 'Centre!' (more like 'Centrrrre!') with all the gravitas of someone announcing the winning host city for the next Olympic Games. The boys got off on it. The interest started at Queensland level and then Symo filtered it through to the national side. Eventually some players started to gratuitously check their guard just to hear Porky, almost quivering with the sheer magnificence of the moment, say the magic word.

Ricky Ponting in particular loved this prank, as he did all pranks. Stephen Waugh was the same. For all the weight of expectation and responsibility they carried as national captains, neither lost his sense of fun. They had to be involved in any form of skullduggery, and preferably somewhere close to the middle of it. After about three years Porky wised up to our silly game, but it didn't stop the frequent requests to check middle stump just so they could hear the 'c' word. Porky reckons that when he was starting out in umpiring he was told that it was important to radiate a sense of authority, and that was the reason he packed such a punch when giving guard.

Interstate teams liked to claim that I was Porky's love child, because he rarely gave me out lbw. After initially rubbishing the suggestion, I found it more fun – and more aggravating to the opposition – to go along with it. When players from other states claimed my pads were a 'Pork-free zone', I'd nod and say, 'Yeah, I wouldn't even bother appealing if I was you. You've wasted your time for 15 years, why bother now?' You don't reckon that used to stir them up! Few people connected with cricket loved the game as much as Porky. I used to talk fishing with him in the middle, and he was always good company and a thoroughly decent bloke.

Martin Whitby was another Queensland umpire whose company

I enjoyed. He was a farmer and a fishermen, so we had a lot in common, and he also owned a sawmill I once visited to see how timber was cut up. A while later he phoned me to say he'd taken possession of a giant red cedar. I bought part of it and he kept it for a couple of years to dry out, before milling it up to become our dining table, my favourite piece of furniture by far because of our connection.

I've been pleased to see a generation of former players, including Paul Reiffel and Bruce Oxenford, rise through the umpiring ranks to international level. Pistol was such a cool, dry character as a player, and he umpires the same way. Watching him on television once, I smiled when a bowler seemed unimpressed by the lbw verdict he'd given. Pistol just said, 'Mate, it was missing leg.' Typical no-fuss, to-the-point Pistol.

I had genuine affection for English umpire David Shepherd, who passed away while I was writing this book. In 2001, he had a really tough series between England and Pakistan, where he gave some English batsmen out on deliveries later shown to be no-balls. He was really down about it and considered quitting. I remember seeing him that year and saying, 'Shep, you're a really great umpire – I love you, everyone loves you, so just hang in there.' He did, and years later he told me how much that support had meant to him at a very difficult time. It struck me that in a lot of ways umpires were identical to players – we all had our insecurities and confidence lapses, and we treasured every bit of heartfelt support that came our way.

24

Waugh Games

I played 103 Tests, yet there are times when I feel lucky to have played one, especially when I recall my opening exchange with the man who'd be my skipper in 40 of those Tests, Stephen Waugh.

Stephen and I first met on a Gabba greentop in a Sheffield Shield match in November 1991. Although he wasn't in the Test team at the time, he was still one of the biggest names in Australian cricket. I was an ambitious 20-year-old playing my second first-class match. He called me 'Fat Boy' and chirped away, 'You're not playing schoolboy cricket now.' I snapped back, 'I don't give a stuff who you are . . . This is our home turf, mate.' I loved that sort of stuff. My philosophy was, 'Throw whatever you like at me, but don't expect me to just sit there and be a passive target. I'm going to come back with something.' I remember next to nothing of the 64 and 43 not out I made in that game, but I do remember every word I exchanged with Stephen. That neither of us backed down forged a lasting personal respect between us.

Stephen loved taunting Queensland. Even when Queensland won the Shield for the first time in 1994–95, it didn't silence him. When the state announced it would erect a special grove at Allan Border Field, with 12 trees planted in honour of the 12 men who'd broken the Shield drought, Stephen claimed, 'We've got one of them too – it's called the NSW State Forest.' Less than two years after our exchange at the Gabba, I toured England with Stephen as part of the 1993 Ashes squad, and watching him at close range was like a four-month tutorial on the art of batting preparation. Stephen was very definite about what he was trying to achieve.

You can feel like you're out of sight playing English county cricket, which is why his phone call to me at Northants in 1999, when I had been in the Test match wilderness for two years, lifted my spirits so much. Asked years later why he'd rung me, Steve referred to the hollow experiences of his own career before he became one of the game's finest players. He said, 'I knew that when you were out of the side and struggling a bit the phone rarely rings. I didn't consider it essential to ring people when they were in good form because I knew they'd have plenty of support. But the game can get pretty lonely sometimes, so I made a point of doing that, not just to Haydos but a few other players on the fringe. I also felt that averaging around 60 at the Gabba, he had to have what it took to play Test cricket. I was never worried about his technique. He made strong contact with the ball, and that was all that mattered.'

The Waughs – Stephen and Mark – were a fascinating duo to play with and I had endless time for both of them. Whenever I missed out on a one-day side and Mark was in it, I never complained, because I always considered him the better player.

And when I was playing in a team with both Waughs I considered myself fortunate. Who wouldn't?

Mark saw life in black and white. He wasn't really into on-field clapping or the other motivational stuff. He appealed when he thought it was out and didn't bother when he didn't. Even his sledging was to the point. When fiery South African spinner Pat Symcox tried to wind him up one day, Mark just looked him in the eye and asked, 'When was the last time you actually took a wicket?' There were no complications or hidden agendas with Mark. He returned to the dressing-room after his Test hundred on debut and said simply, 'I should have been playing for years.' He'd dismiss rivals airily, especially spinners, saying, 'He's rubbish, that bloke.' Stephen would do the same and try to justify it; Mark just said it.

The twins couldn't have been more different than if they were the positive and negative ends of a battery. Stephen had no interest in racing. Mark loved a punt. Stephen loved photography and has thousands of shots in his private collection. I'm not sure whether Mark even owns a camera. Stephen had the desire to go to war for the players in the formative years of the Australian Cricketers' Association. That just wasn't Mark's bag. Stephen was so structured he knew precisely what he wanted out of a net session and would count throwdowns. He'd say, 'I want 20 good ones.' Nineteen good ones would not suffice. He wanted 20, and would wait until he got them. (Strangely, for a player who was so diligent with his preparation, Stephen's kit was always a total shambles. In fact, there were times when it took two or three of us to sit on his gear coffin before he could lock it.) Mark never bothered much with plans – and he wasn't huge on net sessions. He was just a much freer personality. It used to amaze me that there was so little conversation and general contact between the twins. If Gaz and I had played in a Test win together, I reckon we'd have been inseparable after it. But the Waughs barely exchanged a word. There was no hostility – it's just the way it was.

Even their eating habits were different. If they were animals on the African plains, Mark was the lion who went straight in for his feast, while Stephen was the jackal, who'd sniff and fuss around in the background before settling on his meal. We only got an insight into their connection when one of them was under the pump. Invariably, the other twin was the first dressing-room voice to stick up for his brother.

In spite of all the differences, there were some similarities between them too. Neither were gym junkies. They did what they had to. Mark loathed gym work because he considered it a waste of time, whereas Stephen didn't rate it because he'd started in an era when no one did it. As far as gym time went, the Waugh boys were the last out of the barrier, but to their credit they were as fit at the end of their careers as they had been throughout. On their specific strengths and weaknesses they worked as hard as anyone.

Stephen may come across as tough and to the point – which he is – but he's also sensitive, thoughtful, emotional and shy. People see him as a serious character but he loved to laugh, which is why he was such great mates with Tim May, who has a fabulous sense of humour. I've heard people criticise Stephen for leaving the game completely since his retirement, but he never wanted to be a talking head on television. That's not him. He contributes in his own way, as part of an international committee that discusses laws and major issues within the game. He has chosen to devote himself to the Steve Waugh Foundation, which has multinational interests, and in Kolkata, where the charity was launched, he is seen as a prince. Given his natural shyness, I often marvel at his achievements in the public arena, and how he handled the high profile of being a sporting superstar. The secret to it was that he enjoyed challenging himself and moving out of his comfort zone. The greatest praise I can give to Stephen is to acknowledge that, without him, I wouldn't have succeeded at Test level. It really is that simple.

25

Alfie and Me

It was a moment frozen in time for me. Late October, 2009: I was driving home from a break on Stradbroke Island when my old mate Justin Langer rang from Perth. 'Dus,' he said to me, 'I will never play another game in my life.' After 360 first-class games spanning 19 years, it was all over. Alfie had arrived home from his final stint of county cricket and packed his whites away for the last time.

I was speechless, though I probably shouldn't have been. Initially I'd been surprised that Alfie had batted on after his Test match retirement, playing three more seasons of county cricket with Somerset, yet I was still stunned that the man who once seemed like he could have batted forever had suddenly stopped for good. He sounded at peace with his decision, though, and I was happy for him. He was finally ready to move on, which is the way it should be.

How different to the first time we met, the day before a Shield game at the Gabba in 1991. When I walked past Alfie in what he falsely claims was a gym shirt with a hearty, 'G'day, mate!' he took me for a groundsman. I think he called me mate as well, which isn't surprising. 'Mate' is a very useful word early in your career, when you're not really sure who you're playing against. It certainly ensures you won't embarrass yourself. The next morning, Alfie couldn't believe it when I came out to bat.

We didn't have a decent chat until meeting at the Cricket Academy a few years later, when I gave a presentation at a coaching course. I was asked what it felt like to be out of form, and replied that, at those times, holding the bat was like holding another man's old fella in your hands. Everyone seemed aghast, but it grabbed their attention. Certainly Alfie liked the line. Almost two decades later, he's still sending the story around at guest speaking nights, but unlike a lot of his stories, this one needs no embellishment. In fact, it's a bit of a rarity among his after-dinner tales because it actually happened!

By 2001 I felt I was reasonably established in the Test team. But when Alfie joined me later that year at the top of the order, things really clicked. Of all the things I achieved in cricket, few gave me greater pleasure than my long-standing union at the top of the order with Alfie. We were united in our passion by our work ethic, but diametrically opposed in other areas. I was always in trouble if I over-thought things. I needed to have a great structure in place, then let my instincts take over. Alfie, however, was really comfortable in 'think mode'. In his shower at home he had for many years a laminated sheet with a checklist of four words: physical, technical, mental and spiritual. He'd give himself a tick or a cross against each one, depending on how he'd measured up for the day.

That would have done my head in. Shower time is chill-out

time for me. The thought of Alfie standing starkers in the shower after a double century and giving himself top marks for the day was too much information, I'm afraid. I'd say to him, 'Mate, what're you on about? It's life, it's not meant to be that hard.' In our on-field communication he'd think a lot about what he said and was very focused, while I was just running on gut feeling. But I could tap into what he was saying because it made sense, and he'd tap into the way I just let go of everything, which he found hard to do.

Our body language was also very different. We were the original good cop, bad cop. He'd be as smiling and happy as I was cold. My philosophy was 'Give 'em nothing'. I'd occasionally leave my bunker, exchange a bit of fire with an opponent, then immediately retreat into my mental cave. But we were in the zone together. We were having fun. Ask any athlete about their purple patch, and I'll bet they'd say the same.

Alfie and I spent a lot of time together off the field, too. Even when he wasn't actually with me, he never seemed too far away. In my gym on Stradbroke Island, he wrote a message (now plastered on the front of one of my exercise machines) that read, *The pain of discipline is not as bad as the pain of disappointment.* The night before my 380 against Zimbabwe in Perth, in 2003, I went around to Justin and Sue's place and sat on his front lawn, and we had a big cigar together to mark the start of the summer. He started with a toast to absent friends, then we puffed on the cigar and looked at the stars. Even now I will occasionally get a text from him simply saying 'absent friends', which means he is having a good time, normally with his family. We started the absent friends toast about the time the Waugh brothers retired.

Connections are hard to contrive. They either happen

or they don't. But from our very first partnership, Alfie and I just clicked, and I felt amazingly lucky to have found such a connection with someone who also happened to be my opening partner for Australia. And as with any best mate, it's not always about talking. When we were having that cigar under the stars we didn't need to talk much.

We were more compatible technically than most people realise. Before we arrived, people used to talk about the benefits of a left- and right-handed combination, because bowlers had to constantly adjust their lines when the strike was rotated. The assumption was that it was easier bowling to two lefties, because you could use the same plan. Not true – at least not with us.

You couldn't bowl outside off stump to Alfie because he'd just nick you down to third man for fun. In fact, I always felt that's when he was in supreme form, when he was playing those cheeky little nudges through slips that looked half-accidental, but were actually the result of beautifully late, soft hands.

In contrast, that wide ball was not my favourite delivery. For much of my career I didn't enjoy the cut shot, and my footwork was programmed to let dangerous balls go, not defuse and deflect them as Alfie so deftly did. My wrists were trained to turn to steel, his to rubber.

We were products of our cricketing education. Because I learnt on seaming decks at the Gabba, balls that were pitched around off stump and moving away set off warning bells for me. But Alfie, like Damien Martyn, had learnt on the high, true-bouncing decks of Perth, where you can use the pace of the ball with soft hands to glide it to the third-man boundary. Our partnership was a great argument for having different wickets in Australia, because you develop batsmen with different strengths.

And it's another reason why I will always argue against 'drop in' pitches, which are more docile and lack character.

There's a certain kind of cricket boffin who likes to visit cricketers' backyards and look for the little things that helped to shape their game, such as the sloping backyard at the Waugh family house that drew the ball towards the legs of the Waugh twins and made both dynamite off their pads. They might well conclude that my reservations about the cut shot were formed by the endless hours of indoor play in our poolroom on the farm – you can still see the white stumps we drew on the wall. A couple of metres away, at point, was our 'no-go zone' – the glass doors. So the cut shot was out, and – as Mum still boasts – the glass doors were never broken.

Alfie's great strength was my soft spot. If I hit the ball behind point it was often a mistake. If we'd been rock groups, I was Hunters and Collectors and he was Nudgers and Deflectors. Bowlers would try and cut off Alfie's strength by bowling at him. When they did that to me, there were runs straight and through the leg side. I loved to murder the straight line. We also transformed our techniques in ways that made it harder for bowlers to formulate plans. Late in Alfie's career, bowlers felt more confident about getting him so they bowled straighter to him, and he developed an excellent cover drive. And bowlers realised that one way to keep me quiet was to bowl wider of off stump, so I developed my cut shot.

Alfie's greatest skill was using the pace of the ball. Mine was being up and at the ball. Alfie could work the ball in a way I struggled to do, and I could vary where I took guard or bat out of my crease to dominate an attack in a way he couldn't quite manage. Quite wrongly, Alfie was accused of being the sluggish one in our partnership. It bugged him a bit, which is why he has a photo up in his poolroom in Perth of a Test scoreboard that reads 'Langer 51, Hayden 1' – photographic evidence that he was never the barnacle. Often he outscored me early and would beat me to 50, because his method – the off-side glides in particular – were more useful than my driving against the new ball. Quite often, I'd catch him when the spinners came on. He was a rotator against spin, whereas I tried to get hold of them.

People often think that because we were so close we shared absolutely everything. We didn't. I was always a little superstitious about my batting cues, key words such as 'Fight!' or 'Full!' or 'Now!' that went off inside my head and triggered me to do something. They were spoken internally when the ball was just about to be delivered, when I'd tell myself to fasten the bayonet and get down the wicket to a spinner. I didn't explain them to anyone, not even Alfie. I have a theory that once you talk about something like that, its power is somehow diminished.

And as great as our connection was, I just couldn't talk much cricket to Alfie because he was so intense. When we did talk about cricket, it was mainly about his game. If I'd talked to him about my game, it would have sent me bonkers. Ricky Ponting was different. I could talk to him because we were agreed on the right way to go about it.

Ponting is one of the greatest readers of batting technique I've ever seen. He knew my game so well that he could tell what I was thinking by how I picked up the bat in my backswing. Sometimes he'd say to me, 'I know what you're thinking but, mate, let's just refocus.' And I would say the same to him. If he played a sweep shot I'd say, 'Mate, why would you play that shot? You hit the ball better than anyone down the ground on the leg side. If you want to play a sweep I'll throw you 500 balls in the nets.'

We didn't often talk technique, but when we did it was all business, along the lines of, 'This is how we're going to do it.' Meanwhile, Alfie was always looking for new entries to the gospel of batting, and in his hands it was a very thick book indeed. I'd say, 'Mate, just watch the ball,' and did my best to talk him out of any new-fangled trends.

One of those trends – I'll never forget it – was this exotic late twist of the head to face up. I suspect the intention was to get your head straight and eyes as square on to the ball as possible at the point of delivery. It made no sense at all to me but Alfie gave it a go, and because he was a legend of district cricket in Perth, the practice spread faster than a new David Beckham hairstyle. When I saw Mike Hussey do it, I decided it was time to save the cricket world from this dangerous new fad. I said to Huss, 'Mate, what the hell are you doing? Just worry a lot less about it, right?' But then when Ryan Campbell started doing it, I knew West Australian cricket was on the verge of producing its own version of the *Star Wars* classic, *Attack of the Clones*. There was nothing I could do.

In retrospect, it's probably no wonder Alfie thought a lot about the position of his head, because during his career it took a fearful drubbing. The worst of all was in his 100th Test match in Johannesburg, when he was knocked down first ball by Makhaya Ntini. 'Mate, we know you've copped one, now get up,' I said, sauntering down the wicket. But my attitude changed instantly when I saw his eyes. They were gone, and so was he.

There was no question at the time – he had to retire hurt. But should he bat in the second innings? As we were closing in on victory, it became clear it could come down to the last wicket. I was simply in my element that day as a scheming, dressing-room double agent winding up my two great mates Ponting and Langer. Back and forth I went, playing one off against the other, deftly probing their sensitivities. You could argue that such a delicate issue should be beyond any form of gee-up, but I have always reckoned if the Anzacs could poke fun at the Turks by hoisting up cans of bully beef in the trenches for them to shoot at, then we shouldn't stress too much about what happens in a cricket dressing-room.

I knew Punter didn't want Alfie to bat, so I went up to Ricky and said, 'What are you talking about? We're going to lose a Test here. You have to let him bat!' But Punter wouldn't budge and was saying things like, 'Mate, he's gonna die, he's been hit on the head so many times.'

Deep down I also knew Alfie shouldn't be batting, because he still couldn't see properly and was off balance. It actually took him several months to fully recover from the blow. But I couldn't help myself, because I knew what it meant to Alfie to place the team before himself. So I said to him, 'Mate, he's going to declare on you,' and he snapped back, 'Dus, Dus . . . I'm gonna walk out there and bat. I don't care. He can declare but I am going to let the world know he's pulling me off because I'm not going down in history as a weak prick. If he declares, I am declaring our friendship over!'

So I rushed back to Punter with the most earnest face I could muster and said, 'Mate, you're going to kill him anyway by not letting him bat, so you may as well do it with a cricket ball. It's his 100th Test – this could be the greatest thing he ever does.' By that stage Punter, whose natural inclination is to get punchy when cornered, had had quite enough of me. I've never seen him so vulnerable. I knew he couldn't get too angry with me because of one simple fact – if he was the man who'd taken the head-blow, he'd have batted.

Eventually we won with two wickets to spare, and the question of whether Alfie should bat or not was successfully avoided. Alfie showed his true colours in the rooms after the match, walking around saying, 'Helluva Test, that one,' and enjoying the celebrations as much as anyone, even though he'd faced just one ball.

Wouldn't you miss that spirit? I know I did. After Alfie retired from Test cricket in January 2007, I never felt quite the same. It had absolutely nothing to do with the calibre of his replacements, Phil Jaques and Simon Katich, who are terrific blokes and fine players. But when you have a partnership that's right, everything just flows. It's like driving from Brisbane to Cairns at your own pace, just floating along. Having a new partner is like making the same trip with a police car on your tail. You're instantly aware of every little detail. Should I be indicating? Am I going too fast? Alfie and I never tried to analyse our connection too much. It was what it was. When Jaquesey came in, I wanted him to do well and build a solid start to his career, and I wanted to be a part of that process. But it takes energy to start a new partnership in any form of life – especially when the old partnership has been so fulfilling.

The bond between Alfie and me was cemented each Christmas Eve, when our two families, the Buchanans and anyone else who wanted to come shared mass together in Melbourne. Father Pat

Maroney, who married Kell and I, had moved to Melbourne and gave us a special service at Mazenod College in Mulgrave. We had a few beers and a bit of a get-together afterwards.

When we were playing together, Alfie and I developed a custom where he would mark centre as he faced the first ball of a Test, then I would cross it with a line when we changed strike to form the sign of the cross. When I was at the bowler's end while he was preparing to face the first ball I would mark centre and he would cross it when we changed ends. It was another anchor in our relationship.

When we marked the sign of the cross at the crease I would always say a silent prayer: *Whatever happens today is in your hands*.

26

No Business Like Shoaib Business

Put Shoaib Akhtar and me together and you had cricket's 'perfect storm'. We pressed each other's buttons. I loved facing Shoaib because everything about him – his pace, aggression and self-indulgent behaviour – roused my competitive instincts to fever pitch. We respected each other's ability, but there was no friendship. And I never thought he had enough respect for the game.

Nevertheless, Shoaib had amazing gifts. In Perth in 2004 he bowled me with a massive hooping banana-like inswinger that I let go. It was one of the best balls I have ever faced – just unplayable. If I had to face that ball 100 times over it would have got me 100 times. As a pure strike weapon, Shoaib was awesome. But he was also a vulnerable character. He had so much bravado and swagger that you wondered what lay beneath. Was it a mask for insecurity? Did he really have doubts about his ability? Deep down we all have fears – I certainly did – and you only know whether you can deal with them when you are seriously challenged.

The first time I ever saw Shoaib was when I was playing for Queensland in 1999 at Allan Border Field. He was bowling like the wind, so I decided to stir him up by provocatively blowing kisses at him. Because I wasn't playing for Australia at the time, Shoaib was dropping taunting lines like, 'You must be a crap player if you haven't been able to knock Mark Taylor out of the Test team.' I followed up with, 'We'll see.' When he celebrated hitting me in the chest as I missed a pull shot, I fired back, 'Is that all you've got?' My batting partner Stuey Law said, 'You idiot! What are you doing? Just remember there're two of us out here and I have to face him as well. Don't fire him up too much.' It was too late to back down. 'Mate,' I told Stuey, 'I don't care if I have to take every ball from this bloke.' I meant it, too.

Although Shoaib was exceptionally quick, my theory was that he only had three top-class overs in him. He was cricket's blazing comet – a bowler whose flame burned exceptionally brightly but briefly. I'd suggest to the boys at team meetings that if you were prepared to batten down, show physical courage and give him nothing early, he would lose his menace. I was more than happy to do that job.

My favourite duel with him came in the fan-forced oven that was the Second Test of a three-match series on neutral turf – Sharjah – in October 2002, a series initially scheduled for Pakistan before the nation was declared unsafe to tour. A few months earlier I'd had a look at the Pakistan side during a midwinter one-day series in Australia. Shoaib didn't play then, and even if he had, I'm not sure I would have taken much notice. My mind was on other things – Kell was about to give birth to our first child, Grace. Kell met me in the days when it was 'no girls on tour'. And when she was pregnant with Gracie, I'd just made it back into the one-day team. So I'll forever be grateful to a mate who called when I was in Melbourne preparing for a game. He asked how Kell was faring, and when I said, 'Good – the baby could come at any time,' he said, 'Well, what are you doing there then?' A bell went off inside my head and I suddenly knew I had to get home. I saw team manager Steve Bernard, and within hours was rushing back to Brisbane, missing the second game of the series. It was one of the best decisions I've ever made: Kell went into labour overnight, and Grace arrived soon after.

Shoaib had taken 4/0 against us in a truly exceptional spell in the First Test, in Colombo, sparking a rare collapse – at this point we were dominating teams the world over. We entered the Pakistan series having just beaten South Africa in five of the six Tests played the previous summer. We then moved to Sharjah for the Second and Third Tests. When I rang Kell during the Second Test and she asked how hot it was, I told her the only possible way to comprehend could be to set our oven to 100 degrees, open it up and let the air blow all over her. I wasn't being flippant either. The official temperature recorded was 51°C, but it felt even hotter, a cricketing furnace the likes of which I'd never experienced before.

As we were walking out for the first innings Shoaib said, 'I'm going to kill you today.' 'Well, mate,' I replied, 'you've got 18 balls to do it, because then you'll have had enough!'

When he bowled, I reinforced the point by loudly counting his deliveries. 'One!' I called with a chuckle after his first delivery had been driven to the cover fence by Alfie. Shoaib screamed, 'What did you say?' I answered, 'You've got 17 left.' He spun on his heel and stormed off.

As the countdown continued I aggravated him further by

following him around. He got progressively more hostile and shouted again, almost hysterically, 'I'm gonna kill you!' Alfie, who always enjoyed the theatrical side of Test cricket, was loving it. He was at the other end laughing as Shoaib and I traded our best insults. At the time I thought each of my arrows struck home, but now I actually think a lot of them bounced off him because he struggled to come to grips with the Australian accent.

Still, I could tell by the third over that he was feeling the stress. He was blowing up a storm, sweating profusely, and his face looked as if it was going to explode. There was certainly no crime in feeling the pinch. It was so hot many of our bowlers suffered heat stress after three- or four-over spells. (Brett Lee was so hot when he came off that officials watched incredulously as layers of steam rose from his torso as ice was applied to it.) Shoaib's adrenalin was peaking, almost overflowing, and I decided to try pushing him even further into his red zone. He had an ultra-long 30-metre run-up, and just before he got to the crease in his third over, I pulled away and refused to face him. I had the perfect excuse – as he was running to the wicket he was repeating his line, 'I'm gonna kill you!' I approached the umpire, Venkat, and expressed my concern that the Rawalpindi Express had run off the rails. Venkat agreed, and not being a man to be trifled with, from that point I sensed any 50/50 lbw call at Venkat's end might just go my way.

Shoaib was still bowling quickly – one ball in his third over registered at 155 kph – but a dramatic thing happened after his final ball of the third over, the last one in the big 'countdown'. He walked off. His spell was over. I was right! By this stage – with the contest and the heat doing my head in – I completely lost it and started sledging him. I gave him a massive send-off and even waved him off, trying to disguise it so people might have thought I was waving at our room for new gloves. We had to be really careful about our on-field actions, as there was a lot of talk in the media about our behaviour, and match officials watched us closely. Shoaib did return later, and bowled 11 more overs in the innings, but that was his contribution for the remainder of the Second Test and he did not play in the Third.

He had one moment of triumph against me late in the first innings when he bowled a short ball that didn't rise as much as I'd expected. It thundered into my helmet and felt more like a brick than a ball. I saw stars and felt groggy. It was the only time I can recall really copping one in the helmet throughout my career. Shoaib seized upon the moment to snatch the initiative with some verbal pleasantries of his own, and our joust reached a new level of hostility. There was gamesmanship aplenty. Several times Shoaib even stopped in his delivery stride to warn me about backing up too far. I told reporters after the day's play that this didn't seem the smartest tactic to me. Any time a fast bowler runs 30 metres to the wicket in 50-degree heat and doesn't bowl a ball . . . well, put it down as a victory to the batsman, I reckon.

I was the ninth man out and scored 119, seven runs more in my first innings than Pakistan made for the match. Fortunately, the whole game took only 12 hours – and 901 balls, the third fewest in history – and we didn't have to bat a second time. The old saying that a quick game was a good game had never rung truer for us, and Warnie made it possible with match figures of 8/24, a golden contribution for many reasons. Had the match stretched a couple more days, people would have started collapsing on the field rather than in the rooms.

I've never really struggled with heat. Perhaps it's a genetic thing. Maybe it was the result of all those carefree hours running up and down the hills in midsummer on the farm, conditioning me for greater challenges. But I felt it in Sharjah like I have never felt it before or since. I was cooked to the point where I had one beer at the end of the first day and felt like a drunken sailor. I could barely walk afterwards, and told reporters, 'If hell is hotter than this, I definitely don't want to go there.'

In these kinds of conditions, I have a trusted routine: I come off the ground, take everything off and jump in an ice bath, submerging myself up to my neck for about 10 minutes before having anything to drink. The aim is always to get your core temperature down.

That day I had to use every tool at my disposal – wet towels, ice vests, ice scarves, drinks – to keep resetting myself. I made it – just – but no one who played in that Test could ever say they felt comfortable with the conditions, or that they beat the heat. I'm convinced that if you'd put four pads on a camel and sent it out to bat for Australia in that Test, it would have eventually come off with a migraine. It seemed ludicrous to be playing any form of sport in those conditions. That match, in fact, led to new rules being introduced about extreme heat conditions. Not before time, we reckoned. Like many scores made overseas, my century didn't create the media splash of a Boxing Day extravaganza, but it remained one of my best, and I will never forget that showdown with Shoaib.

Shoaib was a powerful athlete and after he took steroids he became huge. You could see the change in him over a period of several years. In October 2006, he tested positive for nandrolone and was banned for two years, yet somehow got off on appeal to a three-man committee of Pakistan officials in December that year.

That riled me then and still does now. At the time I was getting drug-tested every other week in Australia. I had no problem with that, but what's the point in testing everyone if you're not going to have a level playing field? That Shoaib somehow managed to duck that drug charge said everything about the International Cricket Council's inability to handle sticky wickets. Can you imagine what would happen if an Australian cricketer tested positive to nandrolone, a steroid that enhances muscle growth? Shane Warne copped a one-year ban for testing positive to a diuretic, which is basically a slimming tablet, yet Shoaib got off for nandrolone. It doesn't make sense to me.

I spoke publicly about Shoaib at the Allan Border Medal night in Melbourne in 2007, just before leaving for the World Cup in the West Indies, and I have no regrets about it. I feel strongly that sport has a responsibility to be globally accountable. I wished one of our sport's senior administrators had had the gumption to address the issue and give Shoaib the ban he deserved. His excuse – that he didn't know what he was taking – was no excuse at all. When asked by the *Sydney Morning Herald* for my thoughts I didn't hold back, even though we'd been warned to be tight-lipped. Asked if the decision by Pakistan to select Akhtar and fellow drug-cheat Mohammad Asif for the 2007 World Cup had been a talking point among the Australians, I said, 'It's a laughable point amongst our players because we've worked very hard to be clean athletes. It's ludicrous and it's not fair. We're all tested equally. So if someone's tested positive for a steroid, then they have to have the penalties of the game. Anything short of that is a failure from our governing body, simple as that.'

It still amazes me that the issue could be any more complicated.

27

380 – a Pinnacle in Perth

In December 2003, I was part of the annual intake of Australian world-record holders for that year's edition of *Guinness World Records*. A New South Welshman called James Harrison got in for donating more blood (480 litres) than anyone else in the world, a tanning salon in Ballarat did more tans in a day (66) than any other, and a group of lawn bowlers from Ballina played the world's longest game (57 hours), exchanging their whites for pyjamas during the night.

And then there was me. I didn't shed a drop of blood, I didn't end up with a tan as golden as the boys from Ballarat, and I wasn't in the middle quite as long as the lawn bowlers. But on 9 October 2003, I scored what was then the highest individual score in Test history – 380 – against Zimbabwe in Perth. It was in the first innings of a two-Test series crammed in at the start of the summer, in a side that had defended the Ashes on home soil the previous summer, then beaten the West Indies away and Bangladesh at home. Our side contained Stuart MacGill, who was making the most of the opportunity afforded by Shane Warne's year on the outer due to a drug suspension, and Darren Lehmann, who had recently scored centuries in consecutive Tests against Bangladesh. We were full of confidence.

So I couldn't have been in a better state of mind for a big innings. The night before, I'd roasted a red emperor in coconut milk for the Langer family. Alfie and I then shared our traditional massive cigar. I'd just spent two months on Stradbroke Island with the family and had trained my backside off, hitting the sand hills like I'd never hit them before. Running up the dunes was wonderful not only for my fitness but also for my running technique, because it increased the length and power of my stride. There's nothing harder than a sand hill. I was tackling them three times a week, 12 to 15 times a session at different intensities. They get you and they gut you. You get halfway up and there's nothing left in your legs. It breaks you down, but when you're tired on a cricket field you know you have something left in the tank – no assignment on green grass is as challenging as galloping up a sand hill.

The only challenge facing me was that I had to go to work with a sore back, which occasionally happened in the first innings after heavy training. I wore a vest to keep my back warm and secure for the first day.

I certainly never had a world record in mind, though. I hadn't put much thought into what sort of scores were possible in Test cricket but I had always supposed there were limits – you need to have ability, sure, but you have to have conditioning, and most crucially, you need to have time. But I did know this – when I got into the zone I could just bat and bat and bat. Someone who had seen the necessary elements aligning was Stephen Waugh. He gave an interview to an English paper about 14 months before my innings, saying I was the one player in world cricket he felt could beat Brian Lara's 375.

Zimbabwe sent us in to bat hoping their unpretentious attack, which included seamer Heath Streak, might be given a helping hand from the pitch, but there was nothing treacherous about the deck. I played watchfully to be 76 not out at tea before deciding it was pedal-to-the-floor time after the break. I added 107 between tea and stumps, including 83 off my last 53 balls.

Obviously, the Zimbabwe side we confronted in Perth was one of the weaker Test outfits I faced, but I don't think I ever hit the ball better in Test cricket than I did in that innings. The force was with me. When I raised my first century of the innings, I decided to wear my old baggy green cap – the same one I'd received for my first Ashes tour in 1993. After stumps on day one, when I was 183 not out, I told Kell over the phone how enjoyable it was batting with Stephen Waugh in my baggy green, the cap he did so much to popularise as an exalted part of Australia's cricketing heritage.

Later I sat beside fitness coach Jock Campbell, who asked how I was feeling after a big day. '180, no problems,' I said. 'I'll turn it in to 380 tomorrow.' Jock was so taken aback by my words he said, 'Mate, you do that and I'll buy you dinner every day this week.' Jock concedes he still owes me a few feeds, but after all the generous help he gave me in cricket over the years I can't complain.

In fact, food was a key part of that innings, because at the team hotel I found the perfect meal – smoked ham and pumpkin soup – which I ate day after day. The two-hour time difference in Perth always threw out my body clock and I'd struggled to get my eating patterns right this time. But that soup was the perfect meal: big enough for me to feel satisfied, small enough not to weigh me down.

Normally after a day at the crease you wake up feeling a little drained, but my extra training at Stradbroke meant I felt as fresh on the second day of the innings as I had at the start of the first. My concentration was still good and I was seeing and hitting the ball just as clearly – sometimes those things can change overnight too, which is why players with big scores often get out early in the next day's play. So I stuck at it, and kept scoring. Certainly the Zimbabwe attack was a bit demoralised, but the breakthrough for me was being able to maintain all the different components of my batting. It's a little like running a marathon – you only know whether you can break through the barriers when you hit them. I faced 438 balls in ten hours and the only shot that didn't go where I wanted it to was the one I got out on. For the rest of the time I felt in total control.

I've never been a stats junkie, so I genuinely didn't know until that day that 334 was a magical number in Australian cricket, the highest Australian Test score ever, held jointly by Mark Taylor and Don Bradman. That's one of the reasons I was pretty restrained when I passed it – it had never been my Everest. Adam Gilchrist, who knows his stats and his history, was at the other end of the pitch spitting out all manner of numbers. For a while he became my milestone mentor. We'd hear the crowd clap and I'd ask Gilly, 'What was that for?' He'd say, 'Well, you've just passed Bob Simpson – 311 – and Sir Garfield Sobers – 365 – is coming up, but you have Wally Hammond and Len Hutton and the boys to contend with at the moment.'

When I passed Bradman and Taylor I thought I might as well

have a crack at Lara's world record of 375, but I wasn't sure if I'd get there because I sensed we were about to declare. With two spinners on and the field out, I just batted normally. In fact, the closer I got to the record, the more embarrassed I felt – suddenly the show had become all about me rather than the result of the game, and that's not the way cricket's supposed to be.

We just had so many runs that I was secretly hoping Stephen would declare. When you're used to playing as part of a team, sure, there are great personal moments, but when the whole shooting match revolves around you – 21 other players, the officials and all the spectators just waiting for you to get something done – you feel pretty exposed. It's not all that different from making all those people wait while you tie your shoelace. 'Come on, let's get out of here and win the game,' I thought at the time. When I got out, caught at deep backward square leg, my first thought was, *Thank God that's over.*

As the innings rolled on, Kell started to receive phone calls at home, including one from Andrew Symonds. At one point they were on the phone together but just watching their televisions in silence. Apparently they were both a bit numb and not sure what to make of it all. In a way, neither was I. Nice things were happening everywhere. Malcolm Speed, the former Cricket Australia boss become ICC chief executive, got his press man to ring the WACA press box from London to pass on the message, 'No reason not to pick you now!' – a reference to the day I'd flown to Melbourne to ask him if there was any hidden reason I wasn't being chosen for the Test team.

I passed Brian Lara's world record of 375 by pushing spinner Ray Price to mid-off, and twirled my bat as I ran through for the record. Stats and grand announcements were flying in all directions. One thing I will always appreciate about that innings was the amazing reaction I received from the Australian public. To hear people say they stopped work as I got close to the mark and that they'd remember that moment all their lives was heartwarming, and I tried to give something back to them by being as open as I could about the joy and pride I felt that day.

I'm told the innings created mayhem in sports newsrooms because it came late on a Friday afternoon, and with the rugby World Cup kicking off later that night around Australia, plans had already been made to fill the back pages with rugby news. These plans were hastily redrawn and I received generous coverage.

The impact of the score went right down to the most basic level – the scorebook itself. For all the electronic advances made in scoring, cricket is still recorded in those famous old green scorebooks, and WACA scorer Charlie Bull actually ran out of room. Three-quarters of the way through my innings, Charlie had filled up all the space in the column beside my name and had to continue by using the space reserved for 12th man, at the bottom of the order.

After it was over, I remember being touched by the gentle warmth of the dressing-room and I felt as if I was glowing. It was a different and more subdued atmosphere to a big Test win, but for me it was very satisfying. I treasure a photo taken of me sitting alone in the dressing-room in my baggy green, thongs on and nursing a glass of champagne, looking down at my gear. It perfectly caught my reflective mood – just quietly soaking up the pleasant aftermath of a great day. It was one of the few times Channel 9 was allowed in the dressing-room as Mark Taylor, commentating, moved around the room getting a few words from the boys. Tubby and I may have had our moments in the past, but there wasn't a shred of tension that day. I was flattered Channel 9 wanted to make a live dressing-room cross, and enjoyed the experience. The boys were very generous in their praise. Steve Waugh said it was the cleanest ball-striking he had ever seen, while Trevor Hohns got a bit misty-eyed in the grandstand when approached by reporters. Ian Healy said, 'I just can't imagine what it's like to score 380 runs – it's more than I dream about in a season. It's like a team score or a summer's tally for a batsman.' It did have that slightly bizarre feel about it.

Brian Lara rang from Jamaica and told me, 'Well done – great things happen to good cricketers. You and your team deserve it.' Lara was always my favourite player to watch – particularly as another left-hander, there was always a lot to learn from his game – and given my profound respect for him, it was fantastic to hear his words.

I returned the favour when, six months later, Lara made a new world record with his 400 not out against England. Even before I spoke to him I could picture the dressing-room landscape. The last time we'd been in Antigua was in 2004, when the Windies had defied all the odds to score a world-record chase against us on the last day for victory. The Antiguan Prime Minister was a huge cricket fan and promptly descended on the dressing-room to hand out giant Cuban cigars. With the cigars blazing, the reggae music pumping and the players laughing and carrying on, the Windies room just went off. And so it would've again the day Lara broke my record.

I knew Lara would be holding court. Much like Warnie, Lara doesn't flitter around the room like a butterfly. Kings don't do that. They just set up camp and wait for people to pay homage.

I could picture Lara at the back of the room, still in his whites with his West Indian cap on, feet up on a chair and regally puffing his giant cigar – out of the side of his mouth, of course. A king in his element – the only thing missing would be veil-wearing women wafting palm branches.

When I called it took me 45 minutes to finally get someone to hand the phone to him. I said, 'Oh, mate, it's Haydos here, and I just want to congratulate you and give you the respect you deserve. One thing I always remember about breaking the record is how significant it was to hear your voice on the end of the line. I know we've been fierce rivals but I have great respect for you.' He said, 'Thank you very much. It means a lot to me as well.' I asked him how he felt and he said, 'Oh, amazing, but you know what it's like . . . you just sort of bat and it happens.' He made it all sound so natural, which it was.

I dedicated my innings to the victims of the Bali bombings a year earlier, and in a way the Bali tragedy had played a role in getting me to that point. During an appearance on Andrew Denton's television show *Enough Rope*, Stephen Waugh had met a Bali survivor, Peter Hughes, whom he had invited to talk to us before the Test. Peter spoke with piercing insight about the horror of being at the Sari Club when the bombs went off, and showed us the scars he would carry for the rest of his life. For three hours, he spoke to us about how lucky we were to be Australian-born, and how we should stick together. His parting message was, 'Make the most of every day.' We did . . . and what a day it turned out to be.

Two months later, Queensland Premier Peter Beattie made a presentation to me at the Gabba before the First Test against India: a montage of photos from my youth, including one of Gaz and me playing together as kids. That did me in. I choked up, as I tend to do when I stop for long enough to take stock of my life. As I looked through the photos and all the great memories flooded back, I struggled to contain my emotions. My cricketing life had been filled with so many wonderful moments – and there were plenty more to come.

INSIDE THE GAME

Bats

I've always felt Ricky Ponting and Justin Langer have a serious problem – they have massive love affairs with their cricket bats. They'd talk about them as if they were family members. I'd think, *Seriously, what are you blokes on about? It's just a bat, you know. Leave it alone!*

Bats are a great talking point in the Australian dressing-room – probably one of the top conversation topics, along with where to go for dinner, who's getting the coffee (and how some people are selfish for just getting their own), football, Warnie, what's happening in the game and any other gossip doing the rounds. It took me about five years to work out that Ricky was a scheming, mischievous bat sabotager. In his eyes, any bat that wasn't a Kookaburra (his brand) might as well have been a picket torn from a fence. When newcomers came into the team, Punter would inspect their gear, take block with their bat, try on their gloves (which are basically the same no matter who makes them) and toss them down with a dismissive shake of the head and that cheeky half-grin that signals a gee-up is nigh. The new boys would shrink. You'd see them thinking, *Is my gear really that bad?* I'd have to reassure them later that it was all a act.

Or a partial act, anyway. For some reason, Ponting and the other 'Kookaburra boys', Langer and Hussey, are all bat scientists obsessed with their blades. It wasn't uncommon in the Australian room to see a batsman playfully testing another person's blade, and their final opinion often rested on their own innings. If they'd gone well, it'd be, 'Glad I'm not batting with this.' If they had gone badly, it was, 'Maybe I should be trying something like this.'

Our fielding coach, Mike Young, tells a story about Punter going to every locker in the dressing-room (finishing with Warnie's in the corner) after failing in a Boxing Day Test, taking out each player's bat and bouncing a ball on it five or six times before putting it back in the locker. Youngy reckons Punter was operating almost on remote control and only half-knew what he was doing. As Punter left the room and went upstairs to join the other players, Youngy said to the only other player there, Glenn McGrath, 'How 'bout that?' to which Pigeon replied, 'He does it all the time.'

The only time Punter's gear obsession left its mark on me was in 2003, when he picked up one of my bats, flexed it and gave it that dismissive shake of the head as if to say, 'Glad I'm not batting with that.' But on this occasion he meant it. I have never been a bat aficionado, but it was always in my best interests to stay at the forefront of bat technology. And the fact was my bats had been left behind. My association with Gray-Nicolls stretched back to the days when I paid to use their bats and not the other way around. At least, Mum paid. The first backyard bats Gaz and I used were Gray-Nicolls, and we still have one of them mounted on the wall in our old bedroom on the farm. But other companies had developed new, bigger bats with flat faces and far more power than my timid weapons.

This was when I was at the top of my game and felt that either Gray-Nic had to catch up with the times or I would have to go elsewhere. It was hard for both of us, because I never wanted to leave Gray-Nic (and never did, until the end of my Australian career). I had a meeting with the Gray-Nic powerbrokers and said, 'You've been the greatest bat company ever, but you're a conservative company, and unless you change you're going to lose me and your foothold in the market. You'll be blown away by the competition.'

To their credit, the company spent a lot of money upgrading its bats by acquiring machines which cut the bats with flat rather than curved faces. The edges of the bats became thicker. Bats had more wood and consequently more power, but were still easy to pick up. When I now pick up bats I used early in my career they seem so inferior. I have the bat I used in my first Test framed at home, and when I look up at it I wonder how I ever got any power from it. And then I wonder about batsmen playing 70 years ago – no wonder Bradman didn't hit many sixes. But bats can feel different from one week to the next. A few weeks before I scored 380 against Zimbabwe in Perth in 2003, I picked up the bat I would use in that innings and hated it. A few weeks and few extra waves at Straddie later, it was love at second sight. It just felt perfect again.

In the final few years of his career, Alfie made at least three Test centuries using Punter's bats and several more batting in his shoes. He'd jump around in Ricky's shoes and say things like, 'I feel like Muhammad Ali.' Many years earlier he used to wear Steve Waugh's shoes, hoping some of the magic would rub off. Every time Alfie and Ricky catch up now, you can bet that within the first few minutes of the conversation one of them will ask, 'Got any decent bats lately?' They're like two old stamp collectors. They were always full of theories. Alfie went through a stage where he had to have an oval-shaped bat handle, which involved bulking up opposite sides of the handle. Then he went through another stage where he'd have the half grip under the full grip, which provided a thicker bottom part of the handle and a thinner top. Then he followed a bizarre trend set by Jacques Kallis who, for some mysterious reason, used to have a little knob on the end of his bat handle. Don't ask me what it was there for. If something worked, Alfie always reckoned it was worth a try.

It all got a bit much a few years ago, when Ricky shaved about three centimetres off his handle and scored some nice runs, prompting

Alfie to do the same. I once secretly borrowed one of Punter's bats and sent it with one of my bats to the Riviera timber company, where they cut the end off my bat handle and used special glue to stick it on the end of Punter's. I saw him testing it out at the Gabba, inspecting it from top to bottom as he does. He even flexed its handle because his handles have a special flex and, being the bat nuffy he is, he then peeled the grip at both ends of the handle where, to his horror, he uncovered my handiwork.

Punter loves his bats, and when he found what he considered to be the perfect bat he sent it to an Indian factory to be used as a prototype for his future bats. Michael Hussey is so obsessed about getting the weight of his bats right he travels with a set of scales. Huss's scales became a source of amusement on tour. Some players like Punter would use them to weigh their bats one day, then the next day would mock Huss, saying, 'Have a look at Mr Cricket with his scales.' As for me, my hands are my scales. I just pick up a bat, shake it and take block. It either feels good or it doesn't.

Over the years we've seen the glorification of some players' bats, invariably heavy ones. The days of the ultra-light bats used by the likes of Don Bradman are gone forever. In 1998, the Australian team that was crucified in India by Sachin Tendulkar became so infatuated with the little master that at least eight of them brought back copies of his famous Vampire bat, and Brisbane firm Gabba Sporting Products even produced a special version of it. Tendulkar's extremely heavy bats were way too heavy for me. In fact, they may have even been too heavy for Tendulkar too. For a time during his career he suffered from an acute case of tennis elbow, and it was widely thought his heavy bats were partially to blame. Michael Clarke went through a stage where he thought bigger was better, but he just wasn't powerful enough to cope with the heavier blades. He was getting late on the ball – and it's very difficult to change your natural technique overnight. Punter, playing the bat scientist rather than the pot-stirrer, went up to Michael one day, lifted his bat, and said straight out, 'That's too heavy. You won't be able to lift it.' He was right.

A memorable experience with bat branding came in the IPL, when I became the brand ambassador for the revolutionary Mongoose bat. The Mongoose handle is 43 per cent longer than normal bats and the blade 33 per cent shorter, so it looks like something between a cricket bat and a baseball bat. I've never seen a brand catch fire like that. Indians are not known for embracing left-field experiments, and our Chennai captain, MS Dhoni, was mortified when he first set eyes on the Mongoose – it was so different from anything he'd seen before. 'Are you going to use that?' he asked me, and when I told him I didn't know, he said, 'I'll give you any bat in my bag not to use it.'

The Mongoose caused enormous interest among my teammates – everyone picked it up and played with it and were all eyes when I trained with it in the nets. When I first pulled it out for a game in the IPL I could sense the knives sharpening. I know how Dean Jones must have felt when he broke more than a century of tradition and wore sunglasses on the cricket field. I must admit I felt a bit anxious, because if I failed, the brand could go down with me. A lot was riding on it. But I liked the project from all angles. I've always thought Twenty20 cricket was about entertainment, and that there was room for experimentation in many areas of cricket gear, bats included.

When I was approached by the Mongoose firm while commentating in England in the 2009 Ashes series, I was open to the idea of using a differently shaped bat. My interest in the potential of an unconventionally shaped bat started at the 2007 World Cup, when Mike Young asked me to hit some balls with a baseball bat. We had stayed back after training one day and spent two hours hitting balls.

I was very sceptical about the power of a round bat when hitting a round ball, but I changed my thinking when I hit a ball 20 metres further than I could have done with a cricket bat. The longer handle and bat speed just seemed to give me more power, as did the fact that the prime weight of the bat – the head – was where the ball was being hit. Basically, the Mongoose design just cuts out the areas of the blade you very rarely use. My first hit with a Mongoose was in the Middlesex nets, and the ball went miles.

When the product was launched in India there was a large degree of scepticism about it – but isn't that always the way with new ideas? I was on 19 when I called for the Mongoose for the first time in an IPL game against the Delhi Daredevils, and I went on to make 93, smacking a swag of fours and sixes along the way. One Indian journalist likened it to the moment in the movie *Scarface* when Al Pacino's character bursts through the door with a semi-automatic gun and yells, 'Say hello to my little friend!' From that point on, whenever I walked out to bat signs would flash up on the scoreboard reading, *It's Goose time*. I think the next generation of players will use the Mongoose without any reservations – the ice has been broken for them and they won't have to worry about challenging convention.

Andrew Symonds' simple theory on bats is that there are three types: those you use in a game, those you use in the nets – and those you probably wouldn't use yourself, so you give them to fast bowlers and tell them how good they are! Fast bowlers are surely the oysters of the cricket world when it comes to bat selection. They pick up any old thing that's floating by and try to turn it into a pearl.

28

Zimbabwe – from Breadbasket to Basket Case

I don't have many regrets from my cricket career, but I do regret not taking a stance against Zimbabwe's rogue dictator, Robert Mugabe. I was a part of Australian Test teams (in 1999 and 2004) and a World Cup team (2003) that toured the once magnificent but now corrupted country, and I wish those visits had never taken place. I'm not irate about it, though, and I'm not racked with guilt. The tours were complicated, challenging scenarios and we were never flippant or hasty in our decision-making. We went with good intentions, but with the clarity of hindsight, I know we got it wrong.

Zimbabwe is the only country I toured where I felt unsafe. During the 2003 World Cup, in particular, I felt we let ourselves and the game down by playing there. I'd seen the country in better shape when I toured there with the Test squad in 1999, when its nickname – the Breadbasket of Africa – was still meaningful. But soon after, the Breadbasket was on its way to becoming the Basket Case. Mugabe persecuted opponents, rigged elections, dispossessed white farmers and caused widespread starvation and disease.

Despite this, I adored Zimbabwe. As an outdoors man, it had everything I loved – water, wilderness, wildlife and fishing. One of the favourite memories of my touring life is of a train journey in 1999 on a loco we christened 'the Bulawayo Express', which took our Australian team on an overnight journey from Bulawayo to Victoria Falls. I was in charge of organising the trip and Stuey MacGill was in charge of organising the grog. We had two carriages to ourselves, and in the middle of one of those was a massive esky. I organised a jukebox and we felt as if the entire train was ours. Every now and then, a random tourist would pass through and be drawn into our group. In the end, it was one great big party. We had a 'worst hat' competition and players were making obscene offers to passengers for their hats. Justin Langer bought a little hat off someone for US$100 – a king's ransom in Zimbabwe. We woke the next morning in a decidedly seedy state, but could still appreciate the glorious sights around us. Peering out across the long, flat savannahs I could see all manner of wildlife. It was like one big game park but, in fact, it was raw nature at its majestic, unchoreographed best.

Zimbabwe's cricketers were always popular on the circuit, and everyone knew they did it hard. There were stories about how many of the players during the 1999 World Cup had sandwich makers in their kit bags because they found the price of room service in English hotels totally exorbitant. Many of them had ties to the land and were among the first to suffer from Mugabe's dispossession of white farmers' land.

In both 2003 and '04 I went to Zimbabwe because of the 'Three Musketeers' principle: all for one and one for all. I tossed the notion around. I grappled with it. We all did. It was the unwinnable argument. On the one hand, we had the Australian government saying we shouldn't go, but it didn't feel obliged to prohibit us from doing so. On the other hand, Cricket Australia wanted us to go, but it didn't want to order us onto the plane, because that would look as if it was trying to undermine the government. By taking the 'we don't want you to go but you make the call' stance, the government couldn't lose. It could make the point that it despised the Mugabe regime, but it avoided getting the Australian public offside by not banning us, and thus not undermining our 2003 World Cup campaign. All care, no responsibility. Our heads spun. Our decision wasn't just about cricket. It was about history, and history has a long memory.

When we landed in South Africa for the World Cup, Zimbabwean Darren Maughan, our head of security, made a very persuasive pitch to us, which was probably the most influential piece of advice we received. He said our visit would provide a ray of light in difficult times for the traumatised people of his homeland, and he urged us to go. Yet we also had Jonathan Brown, Australian High Commissioner to Zimbabwe, taking the opposite view. He said Zimbabwean people had little interest in cricket and would like to see us defy and embarrass Mugabe's regime.

After seemingly endless meetings, we decided to go, reasoning that we were there to win the World Cup and would be in and out in a day. England pulled out of their visit to Zimbabwe and suffered badly because of it, as the points they surrendered to Zimbabwe meant Zimbabwe ultimately progressed to the next stage of the tournament at England's expense, but England should be commended for their brave stance. I'd love to go back in time and do one of two things – forfeit the match, or wear black armbands in protest against Mugabe as Zimbabwean players Andy Flower and Henry Olonga so courageously did. But we did neither.

Before leaving for the World Cup, I made major news by mentioning in an interview that I wouldn't shake Mugabe's hand if our paths crossed. I said, 'In my opinion . . . a handshake would seriously compromise the values and traditions of what I'm about, and I wouldn't like to do that – no. What I'm going to do is rely on the fact that we have a terrific ground staff and support staff behind us to hopefully not put us in any position where that can happen.' I never actually said I wouldn't shake his hand. I said I wouldn't like to, and hoped I wouldn't be put in that predicament, but many media organisations took it a step further and declared that Mugabe and I would not be pressing the flesh. They were right. Had push come to shove, I would not have shaken his hand, but I didn't mean to cause a noise about it before the situation had even occurred.

Our in-and-out visit to Bulawayo felt like a military operation. We landed in a specially chartered aircraft and were ferried to our hotel under escort from a military helicopter. Our officials took no chance that we'd be involved in unsavoury handshakes. Chairman Bob Merriman told us he'd be first off the plane and would do the meeting and greeting. There were dancers and drummers there to greet us, but the mood was grim. Fortunately, there was no Mugabe. We were taken to the hotel along Robert Mugabe Way, and Jimmy Maher made the crack that it was 'bound to be a one-way street'. Punter thought we might've been taken the back way at one point, to shield us from uncomfortable sights such as lengthy queues for bread and petrol. We saw them in the distance anyway. We weren't there for long but I didn't enjoy a minute of it. It was a nerve-racking trip.

In May 2004, we made a Test tour to Zimbabwe without Stuart MacGill – he took a stand and refused to tour. It was a shrewd as well as principled decision for many reasons – the tour was a complete shambles. The Zimbabwe players were in a bitter dispute with the board and 15 of them, including long-serving anchormen Heath Streak and the Flower brothers, who were genuinely respected by our team, were sacked before we got there, leaving us to play a bunch of kids in three one-day matches. The one Test we were supposed to play was cancelled amid fears it would be a complete farce. We knew what sort of mess we were getting into to when, while waiting for a connecting flight to Harare at Johannesburg airport, we ran into Zimbabwe all-rounder Sean Ervine. He had just announced his retirement from international cricket at age 21 and was leaving the country for good.

Soon after landing in Zimbabwe I gave an interview to the *Courier-Mail*'s Michael Crutcher and I found it difficult to sound anything but deeply concerned about what lay ahead. 'It is never a good sign to see one of [the Zimbabwe] players heading in the opposite direction,' I said. 'Hopefully what we saw in Johannesburg won't be a sign of the month ahead or I will be very, very disappointed.'

I admired Stuart MacGill for his decision. When you're selected for the Australian team you're 'invited' rather than ordered to play. You do have the right to turn the invitation down, but there's always the risk that it will count against you later. Warnie was coming back from his drug ban, so it wasn't as if MacGill or anyone else was indispensable, and he risked his career to follow his conscience. Fortunately, there were no long-term consequences for him, and nor should there have been.

During the 2003 World Cup, an Australian journalist doing a lap of the cricket ground the day before the match asked a woman preparing a corporate suite how much daily life was affected by the decline in the economy. She simply held up a sachet of powdered milk and said, 'Can't get the real stuff at the moment,' and got on with her work. She couldn't even buy fresh milk. The breadbasket was all but empty.

29

India 2004 – Cockroach? What Cockroach?

As any self-respecting chef will tell you, there's nothing quite like seeing a queue at your door, with people all lining up for your food. It's one thing to have people enjoy your best efforts, but quite another to have them shamelessly clamouring for it. So it was on the 2004 tour of India in October, where Hayden's Kitchen opened on the third floor of the Pride Hotel, Nagpur, and did a roaring trade for the entire Test match.

Marto and I had planned well. We'd just toured England for the ICC Champions Trophy and knew there would be a time in India when the boys needed home-cooked meals. So we'd bought a gas stove, a breadmaker, some high-quality olive oil and general condiments, as well as some bread flour and tomato paste for mini pizzas. We carried all this around India for several weeks but decided Nagpur, venue of the Third Test, was the perfect place to break it out.

There was certainly no objection from Marto, because it was in that very city a few years earlier that he'd suffered the only case of instant food poisoning I've ever seen. He ate a bowl of tomato soup that was an intimidating shade of green, and by the time he'd finished he was sweating profusely. He promptly turned the same colour as the soup and was out of action for the next few days.

Downstairs in the main buffet of the Pride Hotel, a similar incident now ensured our popularity. Some of the boys were having lunch when a cockroach popped its head up out of the middle of a rogan josh and started to run for safety. A waiter heard the groans of Gilchrist, Kasprowicz and Ponting and swiftly grabbed the insect and – for reasons we still haven't got to the bottom of – put it in his mouth.

'A cockroach!' was the collective cry from the boys. The waiter shook his head. 'No, sir, no cockroach.' The boys were having none of it. 'It's a cockroach!' they protested, to the waiter's further denials. 'Fair enough, then,' said one of the boys finally. 'If it's not a cockroach then eat it!'

And the waiter did – a great effort for his team, I think.

From then on, it was as though I was handing out gold bars in my room. The downstairs buffet emptied as the queue at my door lengthened; I reckon I could've sold a loaf of hot bread for US$100. As well as baking a lot of bread, I was also brewing coffee – two wonderfully enticing aromas.

I'd set the breadmaker before leaving for training so that the bread was piping hot and ready to be devoured when we returned. It was very much a batsmen-only occasion. Justin, Ricky, Marto and Brad Hodge were regulars. We'd actually tell the bowlers to leave – all good banter between the team's left and right flanks. Kasper has probably never forgiven me for it and still tells people that he's known me since we were 16, has bought all my cookbooks . . . but has never enjoyed a meal cooked by me.

That stop in Nagpur was the joyful punchline to a wonderful tour and an epic series win. The curator, a famously single-minded character with no love of the Indian hierarchy, ignored pleas to shave the deck and left a healthy covering of grass. It reminded me of the Gabba. To have that sort of wicket for the deciding Test of an away series – particularly in India – was the most pleasant surprise imaginable. Our joy was matched only by India's utter bewilderment. When Sourav Ganguly and Harbhajan Singh went out to see the deck a couple of days before the game, they looked like farmers inspecting crops after a hail storm. We predicted neither would play, and they didn't. Ganguly withdrew with a leg-muscle injury that flared up suddenly, and Harbhajan had an even more sudden dose of food poisoning. We put their ailments down to acute cases of 'greentrackitis', where you develop a severe intolerance to green wickets likely to give you nothing as a spin bowler and plenty of headaches as a batsman.

That tour we broke a 35-year hoodoo in India. Not since 1969–70, when Bill Lawry's side won a five-Test series 3–1, had an Australian side won in India. In 2001, when we were pipped 2–1, we were still very much coming to grips with the conditions, but we learnt well. India was losing its mystery for us. Teams were regularly touring there for one-day tournaments and we had just beaten Sri Lanka in Sri Lanka. We realised we should and could play better in India, and we did, simply by revising our bowling strategy. Gilly did some work on it and Dizzy and Kasper spent hours talking about it on the plane trip over. The rest of us agreed with their plan to bowl much more conservatively than we had three years earlier. In 2001, Stephen Waugh had such a sensational group of bowlers it was difficult to consider any possible strategy other than full-blown aggression, but we'd learnt that it didn't always work. When we'd visited in 2001, we were on a roll, completing a 16-match winning streak. Teams did well to take Tests to the fourth day against us. It all seemed so simple. Stack the slips, wait for the edge and trample the world. But in India we'd realised the ball just didn't go to slips. We'd bowl wide of off stump and get picked off, then when we adjusted, there weren't enough fieldsmen on the leg side to cope.

So, instead of bowling to what we thought would be India's weakness (but wasn't), we changed to bowl to their strengths. We were saying, 'You're too good, we'll bowl at the stumps but you'll get one, not four,' as we set fields that had cover on both sides of the wicket. It worked brilliantly, and we saw the absolute peak of a wonderful generation of Australian bowlers. Collectively, no pack of bowlers in my time beat the efforts of McGrath, Gillespie, Kasprowicz and Warne on that tour. They were just spotless – so good that Gilly barely had to ask anyone outside the four to bowl a ball in the first three Tests. Pressure, pressure, pressure: none of them conceded more than three per over for the series. India managed one century in four Tests. Tendulkar and Laxman averaged 17, Dravid 27. The entire Indian top order was shut down. Brett Lee was training like a man possessed on the sidelines, but couldn't get a game. As good as he was, he wasn't the man for that tour. There could be no extravagance. Once our game plan was cracked and the crowds got going, we knew there would be no coming back. But it never happened.

In the First Test at Bangalore, when Michael Clarke made a memorable debut century, Virender Sehwag was shocked to see five men on the leg side when he emerged to open the Indian innings. We bowled at his body and ball after ball went to the field until finally he self-destructed. We won and went to Chennai, where we played a Test that was washed out and drawn, before heading to Nagpur for what proved the decider. Thanks to a groundbreaking initiative from Buck, we hit the ground with much gusto – we'd all freshened up by taking a mid-tour holiday between the Second and Third Tests.

There had been great excitement when the break was discussed at the start of the tour. Some blokes asked whether they could fly home and Warnie suggested a quick trip to England, but we decided a four-hour flight was about the limit. Gilly met his family in Singapore and I went off travelling with my good friend Jacob Cherian, an Indian who'd been living in Australia for two decades. We had some wonderful experiences cruising the backwaters of Kerala on a houseboat and meeting people of the waterway who go to school and church – and everywhere, in fact – by boat. We also went up to the mountains, where Jacob's family own a 3000-hectare tea plantation. I ate as the locals did – with my fingers – and drew the occasional compliment for doing so. I still believe it's the best way to experience the different textures of the curries. When the team got back together we felt completely rejuvenated. We were ready for India, but India wasn't ready for us. We made 398 in the first innings then went into suffocation mode against India, which worked beautifully. They were shut down for 185 as McGrath bowled 25 overs for 27 runs.

The second innings followed a similar theme. So brilliantly did our bowlers apply the choker hold that five of India's top six – Tendulkar, Dravid, Laxman, Chopra and Kaif – managed just 14 between them. The tail batted with more freedom, but they were still bowled out for 200 and we won the match by 342 runs to clinch the series.

I discovered one great resource unexpectedly on that tour – young South Australian batsman Tom Cooper. When Shane Warne was suspended for a year for taking a diuretic, Cricket Australia was in a quandary deciding what to do with his contract money. The wise decision was made to put it back into the game by sponsoring a young player to tour overseas with the Australian side. Tom, only a teenager at the time, won the scholarship, and I felt like paying for him to come on every tour after that. I don't normally rate net throwdowns, because they never seem to have the pace to replicate match conditions, but Tom had a strong, tireless arm and helped all of us – a worthy scholarship winner if ever there was one. It was a joy six years later to captain him in the Prime Minister's XI, when he made a wonderful century against the West Indies.

I was rapt for a lot of people on that tour, but especially for Gilly, who captained the side during the first three Tests while Punter was injured. The triple burdens of captaincy, batting and keeping wicket were enormous and pushed Gilly to the brink of exhaustion. He was also very upset – rightfully so – about a column Darren Berry wrote saying that the efforts of the two keepers in the series, Gilly and Parthiv Patel, had brought the art of keeping to a new low. You could have a crack at Gilly about his batting and generally he'd shrug it off, but taunts over his keeping really hurt him. I urged him not to mark himself too hard, because India was just a nightmare place to keep. Deep down I was furious at Berry.

Gilly had the last laugh, though, when he raised the

Border-Gavaskar Trophy, which he playfully renamed the Gilchrist-Dravid Trophy in honour of the two stand-in captains of the Third Test. Gilly considered the victory the highlight of his career, and we all agreed it was a hard moment to top.

30

Sri Lanka – Tsunami

Of all the millions of words written about the Asian tsunami on Boxing Day 2004, a line from Sri Lankan batsman Sanath Jayasuriya probably best summed up the shock waves that reverberated around the world. 'I had never even heard of the word before,' he told us. 'I didn't know what a tsunami was.'

News of the tragedy broke late on the first day of our Test against Pakistan at the MCG. Natural disasters do unusual things to the human brain. There might be thousands of lives lost, but for each person the disaster is often encapsulated by just one life lost or one single image. My image was a vivid one and I couldn't get it out of my head – I just kept picturing the wonderful staff of the Lighthouse Hotel in Galle, Sri Lanka. It was my favourite hotel, one which had seen me come and go as a young fringe player in 1999, and as an established one five years later when I toured Sri Lanka in February 2004 for a three-Test series and five one-dayers. I feared for the lives of my friends on the kitchen staff, in the kitchen located a floor underground, realising they'd have had next to no chance to escape. Several perished.

In some ways the Lighthouse was perfectly equipped to handle the whims of Mother Nature. Carved into a stone face on the spectacular Galle cliffs, no cyclone could bowl the place over. You wouldn't have felt safer in a raging gale than if you were standing in the Taj Mahal. But wind was one thing, water quite another. The hotel was so close to the ocean, literally 20 or so metres above it, that when you were having lunch on the main deck your conversations would inevitably be broken by sideways glances to admire the foam floating skywards after the waves thundered onto the cliff face. Watching the ocean from the deck was an exhilarating experience, but I can only imagine what the guests sitting in the chairs we'd occupied just nine months before must have felt when they saw the tsunami coming.

I feel my spirit is closely connected to the water, and I love that hotel and its location so much that I flew Kell over there once so she could experience it too. It took us seven years to design our house in Brisbane, and I modelled our master bedroom on the rooms in the Lighthouse Hotel, designed by one of Sri Lanka's top architects, Geoffrey Bawa, who blended a Dutch colonial style with modern design. As a cricketer you stay in a million hotels that look and feel the same, but the Lighthouse is unique. When I stayed there in 2004, I even took an architect's drawing pad with me to note down the special features I liked.

I have treasured memories of Galle from 1999, when I did some fishing there with my new Shimano fly rod. After catching some small mackerel I soon had a crowd around me and I thought, *No doubt about the Sri Lankans . . . they love their cricket. I wouldn't have thought they'd have known me.*

In fact, they didn't. What they were intrigued by was my fishing technique, or more specifically, my magical wand – a brand-new carbon-fibre fly fishing rod. They were used to fishing by standing on poles in the water, using a giant bamboo stick with strings on it to snare their catch.

In 2004, I returned to score a century in the First Test at the beautiful Galle ground, which is flanked on two sides by the ocean and on another by the famous Galle fort. Between times, I talked cooking with the chefs at the Lighthouse, and had photos taken in their kitchen for my first cookbook. The idea of doing a cookbook had come out of conversations with Kell in which we'd realised it was a great way to combine some of our passions – cooking, travel, cricket and family. I will forever appreciate the chefs' generosity in sharing their culinary skills with me.

There were apparently some strange scenes around Galle the day the tsunami hit. Early in the morning, the concierge of a local hotel reported the extraordinary sight of an elephant appearing from nowhere and walking up towards the hotel foyer, roaring and stamping its feet in distress, before rushing off into the hinterland. It was as if it was trying to trumpet a warning signal. Reports say that very little wildlife was claimed by the tsunami. In Sri Lanka's second largest wildlife preserve, Yala National Park, people watched three elephants run away from the shore area to higher ground an hour before the tsunami hit. Galle is a city full of stray animals yet one wildlife official inspecting it in the days after the tsunami found only one dead cat. It was almost as if the animals knew that trouble was coming. On one game reserve, visitors who took refuge up trees when the waters hit found that lizards and snakes not normally renowned as great tree-climbers had beaten them to the best positions.

The first people near the Lighthouse to sense that something strange was happening were a couple of taxi drivers, who had gone down to the shore to look for sea urchins. They saw that the tide was further out than they'd ever seen it, but noticed how, in the space of a few minutes, the waves had gone from being nowhere near them to suddenly slapping on their backs. When they looked in the distance, to their horror, they saw massive waves approaching. They fled and somehow survived. In the middle of the mayhem someone from the Lighthouse had the presence of mind – and the selflessness – to think of people further up the coast and make frantic phone calls to several other hotels in the region, giving them a precious 20-minute warning that enabled them to evacuate guests.

After the initial flooding, there was a two-hour break before the next batch of giant waves arrived, and by this time all guests at the Lighthouse had been evacuated to the third floor. Located in a relatively high position on the top of a promontory, it was still eventually swamped, but there was time to flee. Sri Lanka's great spinner, Muttiah Muralitharan, was almost a tsunami victim. He'd spent a few days in Galle handing out cricket bats to underprivileged children, and left only 20 minutes before the tsunami hit. Murali's manager lost his house, and very nearly his life.

Such was the indestructible nature of the Lighthouse that it was one of the first major hotels in Sri Lanka to open again after the tsunami, but the scars were deep. In the weeks after the tragedy some of the staff, all grieving for lost loved ones, cringed at the sight of guests laughing and having a good time at the bar, but tourism also provided a way for the people and the region to move on from the heartbreak. The tsunami came at a terrible time for Sri Lanka, which was just starting to rebuild itself as a peaceful, enticing tourist destination after years of civil war.

The beautiful Galle cricket ground is one of the most distinctive in the world, and seeing footage of buses and cars floating around on it after the tsunami became one of the defining images of the disaster. It was feared cricket would never be played there again. The ground became a temporary refuge for tsunami victims, and there was even a helipad constructed near the centre wicket block. Thankfully, the Galle ground did reopen in 2007.

I was given further insight into the ravages of the catastrophe when I played in the tsunami relief match at the MCG in January 2005. Over the years the Australian team has had a range of motivational speakers, sportsmen and inspirational figures visit us, but none affected me as deeply as Trisha Broadbridge. Trisha and her husband, Troy, an AFL footballer, were on their honeymoon at Thailand's Phi Phi Islands when Troy was claimed by the tsunami. Our match was held just two weeks after the tsunami and the shock was still sinking in. Even though Trisha was with us in body, you could see that in spirit, she was numb. It is an enormous credit to her that she has rebuilt her life since then. On TV recently she said strong winds, the sound of helicopters or people screaming take her back to the horror of that day, but she has done brilliantly to complete a Masters degree and has set up an education centre at Phi Phi to teach local children in one of the worst-hit areas of Thailand.

31

The Recession We Had to Have – Ashes 2005

There are two simple but telling reasons why Australia dominated England during my career as an international player. We were a team in every sense of the word. They weren't. We watched each other's backs. They didn't. But something changed in the epic 2005 Ashes series. They became more like us and we became more like them.

I saw it coming early in the tour, in a one-dayer against England at Edgbaston. Simon Jones was bowling in the sixth over when I defended a ball back down the pitch. There was no suggestion I was even contemplating a run, but he threw the ball back and branded me on the left shoulder. I was livid. I smacked the crease with my bat and stormed towards him, giving him a heated serve as he held his arms up to apologise.

Normally, Jones would have been left to fight his own battle, but Paul Collingwood rushed in to deliver some sharp-edged words to me, and Andrew Strauss jogged over with words of encouragement for Jones. That was the moment I knew we had a fight on our hands, for it wasn't the England I knew. They were hunting in a pack and watching out for each other, rather than being motivated by self-preservation.

Australia lacked momentum right from the start of that tour. In a Twenty20 game against England at the Rose Bowl, we lost seven wickets for eight runs and the home nation went crazy, believing the victory might signal the start of an English renaissance. Sadly for us, it did. Australian teams of my era had always been great at smashing county teams, yet Somerset chased down 342 against us. The fact that imports Graeme Smith and Sanath Jayasuriya did the damage was small consolation.

The infamous incident in Cardiff, when a group of players went out for Shane Watson's 24th birthday and Andrew Symonds stayed out later than the rest, didn't help at all. We played Bangladesh the next day, and during the warm-ups Symo was clearly struggling. At one point when we were doing stretches he lent on a wheelie bin and it just started wheeling away as he trailed behind it, head down. Very funny now, not so funny then (though I can recall smirking). It takes a bit to get Buck revved up, but he was that day.

To add to his woes, Symo was too cheeky for his own good when he spoke with Punter, who was definitely not in the mood for wisecracks. I heard the end of the conversation as Symo said abruptly, 'Well, don't pick me then.' Punter snapped back, 'Mate, you're not picked – you're dropped.'

We went on to lose to Bangladesh, thanks to a brilliant innings by Mohammad Ashraful. After stumps we felt like a side in disgrace. We *were* in disgrace. There were no excuses for the loss. As well as that, we were disappointed for Symo and in Symo.

At our post-match crisis meeting – for once the term was not an exaggeration – Gilly asked, 'Mate, what were you thinking?'

'That's the problem,' said Symo. 'I wasn't.'

It was tense and awkward, as meetings always are when some people are searching for the whole truth and others are trying to make sure they don't get it. Symo wasn't the only one out late that night, but no one else wanted to put their hands up in case they were sent home. As hard as it is to defend their behaviour, I understood their fear. You've sweated your whole life to earn your stripes, and if you put your hand up it might all be thrown away – even if you weren't playing – following one night on the tiles.

At that point it seemed things couldn't get any worse, but they did. We left Cardiff for a one-dayer against England at Bristol, and when we arrived – late – our bus had parked on the wrong side of the ground, which meant we had to do a lap of the already full ground dragging our kitbags and sorry backsides. It was probably less than a kilometre but it felt 10 times that distance and we were about as organised and dignified as the Keystone Kops. I've seen baitfish swimming through a school of sharks that had a better chance of escaping unscathed than we did that day on our little walk of shame. The crowd relished every vitriolic second of it. Sledges rained upon us and, as so often happens, once you're down, the insults and indignities just keep flowing.

Our lateness to the ground that day was symbolic of our shoddiness throughout the series. It's always a bad feeling turning up late. You can almost sense the opposition thinking, *What about these cowboys?* We'd spent many years being the focus of other sides' attention on the training paddock. Now, whenever we turned up it seemed as though England were there before us and we were looking at them. It was a bad place for us to be mentally, because we needed to focus on ourselves, not get distracted, even if only for the blink of an eye. Mike Young, our fielding coach, always said, 'In a dog fight, the dog that blinks first loses.' We blinked that tour, and that was the opportunity that England needed.

We lost our perspective, individually and collectively. We looked in the wrong places to find answers. At one stage, Buck was looking to break up the top-order 'coffee club' because he thought it was too much of a clique. Marto, myself, Justin and Ricky would often meet for coffee, but this ritual was actually a form of bonding. In the old days, players used to meet over a beer. Times have changed. Coffee was our thing in common. It was where friendships were strengthened and plans were made. Claims it was a negative for the team were complete rubbish, but the mounting examples of our lacklustre tour weren't. As Justin always said, 'Your only currency is runs.' And while the team was out of form, so was I.

Despite the early signs of a team cracking, we won the First Test by 239 runs at Lord's, and we felt like a unified force when we sang our victory song inside the England dressing-room. Disaster struck just before play at Edgbaston in the Second Test, when Glenn McGrath stood on a ball during our warm-up and did his ankle. I was right next to him when he went down and initially thought he was foxing. 'Get up, nuffy!' I said to him, but the banter stopped instantly when I saw his face – it was ghostly pale. The loss of McGrath was a mortal blow for us. Michael Kasprowicz was called into the side, but I'm sure Kasper would admit now he was struggling at the time.

On top of the world on 9 October 2002 in Perth after breaking Brian Lara's Test world batting record of 375. Having my old baggy green cap with me made it even more special.

GRAY NICOLLS

Left: Sweet solitude in Perth, 2002, after my world batting record. This is one of my favourite photos.
Top: Yes, it really did happen – here's the Perth scoreboard to prove it.
Bottom: Mum and Dad scan the news in the next day's *Courier-Mail*.

Above: A chair for a champion. Alfie and I carry Steve Waugh off the SCG after his Test career ended with a draw against India in the Fourth Test of the series in 2004.

Right: Grace loved Christmas Day in Melbourne. Here we share a tender moment on the Test deck in 2004.

The expressions say it all. The 2005 Ashes series in England was a rugged test for anyone wearing a green and gold cap. England deserved their victory and there was nothing much we could do but stand there and watch them celebrate.

No, it's not a bird or a plane but Symo flying high at the MCG after his breakthrough century against England in the 2006–07 Ashes series. My helmet cut into my forehead during our embrace but I felt no pain.

Left and below: It's over – Alfie Langer and I embrace after our final innings together at the SCG against England in the 2006 Ashes series, walking off after securing a 5–0 triumph. I felt as if someone had cut my leg off after Alfie left the game.

Smack! The 2007 World Cup was the time to 'be free', as Ricky Ponting told us. I'd spent the summer planning to launch a head-on assault at rival bowlers, and it was a thrill to see it come off.

Top: Punter, Gilly and I celebrate after our win in the 2007 World Cup final against Sri Lanka in Barbados.
Bottom left: I salute a century during the World Cup.
Bottom right: To top off a great tournament, I landed a 136 kg marlin off the coast of Grenada. Big hits, big fish and even bigger celebrations – life doesn't get much better.

Grace helps me with my bat selection before my 100th Test, against New Zealand at the Adelaide Oval in 2008–09. I survived an lbw appeal but made just 24 before being run out.

My wife Kellie always looks beautiful, but this dress at the 2008 Allan Border Medal presentation evening was my favourite – stunning!

I hope the colour pink will forever be a part of SCG Tests in memory of the late Jane McGrath. Here the Australian team is pictured in pink caps before my last Test, against South Africa at the SCG in January 2009.

Like father, like son. Thomas tries on my helmet after my last Test, taking me back to those days in the backyard where I used to don a helmet to protect myself against Gaz's best work – and the magpies.

Going down swinging. Plenty of effort in this cover drive in my last Test, against South Africa at the SCG in January 2009.

Above: And it's goodnight from me. Gracie and Josh soak up the atmosphere on our emotional lap of the Gabba on my retirement night in January 2009.

Left: Proud to be Australian. With Dad and Mum and our family after receiving my Australia Day medal.

Left: Meet the two Mr Crickets. My Chennai Super Kings teammates Muttiah Muralitharan and Mike Hussey are the two biggest cricket nuffies on the planet.

Below: You never know who you are going to meet in the IPL. During the 2010 season we visited Dharamsala, home of the Tibetan spiritual leader the Dalai Lama, who came to our game against the Kings XI Punjab.

After the final of the 2010 IPL tournament, which the Chennai Super Kings won against the Mumbai Indians. What a victory. We spent most of the season floating around midtable, so it was a great feeling to storm home and win the tournament.

In retirement, I now have so much more understanding and appreciation of what Kell did and does every day to keep the family unit going. I can tell you that facing a little red cherry coming down the wicket at 150 odd clicks is a walk in the park compared to what she does!

The other challenge we faced at Edgbaston came from the reaction by some to 'that toss'. The wicket had been drenched by heavy rain for much of the previous week and the curator had been talking for days about how underprepared it would be and how the covers had blown off at a crucial time. After McGrath was ruled unfit, we went ahead with our original plan to bowl first. Warnie was livid that we put England into bat and he did not handle it well – there was a bit of an underground protest over the decision. I saw him out the back of the dressing-rooms soon after and he was very angry.

You could argue in hindsight that he was right in a cricket sense – but not in a team sense. Our bowlers were so out of sorts I didn't think it mattered who won the toss. We were probably always going to concede a 400-plus total no matter when we bowled. What we weren't prepared for was conceding so many runs so quickly – England made a staggering 407 on the first day. We bowled them out in that time, but the total was still a jaw-dropper. At one point in the middle session, Andrew Flintoff and Kevin Pietersen put on 100 in just over an hour. Everyone was talking about the toss, but our captain had made a decision and that should have been that. Warnie's belligerent state of mind didn't help us. It polarised the team at a sensitive time.

During that series I was also tested by Warnie's fraternising with the opposition. Top players in the opposition sides like Sachin Tendulkar and Brian Lara often chummed up with Warnie, and that summer it was Kevin Pietersen's turn. It probably shouldn't have annoyed me, but our strength had always been our tightness as a team unit. I look back now and realise maybe my own insecurities were to blame. When Warnie mingled with guys like Pietersen, I was asking myself, *What's he doing?* In fact,

Warnie was doing fine. He took a phenomenal 40 wickets for the series. If the rest of us had been firing anywhere near as well, we'd have won the Ashes at a canter.

Given the disruptions to Warnie's personal life, I am even more in awe of what he did in that series. Before the First Test, he'd just separated from his wife, Simone, and he'd been out of form at county level. He called in his coach, Terry Jenner, to help him at Lord's. Before the coaching session, Warnie told TJ, 'I'm bowling crap.' After the session, TJ said he thought that, in the circumstances, a 20-wicket series would be a huge result for him. But just like Warnie's poker bets, he doubled it.

Despite our horrendous first day at Edgbaston, we rallied strongly and went down by only two runs in that famous finish – when Kasper gloved Steve Harmison behind – after needing 107 for victory with just two wickets remaining at the start of the last day. Kasper's glove was off the bat at the time, but even he admitted it would've been almost impossible for umpire Billy Bowden to realise that. Kasper still jokes at sportsmen's nights that he 'single-handedly revived Ashes cricket . . . although unfortunately that hand was off the bat at the time'. The photo of Freddie Flintoff consoling Brett Lee after Kasper's dismissal became one of the most famous in Ashes history, and cemented an enduring bond between them. Before Brett made the decision to quit Test cricket and become a short-game specialist, he sought advice from Freddie, who'd done the same.

Controversy shadowed our every move. I was accused of swearing at a young flag-bearer as Gilly and I walked out to bat at Edgbaston. The story – a total fabrication – made the papers the next day. As a devoted family man, I found the accusation very hurtful, and it unsettled me at a crucial time. The fact that it upset my mum back at home distressed me even further. On top of this there was another incident when we were staying at Lumley Castle in Durham. We'd been tipped off that a tabloid newspaper had arranged for two scantily dressed girls to emerge from behind a wall just as we entered the castle and be photographed with us in a 'look who the boys are with' type of sting. We foiled it by coming in a different entrance, much to the annoyance of the photographers.

Reverse swing was a nightmare for us in that series. Our team meetings went around in circles talking about it. Whenever someone raised the problem, I would raise my arms in mock alarm and shout, 'Fooff!' as if a cork had popped off a magic bottle and a genie had appeared before our eyes. It was that sort of issue – immediate, bewildering, full of theories, short on hard facts. There were a million ideas about how England were getting reverse swing and we weren't. Warnie had a theory about the best way to polish the ball. Brett Lee had a different one. None of them seemed to work, not for us anyway. We felt even more frustrated because England could not only get the reverse swing, they could get it early (the 11th over at Old Trafford); amazingly, they even knew *when* they were going to get it. As soon as I saw Freddie Flintoff heading off the field to have a couple of cans of Red Bull to spark him up, I knew trouble was on its way.

I found the reverse-swinging ball almost impossible to face that series, and I seemed to get out whenever it started. Five times I was dismissed between 26 and 36. One of my problems was that I was often at the crease at the delicate stage when the ball started to reverse. Once you knew it was reversing you could develop a strategy for it. But the changeover period was a devilishly tough time. I had a bizarre experience facing Freddie at Old Trafford, one I've never had against any bowler before or since – I just couldn't see him. It was gloomy, and his arm was propelling reverse swing out of a backdrop of near-black windows – the triple whammy of a dark background, a dark day and a dark art overwhelmed me. It was almost comical. In fact, we did laugh. We never sledged each other but we each knew what the other was thinking. He bowled me one absolutely unplayable ball and just winked, and I looked at him as if to say, 'I can't see what you're bowling and it's quicker than anything I've faced.' He just smiled back.

You can go from hero to villain and back again in the one day in England. The secret to handling this is to let it go and not take it too seriously, but we struggled to do that. For a lot of us, our only experience of losing was to India way back in 2001, and even that series went down to the wire so we weren't routinely ridiculed for being sadly off our game. We had no connection with the heartbreak years of the mid-1980s, no survivor from that team around to say, 'Hey, you think this is bad . . .' It felt much worse than it was – a 2–1 victory to England, and a shaky victory at that.

But the boisterous crowds savoured our every false move. They really targeted Dizzy Gillespie during his barren run. English crowds are the worst winners and the worst losers on the planet. When they're winning, there's unrestrained joy in the world and they delight in rubbing your noses in it. When they're losing, they view their own side as rubbish.

In the midst of the gloom on that tour, there was one interlude that revived my spirits. We'd just drawn the Third Test and were feeling totally harassed in a nation that could sense impending salvation after 16 years of Ashes torment. I was craving a total break from the game when my old mate, Allan Lamb, organised a salmon fishing expedition on the River Spey. A brief visit to Scotland, where cricket isn't the headline-making attraction it is in England, was a timely respite from the suffocating pressure. I caught my first salmon and was introduced to a local tradition: the fisherman who catches his first fish – it's called the virgin fish – must smear its blood over his face. Everything about the trip relaxed me, even Lamby's micky-taking attempts to ease my gnawing concerns about my lapse in form. 'Maaaate,' he'd say in his terrible attempt at an Aussie accent. 'Relax. It's gonna happen.'

As the tour progressed, Warnie was sensational, and McGrath took 19 wickets despite missing two Tests (we lost both), but we struggled to contain England, and our muddled lines and lengths caused a lot of frustration. I recall Damien Martyn saying, 'How dumb are our bowlers? These are small grounds. Set off-side fields and bowl one side of the wicket. It's not rocket science.' It wasn't, but we just couldn't get it right. We weren't solid enough to stick to game plans. We were fractured. We lacked patience. Ricky couldn't captain the way he wanted to because we couldn't execute. Perhaps our tactics revealed the lingering after-effects of the Steve Waugh era, when we simply steamrolled the best and worst of our rivals and rarely ever needed a Plan B. As Marto said, we should have gone back to bowling one side of the wicket and setting defensive fields to cut off boundaries. Many fans fail to appreciate that defensive fields can be used as an offensive weapon. But, Warnie aside, we couldn't find any weapons because we couldn't stick to our plans.

Each of the Tests were classics in their own way. We went 2–1 after the Fourth Test at Trent Bridge, but it was an almighty struggle. We seemed all but out of the game when we scored just 217 in response to England's 447 in our first innings, but we scrambled to 387 in the second, and Warnie grabbed four second-innings wickets before England wobbled to 7/129, and victory.

My series returns approaching the last Test of the tour were 180 runs at 22. Not good enough – I needed a fresh strategy. Some advice came my way on the team bus during the trip to Essex for the tour match before the Fifth Test, when I walked passed our assistant coach, Jamie Siddons. He was looking at footage of me on his laptop and I asked him what he thought. He said, 'Actually, what I think is that you're getting out a lot outside off stump. Mate, you've just got to bat time. You're over-attacking balls that aren't there to hit.' I felt like a man who'd been fumbling around in a dark room, then finally found the light switch. Everything suddenly seemed so clear. 'Mate, you are bang on!' I replied. Simple. I'd been thinking in a certain way which just wasn't working and needed to change. There and then I changed. 'I'll play straighter for longer.'

Jamie was brilliant. He didn't try to force-feed me any fancy theories. He just gave me some simple facts and left the decision-making to me – that's good coaching. People sometimes think solving a form slump involves splitting the atom, but often it's the most basic piece of advice that hits the bullseye. I wondered what would've happened if I hadn't walked past Jamie on the bus. Would he have been bold enough to pass on his advice? Was I regarded as someone who was too strong-willed to be told?

I had my new strategy, but I soon realised it was actually an old one being dusted off. Before leaving for my first Ashes tour in 1993, I'd spoken to former Test opener Bill Brown, a wonderful man I adored, and asked him for advice. He'd made three trips to England – in 1934, 1938 and 1948 – and knew his stuff. 'Just make sure you play straight until you get settled,' said Bill. Great advice from a great man. I wish I'd followed it sooner!

My spirits were further boosted when my doorbell rang at 5.30 a.m. the day before the Test. At first I thought it was housekeeping and was a bit grumpy getting out of bed. But when I opened the door, I saw Kell standing there with Joshua, who'd been born just before the tour. The sight of my beautiful wife with our second child is one I will never forget. I almost cried and laughed in the same instant. It was the best surprise I could have imagined. Kell, who'd been on the tour earlier but had gone home, has always had an innate ability to know when people need her most. We were about to lose the Ashes, which was unchartered territory. I had feared being dropped, or that the game could have been my last Test, but Kell's return completely changed my mood. I started breathing again. Life regained its perspective. I thought, 'Oh well, the worst thing that can happen is I get dropped.'

I still marvel at how well Kell ran the show when I was away (and while I was there for that matter). She is so great about thinking of others. She is a selfless and amazing mother, but long before that it was her kindness I fell in love with. My uncle Gary was an amazing support to me when I was a little fella and is one of two remaining siblings on my mother's side of the family. Kell often had Uncle Gary over for lunch or dinner while I was away. She always organised for me to have my parents to Melbourne for Christmas Eve, and she'd be travelling with three children and eight bags of presents! She always made sure my parents were looked after and had everything and everyone organised. She was truly inspirational.

I made 138 in the final Test at the Oval in a marathon

innings, during which I absorbed some high-class bowling and weathered tough conditions. I stayed true to my revised game plan and stayed patient, letting the attack come to me. There was one moment when I smacked a four off Steve Harmison in fading light when I could barely see the ball. I remember Michael Clarke saying, 'Great shot,' and I said, 'Didn't see it, mate.' He replied, 'Well, keep on not seeing it then.'

As I look back, though, it's fair to say I never played my best Test cricket in England. I can see that my failure to play a Test on my first Ashes tour in 1993 might have made me too keen to do well on the next two. I was trying too hard, particularly at the big name venues, where each Test seems to have major historical significance. To overcome problems in professional sport you need to let go of your ego. In cricket, you're alone with your thoughts a lot of the time. It's both a team game and an individual one. Whenever I got ahead of myself, I never quite nailed it. Maybe my ego was too big for my own good and I simply wasn't prepared to bow to England's best work. I'd watched guys like Michael Slater go out and carve them up on previous tours and I had done the same in Australia – I wanted to be in that place again. England is a team you can beat into submission, and when you get them to a certain point they will break. But in 2005, I never got to that point.

It was such a close series that, midway through the final day, the Ashes were still in the balance. Beneath the inevitable sadness and regret, I had one sobering thought – England deserved to win. They were better prepared, they had better plans, they stuck to them and executed them well, while we were a bit all over the shop. And beneath that feeling was an ever stronger resolve that in my era, this was not going to happen again. We would be more disciplined, more organised and more united. No cracks. Even though both Alfie and I made centuries in our first innings, it was far from enough. On the last day of the Test circumstances still could have swung our way, but the afternoon session was underpinned by Kevin Pietersen's maiden century and solid batting from England, with only two wickets falling. For the first time since 1987, England won the Ashes, 2–1.

It had not been a great tour for many of us, but it did have an unforgettable ending. On my last night I went to a reception at the Royal Garden Hotel in Kensington. Marto, Kell and I were about to catch a taxi when we were held back by the concierge, who informed us that Mr Ponting had arranged a special car for us – and up the ramp came a sparkling Rolls-Royce Phantom. That was Ricky's first surprise. The second came when the Phantom took us to Zuma, one of London's top Japanese restaurants. There to greet us was Ainsley Harriott, celebrity chef and host of the *Ready Steady Cook* TV show in England. What a moment! But there was more.

The last surprise of the evening had nothing to do with Ricky. Soon after us, the England side arrived at Zuma in an understandably celebratory mood after a day of presentations in Trafalgar Square. I shouted Michael Vaughan and Matthew Hoggard a beer. Vaughan impressed me. Even in celebration you could see he was the team leader – a responsible, good-natured man. Hoggy was good fun. He eyeballed me, then got me into a headlock and said, 'Aw . . . to be honest, I thought you were a righteous, arrogant twat. But now I think you're a real good bloke.' What could have been an awkward night turned out to be a memorable bonding experience. I could pay rightful tribute to the English boys and say how I genuinely admired their pace attack and the way they worked as a team, where previously they had seemed like a collection of individuals. They acknowledged that they'd observed how our team wanted to be together all the time – they loved that and learnt from it. They told me how characters in their camp had fallen out of favour because they failed to embrace the new culture. Michael Vaughan created a strong team bond, and I sensed that even though players like Darren Gough and Andy Caddick had faded from international cricket, they may not have been chosen anyway because they had a more individual focus.

It was reported in the Australian press after the tour that a feud between the wives hadn't helped our cause. I didn't know much about that, but what I did know was that ours was a diverse group as far as family situations went. There were young unmarried guys like Michael Clarke and Shaun Tait, players who were married without children like Ricky Ponting and Simon Katich, and others like me and Gilly with young families. You just can't survive in an English hotel with kids, so Gilly and I hired family-sized units near the team hotel, which had their own little backyards and washing and cooking facilities. But it wasn't ideal. We faced the occasional, 'Oh, why aren't you staying in the hotel?' and I felt like saying, 'Well, if you spent an instant thinking about it you'd understand.' Small things become big things when you're losing. Gilly admitted that when he got off the bus after we'd had a bad day and started walking away to his family unit, he was jolted by the thought that it didn't feel right to be away from the team. In contrast, England had a group of players mostly in their mid-twenties and on the way up, just as we had been a few years before, and they could spend more time together.

When we came home to Australia something happened that had never occurred in my cricket lifetime – a post-Ashes inquisition. You couldn't argue with it, yet a part of me thought, *I wish we'd done our inquisition before we left home . . . Isn't that called research?* The loss proved a cathartic experience for Australian cricket. Our team was accused of being too friendly with the opposition, and there was some truth to that. The friendliness had its roots in an increased respect for a side that had gone missing in the past, but was suddenly standing its ground. You can analyse stats and consider what-ifs, but the fact was that we lost because we didn't prepare well enough.

Before that 2005 Ashes series, we'd had too many distractions. Players were squeezing in team sponsorship duties on the days and nights before Tests. The day before one Test at the Gabba, four players were flown over to Stradbroke Island to film a Cricket Australia-sanctioned commercial. After the Ashes loss, small but significant things changed. Rules were set that ensured the bulk of the sponsorship work would be done at the start of the season, which cleared the decks for us to concentrate on our cricket as the season progressed. The only diversions we'd permit ourselves in future would have to be very special indeed.

32

Dinner with Mr Packer

I first met radio guru and former Wallabies coach Alan Jones when he visited our Queensland training camp in 1991 and delivered a stirring address. As a young, ambitious greenhorn, I was gripped by his charisma and soaked up every word. For the rest of my career he gave me his strident support and we became friends.

One night Kell and I invited him to our place for dinner, and when the conversation turned to one-day cricket, World Series Cricket and the inspiration behind the initiative, it inevitably drifted to a giant force in the game – Kerry Packer. Packer was a great friend of AJ's, and the more stories I heard that night about the man who had shaped modern cricket, the more fascinated I became. 'Mate, I'd absolutely love to meet Kerry Packer,' I said to AJ, and in that emphatic, categorical way of his, he responded, 'Consider it done!'

The night before a big game you'd never normally see me far from my hotel room. But when the invitation came the night before the Test match against the World XI at the SCG in 2005, I jumped at it. Dinner with Kerry Packer was truly a one-off, and I managed to expand the guest list to include Stephen Waugh, Justin Langer, Shane Watson and Brett Lee. We were told to dress casually, and the group was split on the lines of the Nerds – traditional types who think gel is something you have with your mum's custard – and the Julios – flash types who put gel in their hair and something sharp through their ear or tongue. Stephen wore a suit and tie, Justin and I the team blazer, and Watto and Binga wore smart casual. Small events became big events that night. At one stage Kerry asked Watto whether he'd like some peas, and hours later there was a moment in the car on the way home when a pensive Watto, staring out the window, dropped the line, 'Kerry Packer served peas for me . . . Kerry Packer!'

My favourite part of the night came when we were talking about Tony Greig's development of helmets. With the subtlety of a sledgehammer, Kerry asked Alfie, 'Son, tell me, why do you get hit on the head so much?' When Alfie said he didn't know, Kerry joked, 'You couldn't be watching the ball,' which drew smirks all round. Soon after, he spoke about the role of luck in the founding of the Packer dynasty, adding to Alfie, 'And, son, you'd know all about luck. If Tony Greig hadn't developed helmets, you'd be dead!' No smirks this time, just unrestrained laughter. The boys rated it the line of the night, one of those instant crackers that spreads like wildfire around the dressing-room the next morning.

Just two months later, Kerry Packer was dead. At the dinner he had looked a little frail but imposing, and his death came as a huge shock. He'd still had a commanding presence and a robust persona, which probably made him seem stronger than he was. We had no idea on the night that he was sick.

I'll never forget the last words he spoke to me. He said, 'Son, thank you so much for taking the time out to come and meet me.' He was thanking me! He inspired the deepest admiration in all of us, not only because he changed cricket but also because it took so much courage to challenge the game's foundations. I left on a high that night, and knew in my heart I would score a century the next day against the World XI.

Sometimes you just get a feeling about your form, and I had a strong one that week, which is partly the reason I let my hair down a little at dinner with Kerry Packer. I had a new, more patient plan to cope with the strategy England had used against me – bowling wide and waiting for me to fall on my sword. I hardly ever talked cricket to Kell, but before that Test I told her I sensed good times ahead.

Good form can sometimes be uncovered in odd places. The day of the Packer dinner, it rained at training and we were forced into the indoor nets, which had already been taken over for a corporate function. I spent some time pushing tables out of the way so I could have a bat – just another entry into the long list of training sessions that were far from suitable for an international team readying themselves for battle at the game's highest level. As Damien Martyn said to Mike Young at such moments, 'Do you think the New York Mets would do this before a big game?'

As I was batting, people were sitting at tables having lunch, and a master of ceremonies was going on about functions and Australia's Ashes loss and even my form. People were lining up beside and behind the net and watching me. It was bizarre – yet, for some reason, it worked for me. It gave me the chance to prove my focus had reached a new peak. It was exactly the sort of challenge I loved. Once I got over my huff at having to rearrange the lunch settings, I slipped into a concentration zone so pure that nothing around me mattered. There wasn't a ball I faced in that session, amid the clattering of dinner plates and glasses, that I didn't hit out of the screws. I felt my new patient strategy, unveiled under extreme pressure at the Oval, would be a winner for me that summer.

Of course, no cricketer would ever be bold enough to announce that sort of thing to the world and put a truckload of extra pressure on himself. It's a shame. I would have loved to trumpet a prediction, then be the genius who went out and made it happen. In any case, the World XI were a fractured unit and we won all three one-day games and the Test in Sydney.

The ICC instigated the World XI series because Australia had been so dominant they felt it would be a promotional dream to have the best players from around the world take on the best side in the world. But teams either click or they don't. The World XI had major challenges from the start. By making the 24-year-old Graeme Smith captain, they immediately pricked the egos of players like Brian Lara and Inzamam-Ul-Haq, long-term leaders of their own countries who deferred to no one. The difficulties confronting Smith were exemplified one day at fielding training, when Inzamam said to Smith, 'I'll take first slip.' The captain replied, 'Actually, I'm fielding there.' And Inzamam walked off, never to return.

I wonder what he would have made of a function room full of tables?

33

Boot-camp Buck vs. the King

Life was never boring in the Australian team when John Buchanan was coaching and Shane Warne was one of the lead players. Some of their jousts were serious, but I look back at many of their exchanges with a smile – and hope they do as well. One of my favourite memories is the day in New Zealand when Buck decided it'd be a great team-bonding exercise to take us to an albatross rookery. Good luck selling that idea to Warnie, who was never much of a nature buff!

It was the morning before a one-dayer and we'd just completed an exhausting training session. I don't think anyone realised the drive to the rookery would take so long, and it had been pure team pressure that got Warnie to drag his sorry backside onto one of the two buses in the first place. He actually drove that bus, and Buck drove the other.

So we set off, and on we went . . . and on and on and on. What Buck had sold as a half-hour journey became twice as long. With every passing kilometre, Warnie's mood grew darker.

I can still see him driving the bus with a cigarette hanging out the corner of his mouth. His lips became more and more pursed. After an hour, he decided the whole episode was beyond a joke and he guided his bus alongside Buck's vehicle. He made throat-cutting gestures as if to say, 'This is ridiculous! Call it off – now!' Then Warnie turned his bus around and headed for home.

Tugga, Alfie and I were stuck with Buck in search of the great white mystical birds, which were apparently going to inspire us to heights we'd never dreamt possible. In fact, the trip was a blast because it was so funny – the timing stuff-up plus Warnie's thunderous mood made it worthwhile. Best of all, when we finally got to the rookery, it was closed. All that was missing was Warnie: the expression on his face when he saw the closed sign would have been worth more than money could buy.

These days, even Buck laughs at the story and tells it at guest-speaking nights. He thought he might be able to draw some consolation from the trip when, after facing the *Closed* sign, he looked up and saw some white birds flying high overhead. Clutching at straws, he said, 'Wow . . . there they go – so natural, so free, so graceful.' I had to break the bad news to him. 'They're seagulls, mate.'

But perhaps the most public clash between Buck and Warnie came during our boot camp in Queensland in August 2006, three months before the final Test series of Warnie's career, when we won back the Ashes. We were picked up at 6.30 a.m. one Monday morning, loaded on a bus and told we'd have to hand in our mobile phones. Some of the boys were a bit anguished over this. Brett Lee's wife, Liz, was pregnant and you could understand his concern.

I thought the phone ban was a tad harsh, but the camp had

its rules. The lesson we'd learnt from the last Ashes tour was that our team was full of big personalities with big workloads, and we needed cohesion and a clear focus to make it work productively. As it turned out, that camp was one of the greatest things we could have done, and it became a key reference point for us throughout that summer. The cracks of the previous Ashes tour were sealed and we became a solid unit again, one which had rediscovered the virtues of teamwork, sacrifices and mutual understanding.

On the first day, we were taken to a warehouse and were divided into small groups under the control of a 'DS' – that's what we had to call them. All we were allowed to take was a backpack, a sleeping bag, a hutchie and a couple of shirts, two pairs of socks, some undies, joggers and other small items. We were told to strip to our undies and stand there in silence. Brad Hodge couldn't stop talking to me so we had to drop to the floor and do push-ups.

At first there was the distinct feeling that we were all a bit too cool for school, but as we tested the boundaries early on, one of the men in charge said, 'Did you ever stop to think that this lack of discipline might be the reason you're here?' Fair point. He continued, 'What part of *no talking* don't you understand?'

We had to lay our clothing out on the floor, as well as medication such as asthma sprays. Predictably, Warnie had too much stuff, including several packets of Benson & Hedges, which were taboo. The man in charge came straight up to him and said, 'What are these?' Warnie said solemnly, 'They're medicinal.' Then he added firmly, 'Just to set the record straight: I'll line up, I'll do whatever you want me to do, but if these don't go, the King's not going.'

The durries went on the camp and so did Warnie.

So the iron-clad army rules were broken – in the first hour of the camp! This had been an opportunity for Buck to break Warnie, but instead the King got his way.

I laughed at the incident – you just had to – because that defiant side of Warnie always cracked me up. Great talent often comes with a bit of rebelliousness. Deep down, though, I had mixed feelings about Warnie getting away with it because the purpose of being there was to knuckle down and rebuild together. And if you weren't going to be part of the solution, you were only creating more problems. The 'my way or the highway' mentality was the reason we were having the camp in the first place. Strategically Warnie might have made a great Test captain, but I'm not sure he'd have been as successful as the two men chosen ahead of him, Steve Waugh and Ricky Ponting, because he would not have been as inclusive as they were.

On our first night in the bush, we were woken up at 2 a.m. from our exhaustion-induced slumber by some sort of bomb. 'Everybody up! We're being ambushed – we have to move camp!' came the cry. We were camped in a swampy area swarming with mosquitoes, and in the mad scramble to move, there were some funny sights. Poor Phil Jaques was in my group and somehow managed to lose his contact lenses. Still half-asleep, he fumbled around in the dark like Mr Magoo. When he called, 'I'm in trouble here, I can't find my lenses,' one of the head men screamed back, 'I DON'T CARE ABOUT YOUR LENSES. WE ARE OUT OF HERE!'

We had only a couple of hours sleep after that before we were up again and on the move. It was freezing and Warnie was starting to look like he'd spent a month on Gilligan's Island. When he came to Queensland he was surprised by how cold it was and he rang me searching for some cold-weather gear. I gave him a bright orange jacket with a personal flotation device, which would inflate the jacket if you pulled a cord. Warnie never had to pull the cord, but he must have felt like sending out a distress signal at times. I can still see his shadowy profile in the semi-darkness, sucking his cigarette so hard that the burning tip stood out like a blazing comet.

As he dragged away, Warnie dropped the line of the camp. 'Well, Buck,' he said with rueful resignation, 'if it's any consolation, I've learnt three things already.' Just as Buck looked up with an expression of mild excitement, the King replied, 'I'm fat, I'm a weak prick and I want to go home.' The rest of us cracked up. That was typical Warnie: 'This is what I think and I don't give a stuff what you think.'

I will never forget the first time I ever saw Warnie. I was playing in a Sheffield Shield game against Victoria at the Gabba in December 1991, in thunderstorm season – a match truncated by rain and plenty of it. It bucketed down for most of the week. Warnie was rooming with Merv Hughes, his idol at the time, and every drop of rain was an enticement for Merv and Warnie to hit the town; they had some massive nights together.

When the game eventually started, Warnie was left out of the team because of the greenness of the wicket, and as Trevor Barsby and I walked out to bat, I noticed this character sitting outside the Victorian rooms in a state of total disarray. Normally I wouldn't say much at all to Tank, fearing I'd distract him, but that day I couldn't help myself. 'Have a go at this no-hoper, would you?' I said, gesturing towards Warnie, who had a fag hanging out the side of his mouth and was about to launch into the time-honoured hangover cure of a pie and a can of Coke.

When Warnie has a hangover, no one in the world looks, sounds or feels worse than him. It's quite a sight. I remember being almost angry with him that day, thinking something like, *I'm training my backside off and have a look at you!*

Warnie and I still laugh about this story. He never takes offence at those old yarns and almost wears them like a badge of honour. I felt in my heart that day that his prospects of making it were not great – but 708 wickets later, I had to change my mind! In fact, he played for Australia just three weeks after he was left out of that match for Victoria.

After Buck retired as national coach in 2007, he said that Warnie's brutal honesty was one of the qualities he most admired about him. As shamelessly rebellious as Warnie could be, it actually made him easier to deal with than some other athletes – you knew exactly where you stood.

One of the interesting things about the boot camp was that it brought together city boys like Michael Clarke and Stuart MacGill with country boys like me. Everyone pulled together, but there was a blow-up when we had to divide up our rations. The boys at the front of the camp column over-clubbed on their supplies, which meant the boys at the back – our group – got nothing. You can talk all you like about the toughness of elite sportsmen, but when they're hungry they're no different to dogs that haven't been fed. There was some almighty growling done by our group, directed firmly at the full-bellied boys at the front. I had to smile, though, thinking back to my first day as a boarder at Ashgrove when I'd drunk that entire jug of milk and copped the fallout from my thirsty fellow students.

The camp didn't go off perfectly. I really enjoyed one exercise in which we were taught how to navigate using the

Southern Cross, but our new skill was soon put to the test when we had to orienteer through a felled forest in the middle of the night – rugged stuff. That was the night Stuart MacGill, who didn't want to be on the camp in the first place, fell down a hole and twisted his knee. The injury proved a major setback to his career. He cracked it and threatened Buck with legal action, loudly proclaiming what rubbish the camp was.

Even though I was in favour of the concept of the boot camp, I thought the night-orienteering stuff was a genuinely poor choice of activity. Although I enjoyed learning how to navigate by using the stars, stumbling through a black forest was another thing altogether. It was pitch-black and we had no torches. To have national athletes stumbling around in a dark forest was just asking for trouble. To steal a line from Damien Martyn, somehow I couldn't imagine Usain Bolt doing it before the Olympics, or Roger Federer before Wimbledon. I fell down holes up to my waist. For me, that exercise was the one mistake of the camp.

I felt Buck was at his absolute best when coaching Queensland, giving structure and firm direction to a culture that sorely lacked discipline. He may have been less effective for Australia but that wasn't necessarily his fault because he wasn't always given the back-up staff he wanted. On balance, the decision to appoint him was a successful one. He made his mark in an eight-year reign from 1997–2007 and I totally disagree with claims by Ian Chappell that the only coach you need is the one that takes you to the ground. Buck often challenged you and was ahead of the game in his thinking. You'd struggle to read from his body language whether the team was winning or losing, and often it was subtly against the flow – upbeat when we were losing, cautious when we were on top of the world. His door was always open and you felt you could communicate with him. He is also a great family man with a good moral code, and he helped make our culture consistent.

He was also right about some remarkable things. The cricket world was stunned by a one-day game we played at Johannesburg in March 2006, when Australia made 4/434 yet South Africa, incredibly, swept to victory with one ball remaining. Buck wasn't surprised at all. He'd been tipping for years that someone would make 400-plus in a one-day game and someone else might just chase it down. Gilly and I used to joke about it. 'Buck's kidding himself,' we'd say to each other and laugh about the likely instructions he'd give us when that day arrived: 'Okay, boys, just see if you can score at 10 an over – but don't take risks.'

Buck never pretended to be a technical guru. If you haven't played at the game's highest level, it's very hard to be an authoritative technical coach. Do you think Buck could have taught/told Warnie how to bowl a leg break? But to his credit, Buck knew this, and his strengths were in other areas. Buck could really get under my skin but, in his defence, I would not have been the easiest player to coach at times; I wanted my preparation to be expertly planned and was really angry when it wasn't. Buck's timing could be poor – such as the day in India when he told the press in the middle of a crucial Test series that Warnie was overweight. And I wasn't completely sold on the idea of computer analysis, feeling that I'd rather spend 90 minutes in the nets than watching videos of a guy bowling outswingers when he might plan to bowl me an inswinger the next day. But Buck still did a fine job, and his exceptional record says as much.

In hindsight, the best coaches in my era were fellow players.

I found the best person to talk to about technique – by far – was Ricky Ponting, who has an acute understanding of the idiosyncrasies of hand movement and its relation to foot movement. His knowledge of all things batting is as good as anyone's I have met. And he has beautifully simple thought processes. Greg Chappell was another one who had this gift, and Steve Waugh was also good, as was Martin Love. Simplicity was the key with all of them. You just got the feeling they knew what it was all about.

INSIDE THE GAME

Team Meetings

Don't get me started. I've always felt team meetings were overrated. There were exceptions, such as the stimulating talks we had with Buck and psychologist Phil Jauncey for Queensland in the 1990s, but routine team talks never seemed to achieve much. Men tend to hold feelings close to their chest; in groups, they take refuge in clichés. Your average sportsman's concentration span isn't built to endure whiteboards and the repetition of basic theories. At school, we were the back-of-the-class boys who spent Friday afternoon looking out the window praying that the grey clouds visible didn't bring rain to wash out the match the next day.

In meetings, I instinctively sided with Mark Waugh, who had a habit of saying what everyone else was thinking and would pipe up every so often with a line like, 'For God's sake, how hard can it be? Just bowl it to hit the top of off stump. There's my tip.' Then he'd doze for an hour. In fact, in all my years of sitting in meetings I never heard a game plan superior to Mark's recommendation. And the longer the meeting, the more truth there seemed to be in Tubby Taylor's adage: if you talk about an opponent for long enough, you'll get to the stage where you think you'll never get them out.

The best team meetings were the intimate one-on-ones. It might be a coffee with Ricky Ponting or a chance meeting with Marto. Jason Gillespie and Michael Kasprowicz plotted India's demise on the 2004 tour with a chat on the plane over. And some of the most important meetings in general are the mid-pitch ones, when your partner is under siege and he hears, 'C'mon, mate, be strong here – four balls left.' Simple but powerful.

A lot of methods have been thrown around over the years to make the team meetings work. There have been focus groups split up to tackle special assignments. There have been group sessions. There have been one-on-ones. Some players thrived on analysis – Adam Dale would cheerfully have analysed every ball he bowled. Others, like Michael Kasprowicz, just liked the general outline. And Warnie was so into what he was doing – and so good – that having the rest of us tell him how to manage his craft would've been like someone from your local stand-up comedy night telling Jerry Seinfeld how to deliver a punchline.

Instead of having team meetings, I wish at times we'd been bold enough to say, 'I've got nothing to say,' because sometimes, when you've won 10 or more games on the trot, you haven't. The reiteration of three points should've been enough: batsmen should watch the ball, bowlers should try and hit the top of off stump, and fieldsmen should be extremely committed. In-depth team meetings can actually mislead you, because their predictions make you look for things that aren't there.

In the 2005 Ashes series, for instance, I was placed on red alert for Matthew Hoggard's big inswingers, yet the first four balls I received from him were well wide of off stump. That's because opponents aren't stupid. They plan as well, and they often know what plan you'll be expecting, so what you end up facing is their Plan B. During that terrible Ashes series we probably had more team meetings than at any other time. What does that tell you? Sounds to me like a vindication of something Alan Jones once said to us in Perth: 'Losers have team meetings, winners party.'

For all that, there *were* moments in team meetings that definitely mattered. One of my favourites comes from the 1994–95 season, the week before Queensland won the Sheffield Shield for the first time.

We needed to beat Tasmania in Hobart in order to host the final, but we were feeling down after being bowled out for 234 on the first day, and Tasmania were 0/30 at stumps. Doing 'anger' wasn't Buck's strong suit, and his rare efforts at tub-thumping never quite rocked us like they were meant to. But this day in Hobart he decided we needed a rocket, and he did his best to fire it. He claimed we'd dropped our heads, and that if it continued we might as well jump on the plane and leave immediately.

AB was furious and said, 'Are you saying we're not trying?' I reckon the conversation was one provocative sentence away from AB dropping the old 'How many Tests did you play?' line, but Buck turned it around and said, 'That's just what I wanted to hear.' The exchange stirred the boys into action and we went on to steamroll Tasmania by 221 runs after bowling them out for 155, their lowest Hobart total in four years.

I think Buck may have underestimated how hard we were trying, how much hosting the final meant to us and how much spirit there was in the group. But the clash between him and AB helped to inspire us to surge through Tasmania and then South Australia at home at the Gabba, and take the title Queensland teams had been chasing unsuccessfully for most of the century.

34

Farewell to the Legends

Over the course of a long career, you suffer some strange injuries. I was pretty fortunate in that regard, but even so I've had hamstrings, headaches and haemorrhoids – and that's just the Hs. However, nothing I'd experienced prepared me for what happened while I was jogging near my parents' home in Kingaroy in October 2006.

It was just a month away from one of the most important assignments for my generation of cricketers – winning back the Ashes on home soil after they'd been snatched from our grasp in England the year before. At the time I felt bulletproof. In week seven of my preseason training, it seemed I could crash-tackle the world. Then I was crash-tackled myself – by the neighbour's cattle dog.

Our neighbours have always had working dogs, who are attracted by movement. I heard the bark of this little dog as I passed the neighbours' property, and was in full stride when he pounced from behind and sank his teeth deep into my ankle.

It was as quick as that. I fell in a heap and couldn't even rotate my foot. I could actually see the Achilles' tendon. Had the wound been deeper still, I'd have been in enormous trouble. As it was, I was in strife, and the injury couldn't even be touched for a week (to avoid infection). I missed about four weeks of practice and game time, and felt totally unprepared for the First Test at the Gabba soon after, managing only 21 and 37. Not that it hurt us, because we won the match by 277 runs, after Ricky made 196 in the first innings. My summer didn't really turn the corner until I made 92 in the second innings of the Third Test in Perth.

The Test of the summer, however, was the Second Test in Adelaide – one of the most astonishing wins of our era. For me, there was also the behind-the-scenes drama of a blue with Damien Martyn.

Marto and I always sat next to each other in Adelaide. On the other side of him was Punter, who upheld the tradition of every Australian captain I played under by scattering his gear around like a scrub turkey sorting its nest. As part of a comic little ritual, Marto would put a line of sports tape down each side of his space, and playfully warn Punter and me that trespassers weren't welcome. But Marto was in a bad place that Test, and seemingly getting worse by the day. When you're under pressure you tend to take it out on those close to you, and Marto and I were – and still are – very close. As with me and Symo, we see the best and the worst of each other.

Many of Marto's great moments as a player came overseas. Nine of his 13 Test centuries were overseas, as was his great innings in the 2003 World Cup final against India in Johannesburg, when he scored 88 not out off 84 balls with a badly broken finger.

None of this was a coincidence. Marto always disliked playing in the home summer because he was back in the 'fishbowl', which meant he was heavily exposed to the media, the public, and all the other tentacles of the cricket world. At home in Perth he particularly felt the pressure. I understood, because home, with all the exposure and sponsorship commitments, often did seem the hardest place to play. Marto was dropped – most unfairly given a string of luckless dismissals – after the 2005 Ashes series and the selectors must have privately acknowledged they made a major blue because to squeeze him back into the side they had to end the career of Brad Hodge, who had an average of almost 56 from his six Tests. Marto returned for the away series against South Africa and his second innings century, on the toughest Test wicket I played on in Johannesburg, was simply a masterpiece. Of his 13 Test centuries, nine were overseas and maybe that said something about the fact he was more comfortable away from the searing spotlight of a domestic summer. And no domestic summer was more claustrophobic that an Ashes summer. After South Africa, Marto was back in the fishbowl and to him it seemed full of piranhas. The press were questioning his form and I know English players were sledging him with lines like 'We got you once and we will get you again.'

I had my own doubts, but I generally left them in the dressing-room. I could actually feel myself growing in stature when I walked out to bat, because I loved the big stage and theatre of cricket. The lesser teams I should have by rights dominated were the ones that tested me, because I struggled to reach the same level of intensity against them as when we were playing the big guns. My record against New Zealand was patchy, and the side I averaged least against was Bangladesh. However, on the big days, whether it was the 50-degree heat of Sharjah or a Boxing Day greentop, I just couldn't wait to get out there.

But Marto never felt that way. In his mind, his position was tougher than mine because, unlike him, I didn't often have to face spin when I came to the crease. We'd talk through his strategy against spin, and his four Test centuries on the subcontinent (two against India and two against Sri Lanka) remain some of the highest achievements of his career and were instrumental in some of the best wins of our era.

We knew at the start of the summer that Marto would probably be a media target. We talked about ways he could handle it, but there are few places to hide in an Ashes series. He was a bit like a coral trout hiding in the coral, worried about a circling shark. He'd sit motionless for an age, then duck out occasionally before scurrying back to shelter.

Marto started the series with 29 in Brisbane and 11 in the first innings in Adelaide, and I also had a slow start after the dog bite. I was starting to realise how much Marto was under pressure because of little throwaway barbs he was tossing in my direction. The drip feed of short, needling comments wore me down. I desperately needed to hit 1000 balls to get my game back on track, but hadn't been able to do so because of surgery. I was trying to put on a brave face and be the strength of the dressing-room, but I was so tense I was struggling just to breathe, and now I found myself thinking, *One of my great mates is starting to seriously annoy me*. He knew it. I knew it.

We had an epic win in Adelaide – one for the ages – when we bowled England out for 129 in their second innings and somehow squeezed in a last-day victory that had seemed a pipedream at the start of the day. Earlier in the Test England had declared their first innings at 6/551, and when we stumbled to 3/65 in our first innings, a draw would have been a big result for us, never mind a victory. There were can-tops cracking in all directions that night, but I didn't drink anything because, sensing things might blow up, I wanted to keep a clear head.

Marto was sitting next to Freddie Flintoff and Geraint Jones, I think, having a beer. He said to me, 'Oh, not having a drink with us?' I ignored him and slipped out of the rooms. I didn't want to be mates with the Poms at that stage. I didn't object to them being in our rooms, but I didn't want to give them anything then either: I wanted to hammer them. Punter had asked us not to be as friendly to the Poms as we'd been in 2005, instructing us, for example, to call them by name rather than nickname. (Kevin Pietersen eventually texted Warnie, asking, 'What's this Kevin stuff?')

I joined Alfie and Pigeon outside and was swept away by the sight of a full moon hanging right beside a church steeple over a fully lit Adelaide Oval scoreboard. We were sitting on the steps outside the room admiring it when Marto came out with that cocky swagger of his, and said, 'What's wrong with you?'

I grabbed Marto and said, 'Mate, you have been the biggest wanker on the planet here, and I'm supposed to be one of your mates. Have you ever looked outside yourself and realised I'm struggling too? A person who has gone out of his way to help you?' At first Marto thought I was joking. But it was no joke. Marto left abruptly, and the news broke a few days later that he'd decided to retire.

I never thought for a second that our exchange had prompted his decision. It had been a long time coming. Gilly revealed after his own retirement that Marto had foreshadowed his exit over lunch the day before the Test. Marto vanished into retirement, and not even Punter – who'd been best man at Marto's wedding – could track him down for a while.

News of my exchange with Marto somehow made it into the media a few weeks later, and we had to confirm there had been an incident, but that there was nothing more to it. Which was true. There *was* nothing more to it. Marto announced his retirement via a media release before the Perth Test and we went on to clinch that match – and the Ashes – ahead of the Melbourne Test.

Later, Marto told us that the one thing he missed about the game was his mates. I can understand that. Most retired cricketers feel the same. Though Marto loathed the spotlight, the three things he really enjoyed – golf, a coffee and a nice bottle of wine over dinner – revolved around the company of his mates. In some ways, his attitude to cricket was similar to that of Andrew Symonds. Both loved the game but hated a lot of things that went with it, such as sponsorship appearances. If you asked them to describe their perfect cricketing life, it would be to simply play the game and enjoy the company of their mates. I'm sure Marto would've liked to earn the big dollars that come with private sponsorships, but to do that you have to put yourself out there as a personality, and that was never his style. He just wanted to be left alone. He was one of the worst sleepers in the team and it didn't do much for his state of mind. When he batted, he was driven to just get to 40 so he could relax. A few years after his retirement Marto moved to the Gold Coast, and immediately felt more comfortable having a lower profile out of Perth.

Symo and I had a great time in the Melbourne Test, adding 261 for the sixth wicket after an early collapse, and Symo's 156 was hailed as a breakthrough innings. Soon after he came to the wicket, Pietersen started taunting him as 'a specialist fieldsman'. Far from being unsettled, Symo got off on it – he always did. He started sledging Pietersen about his penchant for wearing tight singlets after dark. 'You're not going to have to worry about any excess luggage, champ, are you, while you're just wearing those singlets around?' It was the perfect reply to Pietersen, who we all suspected was a little more sensitive behind his bravado than he let on. Alfie Langer always said that it was never the loudmouth you had to worry about – it was the quiet guy who knew what he was about.

The final Test, in Sydney, was a very emotional time. It involved Test farewells for Alfie, Warnie, Pigeon and Buck, who I gave a big, tearful hug as we left the ground after Alfie and I had steered us to a 10-wicket victory. As victory drew near, Alf's emotions were rising. 'This is getting a bit much,' he admitted, with seven runs to go. 'How about a six and one to finish it for me?' I laughed and said to Freddie Flintoff, 'He doesn't want much, does he?' But I duly hit Sajid Mahmood for a six and one – and so ended my unforgettable batting partnership with Alfie as we sealed a 5–0 victory in the Ashes.

Alfie's retirement obviously affected me the most of all. It was as if someone had cut off my right leg, and life was never quite the same for me at Test level after he left. I missed him almost before he was gone, because I'd known that season would be his last. I sensed the same of Warne and McGrath, to the point where I can't even remember the precise moment when someone confirmed their retirements to me. It was like the setting of the sun. I felt deeply honoured to have played with these two absolute legends of the game. They could have come along at any time in the history of cricket, yet Australia had them together for 13 years.

The departure of our champions was a bit like an earthquake: the quake itself is damaging, but sometimes the aftershocks can be worse. The full impact of Warnie's exit really hit me in Sydney a year later, when India waltzed to 532 in their first innings, with Tendulkar and Laxman making centuries. There were long periods in that innings when nothing was happening for us on the ground Warnie had dominated for so long. Punter, standing beside me, quietly dropped the line, 'So this is life without Warnie.'

It was indeed. And a suddenly challenging one at that.

35

Murali

I never thought I'd find a bigger cricket nuffy than Michael Hussey, but I have – Muttiah Muralitharan. It was during a flight for the Chennai Super Kings in the IPL that I found myself the meat in a cricketing sandwich made up of Huss and Murali. They went at it incessantly, reeling off cricket facts great and small, until Huss finally faltered and fell asleep. 'Congratulations, mate, you've done it – you've out-nuffed the nuffy!' I told a smiling Murali. 'That makes you the new Mr Cricket.'

Murali has an unquenchable thirst for cricket knowledge. When Tasmania's George Bailey joined the Super Kings, he couldn't believe how much Murali knew about even minor Australia first-class players. Murali's mind never rests. He has a theory on everything. And he's never afraid to let you know it, either. There are times when I've been dismissed for the Super Kings and am in that sensitive cooling-off period after an innings, and Murali (Test batting average of about 11) will come up and say, 'Your go is playing straight. You hit the ball miles.' But he can say anything to me and get away with it: he's a very special bloke.

Murali only started bowling spin at age 12, when he was struggling to take wickets as a medium pacer. His parents run Sri Lanka's third-largest biscuit factory – Luckyland Biscuits – which Murali visits whenever he goes home to Kandy. After playing with him for the Super Kings I rate him easily the quirkiest spinner I've ever come across. Give him a ball and everything about him radiates aggression and confidence. From his bouncy little stride to the clinical, businesslike way he looks around the field, and even the purposeful way he fizzes the ball from hand to hand – it all sends the message that he just can't wait to bowl.

Yet beneath the imposing aura lies a man who has more doubts than the outside world realises. You could not believe that a man who has taken more Test wickets than any other bowler could have so many doubts. He worries about absolutely everything. A wet ball, a fast outfield . . . you name it and he'll find something to fret over. His demeanour also changes starkly when he's batting. You can see by the way his big eyes peer out from under the helmet with trepidation that batting is not his domain. I don't think he likes the fast stuff.

It's hard to believe that a bowler who's taken more wickets than anyone in the history of the game can be so paranoid about so many things. When I discovered this about Murali while playing for the Super Kings, it reinforced a theory I have that most spin bowlers – no matter how great their achievements – have a layer of insecurity that makes them vulnerable to rampant aggression. I've always felt the key to beating spinners was to attack them and get their bat-pads to retreat so you could hit singles and rotate strike and the fours will come. Once you got the men away from the bat, you really did think, *How is this guy going to get me out?*

One of Australia's most underrated series wins was against Sri Lanka in 2004: an epic showdown between the two most successful spinners of all time, Murali and Warnie, who, like poker hustlers, just kept slapping big hands on the table. They took 54 wickets between them (Murali 28, Warne 26), and were so clever in the way they mentally worked batsmen over. Rather than start with men around the bat and run the risk of having to move them back, thus conceding to the batsman, they preferred to gradually move the field in as their bowling spell – and their spell over the batsman – intensified, as if to say, 'I am taking control now.'

We managed to win that 2004 series 3–0, but it was heavy-duty cricket all the way. In each Test we trailed on the first innings, only to somehow rally and win. That was never easy in Sri Lanka, a place where everything seemed to be against you – the crowds, the wickets, the humidity. You felt under pressure the whole time.

That Sri Lankan tour was a watershed in Warnie's career because he learnt how to bowl on the subcontinent, getting over his infatuation with the big leg break, which gave adept players of spin the time and room to cut. Instead he used sliders and other balls out the front of the hand, and fast leg breaks to attack the stumps. Had he tried this strategy against the Indians, most particularly in India, it might have erased the only spot on his otherwise magnificent record.

For the same reason, I always felt far less threatened by Murali on big-turning wickets in Sri Lanka than I did on flat wickets in Australia. If the ball turned too much, it would drift towards the leg stump or down the leg side and could therefore be swept. And if he allowed for turn and didn't get it, then the cut came into play. But if the ball doesn't turn in Australia, then most times it's heading towards the stumps, which means the cut is out of play, the sweep is dangerous and there's just not much to do with it.

So could I read the greatest wicket-taker of all time? Hand over heart, I must answer no. Most of the time I could. But not all the time. Murali's action is such a whirlpool of movement I tried not to concentrate on it, almost for fear of being mesmerised. I just watched the ball as closely as I could. Murali bowled very quickly to me because he knew I'd try to get to him on the full.

Murali was like a magician, trying to lure your eyes in one direction with his whirling action while performing something deft with his hand that you didn't even notice. Murali dominated the cricket world because of two great skills – he could spin the ball as far as any finger spinner who had played the game, and he could bowl with freakish accuracy. These two talents rarely go together. He had the flair of an artist and the frugality of an accountant all rolled into one dynamic package. We prospered against him because we tried not to sweat about his arm, his elbow, his fingers and another major distraction that no one ever talks about – his eyes. At the moment Murali delivers the ball, his eyes pop out like those of a goldfish that's been squeezed. I'm sure this expression is the result of the amount of effort he is putting into his bowling rather than a playful piece of choreography, but it's distracting nonetheless. Murali's eyes were like Curtly Ambrose's quivering lips – you know they're irrelevant to the bowling, you'd tell yourself there was no way you could afford to look at them, but somehow they drew you in all the same.

On the 1999 tour of Sri Lanka, the Australian team had

privately whinged too much about Murali's action. It was four years after Murali had been no-balled out of the Boxing Day Test at the MCG and we had become consumed with the bona fides of his action. It was negative stuff and – more importantly – didn't solve the riddle of how to play him. In 2004 we were far more positive and played the ball, rather than worrying about the arm that delivered it.

36

Man on a Mission – World Cup 2007

Picture this: it's after midnight on a beautiful Caribbean night. An Australian cricketer is the world's most contented man as he sits alone on an exotic island under a coconut palm, the stars shining like diamonds on black velvet. He's had five or six rum punches (actually he's lost count) and good vibes are coming from all directions at this little one-man party. As a gentle sea breeze wafts in and waves lap softly on the shore, our man has a rum punch in one hand, a giant cigar in the other, and the satisfied look of someone who has attained his heart's desire.

This was me at the 2007 World Cup, when Australia won the tournament for the third consecutive time and I was fortunate enough to score the most runs out of all nations. It probably won't surprise you that I was celebrating, but if you guessed the occasion was a post-tournament victory party, you've got it wrong. It was the first night of the tour and we hadn't even played a game.

We'd arrived jet-lagged after almost two days of travel, as

there is no short route from Australia to the West Indies. At the hotel on St Kitts we were greeted by the mandatory hostess serving rum punches. Many is the time I have politely declined on these occasions – I've always been a light drinker – but I was in the mood to celebrate that afternoon, so I had a couple. Then a few more. And actually . . . a few more after that.

We all sat around outside the hotel with only a giant mango tree between us and the Caribbean. One by one my teammates went to bed, but I just didn't feel like turning in for the night so I went for a stroll up the beach to contemplate what lay ahead. As I sat under a coconut palm and puffed on the cigar, I made myself a promise – a drunken promise, but a sincere one nonetheless – to enjoy myself no matter what happened. Therein lay one of the key ingredients to my success that tour. Ricky's motto for the tournament – 'Be free' – dovetailed perfectly with my own game plan. Punter's message was not to hold back or second-guess yourself, but to back yourself, liberate your talents.

I had prepared hard, had a super game plan, knew the conditions well and loved the idea of being near the water for the entire tour. Even my cavalier first-night foray went my way. Adam Gilchrist had always said the best way to tackle jet lag was to have a solid drink the first night of the tour and then you'd be away the next day. Worked for me! I woke up fresh as a sea breeze the next morning (actually it was about 1 p.m.) and plunged into the ocean. But the boys who'd gone to bed early and tossed and turned all night looked as if they'd fallen head-first out of a coconut palm.

Several key elements came together for me at that World Cup and produced a form explosion, the highlight of my one-day career. Almost a year before, I'd come 19th in Australia's list of one-day rankings. In assessing these, the selectors review your form for the last year and combine it with their expectations of you for the next year, so being ranked 19th didn't say much for my World Cup prospects, particularly as they were only taking a 15-man squad. Put bluntly, the selectors didn't expect me to make the tour.

The widespread feeling that my one-day career was over was embodied in the expression on a journalist's face at a preseason press conference. Ian Eckersley, from the ABC in Brisbane, asked me whether I had hopes of resuming my one-day career. I can still see his look of disbelief when I said, 'I am going to . . . I definitely want to keep playing one-day cricket – remember I made that statement.' The general feeling that my one-day career could be over – or at the very least in serious decline – inspired me to prove it wasn't.

That summer had been a struggle. I was working hard to maintain my place in the side, but also trying to formulate a plan that would work in the West Indies. The retirements of Langer, McGrath and Warnie didn't have much impact on the one-day tournament, because Warnie and Alfie had no longer been playing one-day cricket anyway and McGrath was with us for his farewell tournament. But I was on the edge and could feel the pressure building. In the Perth match of a crucial warm-up series against New Zealand, I slashed a ball to Dan Vettori at mid-off while still on nought. He grassed the catch and I went on to make a century. To this day Dan still ribs me about saving my career.

My problem was I didn't have a clear idea about what was expected of me in the one-day game. If I was expected to average 45 or more, I could do it easily by reining in my strike rate to late 70 or more – the Ricky Ponting mode of one-day play. But if I was expected to crank it up to a strike rate of around 100 – the Gilchrist way – my average would have to take a hit. The late David Hookes had a theory that Australia no longer needed a bat-through-the-innings man like Geoff Marsh, because we were batting a lot deeper than we had in the bad old days of the mid-1980s. He claimed the role of the opener had changed to become more cavalier. I reckoned this was a fair point, but not everyone agreed.

Before the tournament, Buck had lit a fuse under me. He approached me in Hamilton, at the end of the New Zealand tour, and said the side wasn't getting enough out of me, repeating that my position wasn't assured for the World Cup. It angered me, as did our difference of opinion on the role of an opener, but I knew any point I made in a private meeting in a hotel room would have little impact compared to one I could make in the middle. It was an argument that could only be settled at the crease.

The next day I went out and made 181 not out, the highest score in Australian one-day history and one of the most important innings of my career. After I made 380 against Zimbabwe, I said I'd never thought I'd make a triple century because I never felt I'd have the time to do so – but I've always felt it's possible to make a double century in a 50-over game as indeed Sachin Tendulkar did against South Africa in Gwalior, India, in February 2010. It's a box I would love to have ticked. One other motive for my 181 was that my toe had been broken after being struck twice in the one over by Mark Gillespie and I could barely move. I just stood and swung like a baseballer, clearing my front leg. My plan to make it to the World Cup was now on the table for all to see.

I had a theory that the World Cup would be won by power

play. I was practising – and at times playing – accordingly. I'd train for two hours with the team, then bat for two more hours after training had finished until I could barely stand up, hitting the ball as hard as I could. At St Kitts I often let the bus go back to the team hotel and would spend time just blazing away in the middle, lobbing six after six over a wall and into a sugarcane plantation across the road.

One of my tactics was to move my front leg towards the leg side, just getting it out of the road to increase my hitting power. It's not the tactic for Australian conditions, but it is Plan A in the West Indies with their small grounds and short boundaries. Buck didn't agree with my 'Big Bang' theory but he was out of step with the thinking of a lot of the guys, who, like me, believed that raw power would win us the World Cup – which it did.

Our Cup squad was beautifully balanced, with the pace power of Shaun Tait complementing the subtle skills of Nathan Bracken and Glenn McGrath – and the tournament's surprise package, Brad Hogg. No one could pick Hogg's exceptional wrong 'un, and it netted him a string of big-name victims including England's Freddie Flintoff, South Africa's Herschelle Gibbs and Sri Lanka's Mahela Jayawardene. Even from first slip I found his wrong 'un challenging to read. Hoggy, a classic unsung hero, had a beautiful moment at the Barbados airport when he briefly crossed paths with the great Muttiah Muralitharan, who said the four words that make a spinner's life: 'They can't pick you.' That from the world's most prolific wicket-taker. A look of total contentment came over Hoggy's face at that instant, as though his life's work was complete.

Just before the World Cup, Australian fans had a rewarding summer as we thrashed England 5–0 to regain the Ashes. But things turned sour before England went home, when they beat us in the finals of the Commonwealth Bank Tri-series. We won our first five matches of the series against England and New Zealand, then lost four in a row, the last three to England. Because we had steamrolled England all summer, it was a finale no one could have predicted. We looked like a team falling apart, but there were other forces at play. Because we knew the practice facilities in the Caribbean would be poor, we'd front-loaded our campaign and were training ultra-hard before we got there, sometimes on the morning of VB series games. Time would prove this tactic a masterstroke, but the cost for long-term gain was short-term pain: Andrew Symonds may even have torn his bicep because of the training load. But we knew that if we waited until we got to the Caribbean to prepare we'd be way behind.

There were interesting moments in our fielding sessions with Mike Young before the World Cup, some of which were even harder than Bob Simpson's legendary ordeals. One day in Melbourne, we were in full swing, playing a fielding game featuring Ricky, Symo, Michael Clarke, Mike Hussey and Cameron White. Young would stand in the middle, we'd stand around him and he would throw the ball to us. You had to run to catch it and then throw it to someone else. It wore everyone out very quickly and for White, new to the squad and unused to its intensity, it was all too quickly. After 10 catches, he pantingly conceded, 'I can't.'

Youngy jumped on him immediately. 'What did you say? There are no such words here, mate. Keep going.'

Sometimes those little slip-ups go unmarked. But at that precise moment, when we were readying ourselves for the monumental challenge of trying to win our third consecutive

World Cup, there were no such words in our vocabulary. That was the worst moment of Cameron's career, I reckon, and it came in front of the national captain. Whether because of this momentary lapse or not, he did not go on the tour.

This tournament was special to me for so many reasons. There was a little island off the coast of St Vincent where the umpires were staying, and I used to swim around it in my goggles and snorkel. I know the boys used to ask, 'What's Haydos doing?' as they saw me float off in the distance. I'd never heard about any shark attacks in the West Indies and deliberately didn't ask the question, in case there was an answer I didn't want to hear. I even organised a surf in St Vincent through a mate in Barbados. Surfing, fishing, sun and sand have always added up to good times for me.

But more importantly, the confidence I felt during the tournament allowed me to bid farewell to that little bogey man on my shoulder – the one who'd appeared all my cricketing life in tournaments and try-outs and one-on-one shootouts. Since my days in short pants, I was often at my worst in major tournaments because I became overwhelmed and distracted by everything except the one thing that really mattered – the next ball.

Before our first big game of the World Cup, I decided it was time to go big-game hunting. We were playing South Africa, and I wanted to take down Shaun Pollock. Although Pollock was no longer captain of the Proteas, he was still their rock and spiritual strength, and his strength was also his weakness. Like McGrath, he was very structured in his play. Knock him off his structure and you could own him.

At the team meeting the night before the game, I decided to

make the big call. 'I think I can get to Pollock,' I said. 'I'm going to wait until the third ball then I'm coming . . . Punter, get ready just in case it doesn't work.' I'd never be this candid with the media because I didn't need the extra pressure, but I would do it occasionally with the team. I always felt it was important to show some leadership and convey a strong, calculated message. (Sometimes I drove my teammates mad with this tough talk, especially after I'd finished batting. In a sense, by then, I couldn't be wrong. Huss and some of the others hated it when I'd be sitting there and a spinner came on and I'd be dropping lines like, 'That's got to go for six . . . surely.')

My plan to torment Pollock got off to just the start I wanted when he bowled a typically neat first ball on off stump, which I drove for four. Two balls later he adjusted his line to middle and leg, and I knifed one past mid-on for four. Now there was no going back. Pollock's third over was my gold-plated jackpot. I had a little surprise for him – a newly developed cut shot. When he fed it first ball of the third over, I cut him for four. Being the percentage bowler that he was, I knew this would prompt him to readjust his line towards my pads. So I took a chance and walked down the wicket at him. Sure enough, his next ball was perfectly in the slot for a swipe over cow corner for six, prompting Mark Boucher to move over the stumps in an effort to keep me in my crease. Next ball I played a similar shot to the same place, and was greeted by the sight every batsman loves – the captain (in this case, Graeme Smith) jogging from slip for an urgent tactical review with his bowler. We reached 50 in the fifth over and had stolen a break they never looked like pegging back.

Things don't always go to plan at the top of the order but they did that day. I finished with 101 off 68 balls, including 33 off 16 balls against Pollock, with four fours and two sixes. It was the World Cup's fastest century, yet I never felt as if the accelerator was pushed totally to the floor. I reminded myself, *Take time to establish your innings and play the percentages – the harvest will be greater*. It was best to take Pollock for one or two boundaries an over, not to try for six in a row, because I knew from experience that whenever I got into trouble in my career it was usually because I was too aggressive for my own good. And this piece of solid advice had come from a crab fisherman from Stradbroke Island. Over 15 years in international cricket, I've been privileged to meet prime ministers, corporate directors and international CEOs, but sometime's life's messages come from the most unexpected places.

In the countdown to the World Cup that year I had been on Stradbroke Island chatting to Bryden Phillips, a professional crabber, about the challenges of sustaining his business despite tough government laws that restricted the size of his catch. He spoke about maximising his catch as increased zoning diminished the number of fishable areas. 'Don't go for the big crabs all the time, cause that's where the greedy crabbers go. Sometimes they'll strike it rich, but other times they'll end up with nothing,' he had said. I thought of Bryden's advice when I was launching my full-blown assault at Pollock during that first big match of the tournament.

As the floodgates opened, something very significant happened. The South Africans began to drop their heads. I'd had a rough start to my international career against South Africa, but had since balanced the ledger and was now pushing well into the black. When you've had success against a side and start well against them, you can sense the life draining from their challenge before your eyes. Australia was the team they hadn't beaten in a major event since apartheid, and there were also two near-misses against us in the 1999 World Cup. History weighed heavily on them that day, and you could see it in their faces and hear it in their chatter – or lack of it. They were thinking, *Here we go again*.

We scored 6/377 then took them down for 294. Their innings was a controversial one – Jacques Kallis made 48 off 63 balls and was widely accused of batting too slowly. There were whispers that Kallis's teammates were frustrated because he just didn't seem to appreciate the need for speed – or at least to lift a gear. The next morning at breakfast someone spotted his team sitting at one table and Jacques sitting by himself at another.

I rate Kallis the best all-rounder of my generation – by a street. He is the man who's got everything: a good arm, great hands, useful medium pace and exceptional batting skills. He's a phenomenal player. But for a lot of his one-day career he was just a gear short of where he needed to be. His career batting stats of an average of around 45 and a strike rate in the low seventies were certainly honourable, but he was better than that. Those figures are in the realms of the 'very good' not the 'great'. There was a fifth gear to him – we've seen it in Twenty20 cricket – but he rarely found it in Tests or the 50-over game, and that could put pressure on his teammates.

Some people called Kallis selfish, but I've never gone along with that. Selfish players are invariably insecure players. You could never say Kallis was playing out of fear of losing his place – he was the first player chosen in the South African side for more than a decade. I saw him facing similar pressures in South Africa as Allan Border had done in Australia a few decades before, when he was the rock of a side during turbulent times. Where Border had to anchor sides missing talent to the Packer revolution and rebel tours of South Africa, Kallis's team was destabilised by the quota system – which ensured the presence of black and coloured players as well as players chosen exclusively on form – and the Hansie Cronje match-fixing affair.

The South Africans were rocked by Hansie's involvement in match-fixing and I couldn't blame them. I barely knew him but it took me aback as well. In limited dealings with him I found him a genuinely nice bloke, good company, and there was no trace of anything sinister about the man or his life. He also impressed me as a player because he was the first batsman I saw – and one of the few ever – who really took to Warnie. One of the strong memories I have of my first South African tour in 1994 was Cronje taking apart Warnie – and the rest of our attack – with a stunning innings of 251 for Free State, of which the last 50 came off just 23 balls with a series of ferocious sixes.

I believe Kallis would've been a different, more expansive player had he been playing for Australia. We would have encouraged him to be free rather than theoretical and conservative, and I guarantee his strike rate would have been 10 runs per 100 balls quicker than it was while he was playing for South Africa.

That win over South Africa set up our tournament, and had a sweet and memorable aftermath for me personally. At the presentation ceremony it was announced I'd become an honorary citizen of St Kitts and that I would be given, of all things, a greyhound – although I've never actually set eyes on it. The greyhound was mentioned as part of the gifts flowing my way, but I never heard any more about it. I just hope I wasn't expected to feed it! I liked St Kitts so much that I returned there with seven of the boys in a private plane during a break later in the tour, telling the locals how nice it would be to host them on 'my' island.

One of the many joys of that World Cup, apart from the cricket, was taking pleasure in the company of teammates like Brad Hodge. In my books, Hodgey is pure gold. He was always fun to be around and definitely my first invitee to any dinner table. To finish his Test career with 503 runs at 55.89 from six matches makes him the hard-luck story of the century, I reckon. Future generations will look back and be struck by the oddness of those numbers. Did he get injured? Did he do something bad? Did he get too old? The answer is none of the above. He was just plain unlucky.

In St Kitts, where we were looked after like royalty, Michael and Sally Marshall, a generous local couple, provided us with Moët & Chandon after every victory. I asked Michael if he could take us fishing, and off we went with plenty of Moët packed. We caught a little barracouta, and Hodgey gave him a sip of our precious bubbly, saying, 'Have a drink, fishy,' before letting him go to swim off happily.

In Grenada a group of us went out marlin fishing. I was conscious of not overheating because we had a game the next day, so I retreated below decks after a while to watch the cricket – South Africa was thrashing England – in the air-conditioning. I was just dozing off when I saw through the porthole every fisherman's fantasy – a huge blue marlin leaping skywards! I darted out immediately, yelling, 'Fish on!' The boys didn't realise what was happening because the ratchet on the rod only starts clicking when the fish heads away from the boat. In fact, it was swimming alongside us, so the rod was yet to feel the impact. Watto was closest, and I asked him if he was taking it, but he didn't sound keen so I grabbed my chance.

When you get in a fight with a marlin, you get your head punched in. Simple as that. They are extremely strong. Fortunately, we had a heavy line and I was able to reel this 136-kilogram beauty in without too much of a battle. Three years earlier in Perth, I'd gone out fishing off the coast the day before a one-dayer against India and had landed some massive Sampson fish, which pulled like freight trains. They pulled so hard they made capillaries in my arms burst and my forearms swelled up like Popeye's after a can of spinach. I even had to wear a compression garment into the match, not that it helped me. I could barely swing the bat, and got out for a fifth-ball duck. I certainly didn't want to go through that experience again!

When we finally landed that marlin, we felt as if we'd won the World Cup. They're incredible fish, and glow with all the colours of a Christmas tree when they're agitated. I wanted to release it but the skipper was adamant it was coming with us, and we soon learnt why: by the time we landed, he'd summoned television and newspaper crews from all over the island, and images flashed around the world. One Australian newspaper worked out our marlin was as big as three Kylie Minogues, or about the same size as Dreamworld's new Bengal tiger, Sita.

Seeing Shaun Tait's success was another highlight of the tournament. We called him 'Carib', after the local beer, and I still call him that when I send him emails. Shaun's career has been cruelly affected by injury. He loved that tour because it was the one time everything went right and he relished Ricky's 'Be free' philosophy. He was built for sheer pace, but it was still a surprise his cardiovascular fitness levels weren't higher. The big fellow would puff up a storm after three overs – but that was as long as his spells needed to be.

Some of Tait's work against the minnow nations was breathtaking. I wasn't old enough to witness Jeff Thomson terrifying teams like Sri Lanka in the 1975 World Cup, but I reckon Tait inspired similar fear at times, and his withering down-wind spell against Ireland was one of those occasions. The Irish boys had trained for Tait by getting their bowlers to bowl from about 16 metres in the nets. But not even that prepared them for his display that day. Perhaps it should have been 12 metres. He was all over them, and his occasional waywardness only enhanced his menace because no one – least of all Taity – was sure where the next ball was going. He bowled nine wides in six overs but took three wickets, and I can still see the agonised looks of the Irish boys on the players' balcony as he wreaked havoc.

I don't mind facing anyone in the middle – the greater the challenge, the more I can draw out of myself. But I simply refused to face Tait in the nets. In 2005, Shaun bowled himself into Test cricket after Trevor Hohns watched him rattle Justin Langer in the nets at Trent Bridge in a spell that included a full toss to the groin. Hats off to Alfie for his bravery – but he can have it. In my opinion, it was a waste of time facing Tait because he was so different to anyone else around. And, frankly, I just couldn't see him. (For the same reason, I was loath to face Brett Lee when he used to come in off 18 yards. Okay, I was scared. There, I've said it.)

The final of the World Cup was a memorable day for many reasons. Gilly stole the show with one of the greatest innings in one-day history – 149 off 104 balls – which left us perched on 4/281 after 38 overs in the rain-shortened match. From the opening ball, Gilly looked magnificent. We knew it. Sri Lanka knew it. I thought, *Don't worry about me today – I'm here to run, hopefully twos, so you can get back on strike.* I heard later that when Gilly pushed forward defensively to the first ball of the match and it raced to mid-off, the man who bowled it, Chaminda Vaas, apparently turned to Murali and said, 'We're stuffed.'

As Gilly's opening partner, my job was to encourage him to have total freedom of expression. Trying to rein him in would've been like telling Jimmy Barnes not to sing too loud. 'Mate, just smash it, smash it miles,' I'd say to him. He enjoyed that freedom. Batting with Gilly was much like partnering my old swashbuckling Bulls teammate, Trevor Barsby. My job with both was to encourage them to keep it simple. Just hit the ball and enjoy it. They had very similar batting personalities.

The only downer of our night of celebration was when we came together to sing our team song on the field and a power-drunk local policeman ordered us off. We couldn't believe it. By that stage we'd all had a few – as you do when you win a World Cup – and it was an understatement to say we were livid. We'd won a tournament which had generated millions of dollars for the local economy. We weren't trying to set the grandstand on fire. We only wanted to sing a song. But the policeman threatened to lock us up if we didn't move off the ground, which we finally did, but not without a hearty protest from Ricky.

When bad light during the match had started talk of continuing the game the next day I started panicking. Our third child was due the day after the final. I'd been there for the births of Grace and Josh, and Kell and I desperately wanted to complete the trifecta. I'd arranged to leave early via the quickest route possible – Miami, LA, Brisbane – as opposed to the team route via London. The morning after we won I left at 4 a.m., leaving the boys to continue celebrating that day, and later on James Packer's yacht. As it happened, our son Thomas was six days late, so I was well and truly home before we welcomed him into the world.

If the World Cup is played for another 100 years, I doubt there'll be a better team effort than Australia's in 2007. It was almost flawless. We had four of the top ten run-scorers and four of the top six wicket-takers. In 11 games, we never lost more than six wickets and our tail never had to bat. The man of the series, Glenn McGrath, could have played the entire tournament without any gear – he never once had to pad up. Extraordinary.

Pigeon was in a similar frame of mind to me at the time, I reckon. It was his last tournament as an Australian player, and just being there was a great achievement – he was going to enjoy himself. Behind the scenes, of course, he was dealing with a far greater challenge. Glenn never shared his feelings about Jane's illness with his teammates. 'Never better,' was his standard cheery reply when asked how he was faring.

But I gained the occasional insight through Kellie, who was very close to Jane. During the Boxing Day Test of the 2005–06 summer against South Africa, I came home from the MCG to be greeted by Kell in tears. Jane had had some sort of seizure while they were together and had been unable to see properly. We didn't know what the problem was, only that it was something serious. Jane was as strong a woman as you could meet, but even she was worried that day. Jane and Glenn's bravery throughout Jane's 11-year battle with cancer, which ultimately claimed her life, was an inspiration to us all.

37

Symo

In August 2008, the 'gone fishin' affair hit the media. Andrew Symonds had missed a team meeting in Darwin before the first one-dayer in a series against Bangladesh because he was fishing, and was sent home. The day after, my mobile beeped. It was a message and photo from Symo. Sporting the blissful smile of an angler who'd filled his creel, Symo proudly displayed a giant barramundi. The photo was accompanied by a message: *What's all the fuss about?* I had to smile. As Symo flew out of a media storm the size of Cyclone Tracy, he still had time to celebrate his catch.

I couldn't be too harsh on him because I strongly suspect that if I'd made the trip, I'd have been in the photo with him. The Northern Territory is adventure land for me. My most memorable catches in Darwin had scales and fins and were taken in estuaries, not at gully. The moment I stepped foot in Darwin I would be met by a mate of John Dunphy, boss of Shimano fishing gear. I'd find myself cheerfully whisked away to a barbecue where we'd eat mudcrabs and talk fishing. Pure bliss.

With this incident, Symo's cricket career had reached a major fork in the road. Soon after he returned, I invited him to my place for a chat. As we sat at my kitchen bench in Brisbane I laid out his options as simply as I could. 'Do you want to play for Australia?' I asked.

'Ummm, yeah,' he replied.

It wasn't exactly convincing. 'There's no half commitment,' I said. 'You either want to play for Australia or you don't. If you don't, put it there' – I offered him my hand – 'because you've made Test match hundreds, won World Cups, Sheffield Shields . . . You've done everything in the game. You've been amazing. You have set the standard for athletic ability. You will never look back. So if you walk away now, know that you'll have people like me saying congratulations.'

'No, I want to play for Australia,' Symo said, more insistently.

I felt it was important to emphasise the non-negotiables of his decision. He still had some goodwill behind him. But you couldn't ignore the potential consequences if things didn't change. 'Mate,' I said, 'the truth is – and you have to grapple with this – if you say, "Yes, I really do want to play for Australia," you won't hear me or anyone else saying you can cut corners, because the culture is bigger than you. You have to work out which path to choose and stick to it. But you can't keep on the same way. It's just not working. You have to build relationships with the media, Cricket Australia . . . everyone. You have to compromise and do things you don't want to do, things you did in the past that made Australia the best team in the world.'

It's also true to say that Symo felt let down by, and never quite got over, what became known as the 'Monkeygate' affair. It had a lasting effect on him. Symo was taunted by chants of

'Monkey' throughout the 2007 tour of India, and I was involved in another incident in Australia, when I overheard spinner Harbhajan Singh calling Symo 'Monkey' during the Second Test in Sydney later that summer. Harbhajan received a three-match ban for racial abuse, but the Board of Control for Cricket in India lodged an appeal against the decision. The appeal was heard in Adelaide by ICC Appeals' Commissioner John Hansen, with the result that the racism charge against Harbhajan Singh was not upheld and the three-Test ban was lifted. Harbhajan was instead fined 50 per cent of his match fee for using abusive language. Hansen later admitted that if he'd known about Harbhajan's other misdemeanours – including a suspended one-Test ban – he may have considered a more severe penalty. The verdict was a sobering jolt to us all.

India is the most important cricket market on the planet, and the truth of the situation was that both countries understood that anything that would adversely their relationship was unacceptable, from a business point of view. We learnt that from 'Monkeygate'. The whole affair was very regrettable and remains a weighty chapter in the development of both countries. I'm pleased to have moved on from it, and to now be playing a part in enhancing the relationship between our two great countries in the IPL.

Symo finally fell from grace during the World Twenty20 in 2009 for drinking outside the team hotel. The team leadership group decided he ought to be sent home and he never played for Australia again. It was a bit like a parent rousing on a child for an incident that wasn't as serious as one that had happened a few days before. After a period of sustained aggravation, the tipping point had been reached. I was never a fan of the idea of a leadership group. The group had been formed on the recommendation of leadership guru Ray McLean, who had set them up in AFL teams like the Sydney Swans, the Adelaide Crows and the Brisbane Lions. But the AFL players appointed their own leadership groups, while ours was appointed by Cricket Australia, and contained Punter, Michael Clarke, team manager Steve Bernard, and coach Tim Nielsen. I simply didn't agree with the concept of peers judging peers on major issues, and said so at the relevant team meeting. But still, I reckon the result was the right thing for Symo. He was out of love with the game and had no more answers. He is now completely comfortable with having ended his international career and I'm pleased that he has made his peace with it.

Symo and I gelled from the moment we first met because we loved to have a crack on the field and a laugh off it, and we both love the outdoor life. We've occasionally been in quite extreme conditions together, aside from sinking boats. I was with Symo on his first pig hunt in 1997. He'd been hunting before, but never pig hunting with knives and dogs, which is primitive and very dangerous. I have mates who've been ripped from knee to groin by pig's tusks, and for that reason I never went hunting like that again after my trip with Symo. But he and I had worked really hard together that year, trying to get his game in order, and I'd been wording him up all year about the thrills of the chase.

So we went away to North Queensland on a month's fishing expedition, and what a trip it was. My brother Gaz was up there, and we had a mate, Alan Parry, who lent us a vehicle. Off we went, occasionally stopping in at ports like Cooktown and Weipa, where we had friends and relatives, and other great little spots like a hippie community at Archer Point.

We'd fish all day – it was like fishing in an aquarium, with queenfish, red emperor and Spanish mackerel all on offer – make a fire and a meal, eat up, go to bed and do it all again the next day. I'd told Symo about the skills required for pig hunting. The dogs hold the pig, but because the pig is stronger than the dogs, it generally sends the dogs flying everywhere as it struggles. But the dogs never had an easier kill than the day they went hunting with Symo. He's incredibly strong, and got carried away and just barrelled the pig himself, then killed it with his knife after a mad flurry. We solemnly smeared his face with blood in the traditional way to mark his first kill.

Symo's also got a very gentle, quiet side. He takes time to look at the world around him, and as a result is extremely observant and thoughtful – the guy who will spot someone alone at a party and make sure they're comfortable. Kids gravitate towards that kind of person, and mine love him. He's always been very considerate of Kell, too – a genuine all-rounder. He's a very private person. I consider him one of my best mates, yet he doesn't give his inner thoughts away easily. And I respect that. After Symo and I had been fishing, Kell would ask, 'How's Symo?' When I'd tell her I wasn't really sure she'd say, 'But you've just spent ten hours with him! What did you talk about?' I'd say, 'Not much,' which must have sounded as if I was hiding something, but it was the truth . . . and a comment about the strength of our relationship.

Symo was missed by the Australian cricket team for reasons people probably would never appreciate. The dressing-room was the poorer for his absence. He was a 'roll up your sleeves, she'll be right, mate' sort of guy. Symo keeps life very simple and you can't bullshit someone who keeps it as simple as he does.

Towards the end of his career he was very good at breaking down barriers with the Gen Y boys, the only guy capable of doing it. He'd say to Michael Clarke, 'Mate, worry less about your hair and whingeing, and more about the team, and you'll be a better bloke for it.' Clarke would respond with, 'Turn it up, Drew,' they would have a laugh and it would be a good result for the team. Symo also had his say in Antigua during the 2007 World Cup when Shane Watson, obviously not impressed by the smell of the dressing-room, lit a scented candle. Symo turned to our manager, Steve Bernard, and quipped in that stonefaced way of his, 'Have a go at this . . . Do I really want to play for Australia any more?' Watto was devastated. I couldn't have too much of a go at him because I'd used candles early in my career to help my erratic sleeping patterns. Watto even had a stylist groom him for one Allan Border Medal, and when I learnt this, my mind drifted back to the 1993 Ashes tour and how life had changed since those simple old days with Boonie and AB at the bar.

The Gen Y culture covered a lot of different areas of our lives as blokes became – how can I say it? – less blokey. Spirit-based drinks replaced old-fashioned beers. Conversation topics would include shoes, hair and clothes. I sensed it wasn't quite my scene way back in London on the 2001 Ashes tour when a hairdresser convinced me to get streaks. He put these silver foils in my hair and even before they came out, I knew it wasn't me, and promised myself I would never get them again, which I haven't. As for clothes, Kell buys all mine, apart from some suits I purchased in India.

Symo never saw himself as bigger than the game, and he never let anyone else become bigger than the game. This might sound strange given the trouble he got into for disobeying team rules, but Symo sees being part of a team as almost a life of service. One of Symo's weaknesses is that he's extremely stubborn (much like myself). I used to tell Jimmy Maher that he was the most stubborn person I'd ever met, and Mahbo would prove the point by never conceding that he was. Symo is almost in the same league. If Symo thinks something isn't right, then his opinion will not waver a square centimetre, no matter how persuasive the counter-argument. I share his opinion that being open about your views contributes to team culture, whereas modern leadership and management is too often about toeing the party line and keeping quiet. I'm not defending his actions in missing meetings and disobeying team rules, but you can go too far the other way, and leave no place in the game for a valuable contributor like Symo.

My one regret for Symo is the way he handled the end. As he was flying home from the Twenty20 World Cup, I caught him by phone while he was in transit and encouraged him to tell the full story, to say something like, 'Sorry, but I just don't want to play any more. The game is moving in a different direction to the way I most enjoyed it, and I still want to have a beer with my mates. I don't want to have sheep stations riding on it. I'm in the process of dealing with my problem with alcohol and I've been diagnosed as a binge drinker. I firmly believe I am that and I am willing to tackle the difficult road ahead of me and see if I can come up with some answers.'

I walked him through the whole process, but his manager took him on a different route and set him up with a *60 Minutes* interview. Symo had to face some awkward questions and did his best to negotiate them as he admitted to being a binge drinker. But the interview never got the right message out – Symo's message.

One of my most treasured memories is batting with Symo against England in the 2007 Boxing Day Test at the MCG, and there's a magnificent photo of Symo jumping into my arms – actually it looks as if he's trying to jump over me – when he scored his century. He hit me with such force that he pushed my helmet rim into my forehead and cut it open, yet I still regard that moment as one of the highlights of my career. The sweetest part of the day came after stumps, when we were sitting together at the back of the dressing-room in the empty ground. He gave me a big hug and said, 'Do you know, I never thought this would happen?'

In some ways, I see Symo as a trailblazer for the international career players may have in the future – shorter than we're used to seeing, but very intense. He was the greatest fieldsman the game has seen, and one of its most entertaining players.

I'm proud to call him a friend.

Me

I've always tried to have a pretty relaxed attitu
Some players devoured everything that was written
press and reacted accordingly. I tried to keep things in
Greg Chappell always said, you knew when you were goin
didn't need to read about it to find out. I tried not to get swept
the good stuff written about me either. I wanted to keep a balanc
didn't want to have my head in the clouds one day then feel und
attack the next. I read my share of press, but I wasn't obsessed by it, and tended to skim articles rather than take out the fine-tooth comb.

There were some fascinating people in the international media whom I remember with fondness. The Indian journalist Lokendra Sahi, who worked for *The Telegraph* in Kolkata, would often give me a silk tie when he saw me at the start of a tour. Once, during the 2003 World Cup, he chased me all over South Africa for an interview. My time had been so restricted in Kolkata that we couldn't manage to do the interview while I was there. So after I left – and finally had some spare time – I offered to do the interview by phone. He said, 'No, no, I'll fly down and see you. To do it over the phone would spoil the romance of the interview.' The romance of the interview! I liked that.

Sahi loved his face-to-face interviews so much that once, when the Australian team had evacuated the Royal Garden Hotel at Kensington in London at 2 a.m. because of a bomb scare, he materialised looking as bright as a spotlight and approached our media man, Jonathan Rose. 'Would this be a good time for one-on-ones?' he asked. Jonathan cast a bleary eye over our dishevelled, half-asleep group before deciding

ıld be better times. At the end of my career, Sahi gave me a a touching article he had written about my retirement.

witnessed many changes in the media during the 16 years ayed international cricket. Clearly, the internet has had an rmous impact. There was a time when interviews given to small-wn papers were a bit like guest-speaking nights in the bush – what you said barely ever left the room. But there came a day in 1997 when I realised it had all changed.

I was playing county cricket in Hampshire at the time, and was interviewed by a journalist from the county's *Daily Echo* about some comments Ian Chappell had made suggesting I was 'suspect' against the game's best bowlers. I always loved a good scrap, and because I didn't think my remarks would go much beyond the county, I fired up and had a few strong things to say about Ian and his thoughts. In these politically correct days, my inflammatory response would definitely have sparked off a week of hostile headlines. It wasn't quite that bad in 1997, but my comments certainly spread around the cricket world more widely than I'd expected. The game's communications had gone global.

We often joked about ways of getting around this, and found the best way of disguising a pointy quote was to say it came from someone else. Dizzy Gillespie did it in India after the last Test of the 2004 series, which was played on a raging turner in Mumbai. He nonchalantly dropped into a media interview, 'A mate of mine rang from Adelaide last night and said, "Isn't the wicket an absolute disgrace?"' Cricket Australia officials pounced on Dizzy immediately, but the boys reckoned it was a nice try.

I played through three distinct eras of cricket – barely professional, semi-professional and professional – and saw significant changes in player–media relationships over that time. In the early years, you were

just as likely to have a beer with journalists as you were with Allan Border. Journalists stayed at team hotels, and you tended to run across each other in the hotel bar at the end of the day and find yourself sharing a quick ale before dinner. No one gave much thought to it, but it was actually a very powerful bonding agent, a natural way of getting to know and respect the media boys. I've always admired Mal Conn of *The Australian* for his strong, considered views, and I invited him to my retirement function in Brisbane just after I left the game. I was delighted he made it.

On my first tour to England in 1993, I'd often see Mal verbally slugging it out in the bar with Boonie, AB and especially our physio, Errol Alcott, who loved a good argument. But you could tell there was great mutual admiration. The players and journalists got to know each other well. Because of that, I knew I could occasionally approach Mal and tell him my concerns about something he might have written. It was a good working relationship. In my last season, Mal wrote a couple of articles in which he said he thought my time was just about up. I know at the time he agonised over it, telling a few people that they were among the most difficult stories he'd written in his 25 years of covering cricket. He shouldn't have fretted. He was only doing his job, and I respect him for that.

In 1993, our Ashes tour was four and a half months long and the tour's many pit stops were great for player–press relations. The three-day county games we played were invariably more relaxed than the Tests. You might be walking down the main street of Canterbury, run into a pressman and spend 20 minutes chatting.

These dynamics changed as cricket became more professional. Tours were shorter and more intense. The sport had become more of a business. In the mid-1990s, Cricket Australia appointed a 'media liaison officer'. This was only a reflection of how the rest of the world was moving, and was a necessary appointment given the ever expanding nature of the media landscape, but as soon as you bring a third party into a relationship, it changes the connection.

In the current era, players sit on one side of a table at press conferences, journalists sit on the other, and they don't really get to know each other. I'm glad to say these changes didn't affect my relationships with people from the media, which I maintained to the end of my career. The demands of a 24-hour news cycle with the internet have made journalists busier than ever. Teams don't drink at hotel bars during Tests any more, and journos don't seem to as much either.

The coverage of our sport has also changed. At the start of my career, cricket reports were moment-by-moment, day-by-day stuff. Now, coverage has become far more sensational and personal. Michael Clarke was snapped by photographers simply sweeping his balcony. Relationships are big news, where once they were private business. It sometimes seems the cricket is the last rather than the first thing that matters.

Cost-cutting measures by media organisations are also affecting cricket coverage. Media companies in Australia that once considered it essential to have representatives at every national tour often don't bother sending their own people to one-day tournaments abroad now. If the tour goes to England, it's often the English tabloid news that gets fed down the line to Australian audiences.

The media demands on the high-profile players are heavy, and I've always felt the workload should be spread more evenly. I remember watching English captain Andrew Strauss doing four interviews after the toss at Headingley in the 2009 tour, when television and radio networks were broadcasting the series. When he came out to face the first ball a few minutes later, there was no way he could have had a clear head, and he scratched around for a while before getting out for 3.

It has been interesting to experience life recently on the other side of the fence – as a commentator. And if I'd thought all my Ashes clashes were over once I stopped playing, I was wrong. During the 2009 Ashes tour, I was contracted by the BBC to join Geoff Boycott, the famously outspoken Yorkshireman, as a guest radio commentator. Boycs gave a five-minute spiel to start, which included his opinion that players like me and Shane Warne would have struggled to perform on the uncovered wickets of a few generations ago.

I couldn't offer much defence on my own behalf – I probably *would* have struggled. But Warnie would've been turning those big leggies from one side of the wicket to the other on those damp decks, I reckon. I doubt whether any other bowler in history has proved more adaptable than Warnie – he was a chameleon of the crease – and one more challenge would not have bothered him. And I said so. Talk about stopping the show – Boycs threw down his headphones and stormed out. I heard him fuming, 'I am wasting my time!' The studio went quiet and everyone seemed terrified.

When he came back in, I think he tried to just blow it all off, pretend it hadn't happened. But I'm not that sort of person. I invited him outside to talk it through. He argued that I was being disrespectful to him, so I offered to come back inside and get the transcripts of the interview to prove otherwise. We had what you might call a spirited debate, each of us standing our ground. I finally suggested we either go back in and listen to the transcripts, or shake hands and agree to respect each other for the remainder of the series. I told him I had no intention of being his lap dog and would've been just as happy to go and sit on a beach somewhere. Fortunately we shook hands, and I must say he was brilliant for the rest of the series.

The big guessing game now is where media coverage will go in the future, and I'm not sure anyone has the complete answer. I've noticed that the new generation of players – the Gen Y boys – don't get much of their information from newspapers any more; they rely more on their iPhones and on TV. And I must admit that I read newspapers less than I ever did. The challenge for traditional media is to respond to the speed with which today's generation is embracing new and constantly changing technology. Cricket coverage must embrace new ways of communication to remain relevant, topical and fresh.

38

Goodbye, Green and Gold

During my last summer of international cricket a random thought kept drifting through my head. I remembered Craig McDermott saying many years before that no matter how you structured your career, you only had a certain amount of runs or wickets in the tank; once you'd reached them, your number was up. You might try to fight it, you might stretch things out for a while, but the end was the end.

Was my number up? The force wasn't with me from the start of an Indian tour before my last season, when I got several poor decisions, including my first of the series – I was incorrectly given out caught behind off Zaheer Khan. Momentum is a strange thing. When you have it, you feel like you're never going to lose it. When you haven't got it, you feel you're never going to get it. Australia had to fight hard for its success after the retirements of Warne, McGrath, Langer, Gilchrist, Gillespie and Martyn. There was never any sense that the side would tumble into a deep, dark abyss, as it had when Lillee, Marsh and Chappell left in the mid-1980s, but life was certainly tougher. My 2007 World Cup form had flowed into the next home summer, when I scored three centuries in four Tests against India, but we only just crept home 2–1 in a spicy series made unforgettable by the infamous Monkeygate exchange in Sydney.

Then in 2008–09 we went to India, where we were beaten 2–0. We came home to Australia and lost a Test series on home soil for the first time in 16 years, a 2–1 defeat by a South Africa who had fast bowler Dale Steyn in wonderful form and a new batting discovery, J.P. Duminy, who'd only played because Ashwell Prince was a late withdrawal through injury. Duminy quickly became a revelation.

There were no excuses for our series loss. In the first Test in Perth we had a 94-run first-innings lead yet they powered to an exceptional victory total of 4/414 after A.B. de Villiers and Graeme Smith made centuries. The agony continued in the second Test in Melbourne where we had them 8/251 chasing our first innings of 394 and they kicked the jail door open again with wonderful lower-order partnership between Duminy (166) and Dale Steyn (76) that saw them seize control of the Test and clinch a deserved series victory. Our pace attack struggled to finish them off and we lacked a frontline spinner. I remember thinking we seemed half the side we once were.

I had no fear of retirement, because I'd been in and out of the Test and one-day teams so often I knew what it was like to not be playing. It wasn't if I was ever going to think, *Wow, so this is life on the outside*. I'd been there and done that, and was very comfortable with my life. I had some great mentors throughout my career and developed some fascinating friendships with people whose paths somehow crossed mine. There was much to look forward to in life after cricket.

As difficult as my last season was, my respect for my old touring mate and one-time wrestling opponent, David Boon, a national selector, increased throughout it. He was different to the other selectors because he'd been a mentor and role model when I first came in to the national side 16 years earlier. As a selector, Boonie was very good at making you feel you were in a partnership with him and the panel. His message was, 'How do we help you help us?' I appreciated that thinking.

After what turned out to be my final Test against South Africa in Sydney on 3 January 2009, Boonie came in the rooms and I thought I saw a tear in his eye. He said to me, 'Mate, you've earnt the right, and I have earnt the right to tell you to do whatever is in your heart. I'll support you because I feel you can still play. I know how important you have been to the baggy green culture. Because you love it so much, like I did, whatever decision you make will be perfect.'

Boonie could have hidden behind the selectors' privilege of saying nothing, but he didn't, and I'll always appreciate his courageous stance. The selectors didn't push me into retirement. Chairman Andrew Hilditch did tell me late in the summer there were 'no guarantees' about my future – but when were there ever any guarantees? I left Sydney genuinely unsure about whether I was going to retire or make myself available for the tour of South Africa in February.

I remember looking around the dressing-room and wondering whether my drive as a player was finished. I had tried to re-energise by throwing myself behind Ricky in a difficult season. But in my most private thoughts, there was a challenging truth I couldn't escape: I'd lost the desire. And desire had been the byword of my cricket career.

There was no single watershed moment when the bell rang, the lightning bolt struck or the neon sign appeared from nowhere flashing the words *It's over*. It was a subtle process. It takes place in your eyes, in your motivation, in your talks with other players. What's meaningful suddenly becomes less meaningful, and once you lose that edge, mediocrity beckons. I've seen it affect others, even the greats. When Ricky Ponting is switched on he can bat as well as anyone who's ever played the game. When he's not switched on, he can be average and vulnerable. I was the same. In Steve Waugh's final Test, against India, he batted brilliantly and we urged him to keep going. But when I looked at him closely, I noticed a certain dullness in his eyes. The gunslinger's glint had gone.

My thought processes were muddled that season, because I started thinking seriously about retirement. Everyone was talking about it and it became a distraction. None of the speculation matters until you start thinking about it yourself. The only time in the series against South Africa when I felt totally switched on and in full gladiator mode was in the second innings of the last Test of my career in Sydney, when I came out to bat with six overs remaining for the day. Alfie used to hate those situations, but I loved them – there was a defined period of intensity, and it really helped me focus. I was supremely pumped up for the occasion and powered to 18 not out at stumps. I rarely got out in that type of situation and was proud that I didn't that time either.

After making 12, 4, 8 and 23 in the first two Tests, I made 31 and 39 in my last Test, which we won in dramatic circumstances when Graeme Smith was bowled by Mitchell Johnson after coming in at number 11 with a broken hand. In the rooms after the match I remember saying to Peter Siddle that this might be the last time I sang the team song as a team member. And it was. It was a long time coming after Michael Clarke and Simon Katich had a fight over when the song should be sung. Everyone knew the next time Australia had a Test victory it would be a time for restoring tradition and there could be no such tension. The team song needed to be put back on its pedestal.

The moment came at Headingley a few months later, after I'd retired. Australia won its sole Test of the Ashes series and I headed to the rooms after finishing BBC commentary duties. I tried to leave as Australia prepared for its victory song, but manager Steve Bernard was having none of it. 'You're not going anywhere,' Brute said, blocking my path to the door. For years I'd been the one doing the urging when the likes of David Boon, Allan Border, Steve Waugh or even Alfie Langer had been in the rooms, and I'd seen the slightly awkward looks on their faces when the invitation came to sing. It seemed the most natural thing in the world to invite any former great in sight to sing the song, yet none of them felt comfortable doing it because they hadn't earnt it on the day. That's exactly how I felt. I sang the song – and it felt great – and I almost felt good about spending 30 minutes in a cab in a beer-soaked suit heading back to the hotel. But drinking the victory toast means so much more if you have actually fought the war.

I came home from the Sydney Test on 8 January 2009, and five days later made the decision to retire. I was picking cherry tomatoes with Grace and we were talking about Santa Claus. I asked her how she'd feel if I retired, and she said that'd be okay so long as Santa could still find us at our home in Brisbane (we'd been in Melbourne for every Christmas of her young life). So that was that. I felt more relaxed than I had for ages and the switch finally flicked. It was stumps.

I walked into the house and said to Kell, 'I'm done.' She said, 'Are you sure?' and I said, 'What do you reckon?' Kell knew me well enough to know that once my mind was made up, it was made up. I then had a great conversation with a close friend, Neil Honan, who gave me the good advice to act quickly. I told my manager, Chris White, and we decided to wait until the day of the Twenty20 match between Australia and South Africa at the Gabba to make the announcement in front of my home crowd.

The next few days were madness. I'd placed the four and a half kilos of cherry tomatoes I'd picked with Grace in a large pot on the stove with the intention of making them into tomato sauce and relish. We were so frantic they stayed on the stove for days and eventually we had to throw them out.

When I told Ricky of my decision he said, 'I don't suppose there's any chance of me changing your mind?' My response echoed my remark to Kell. 'We've played together a long time – what do you reckon?' Later that day he rang back with a very generous idea. He'd step down as Twenty20 captain and let me lead the Australian team that night before my home crowd, in a grand farewell. I turned him down. It just wasn't me. Ricky's a cricket tragic who'll play the game until his last breath. He'd relish a big playing farewell, but my ideal way of retiring was to do exactly what I did – share a few jokes with the boys, have a few beers and enjoy the day. I did a memorable lap of the ground and am forever grateful that much of my last day was caught on film, because I realise now your retirement day's a bit like your wedding day – there's so much emotion in the air it just flashes past you.

I felt quite overwhelmed the whole day of my retirement. Kell had arranged for Gaz to come down from North Queensland and he provided soothing company on a memorably madhouse day. The phone rang off the hook with the likes of McGrath, Gillespie and Gilchrist on the line. Then prime minister Kevin Rudd even called and we had a quick chat about our collective desire to improve the lot of indigenous cricketers.

It was suggested to me the best way of handling my press confererence was to just let it happen naturally, but I knew I had to write down what I wanted to say because I was certain to become highly emotional and could hopefully centre myself by referring back to the notes. So it proved. A couple of times I got misty-eyed and felt an elephant-sized lump in my throat but I got by. There was one point when I was just about to lose it when, from the back of the room, my young son Thomas nonchalantly came up and joined me. We all had a good chuckle and it broke the tension.

I was also rapt having my old mate Punter sitting beside me on stage, and when I entered the room I had no idea the entire Australian Twenty20 side would be standing up the back.

The lap of the ground was a wonderful experience and I saw many faces from my life in cricket . . . old mates, former teammates and fans. The next morning Brisbane's *Courier-Mail* reprinted the first-ever mention of me in the paper – when I made 187 in a grade game for Valleys in 1990 – and said there had been 6000 mentions of my name in the *Courier-Mail* over the following 18 years.

I am relishing my retirement and have found myself very

busy. I've set up The Hayden Way. The company promotes a lifestyle centred on family and community, sustainability and social responsibility through the celebration of sport and leisure pursuits. In short, I subscribe to the theory of 'make your vocation your vacation' and my company endeavours to bring together all my passions in life: family, food, travel, fishing, cricket and surfing. We encourage people to get outdoors and lead an active life.

I've also very much enjoyed making a documentary series, *Matthew Hayden's Home Ground,* for the Lifestyle Channel on Fox, featuring interesting people who do great things. We visited a lot of country folk for the series, including two ex-naval officers who have a fully sustainable farm outside Coolum on Queensland's Sunshine Coast. They have a deep connection to their land and don't need to do anything else to survive and be happy. The more time I spent with people like that, the more I could relate to their priorities in life.

A really special moment for me was when Dad and I did a walk-through on the family farm. It was probably something I should have done 15 years beforehand but I had been boomeranging around the world and time had flown. It was a beautiful reconnection and I am sure it is one piece of footage I will always look back on and feel nothing else we did topped it.

A year after I retired from international cricket, I was appointed a Member of the Order of Australia. To receive an honour that comes from doing something you truly love is both wonderful and humbling, and has provided me with even more incentive to give something back to the game that has given me so much.

39

Imparja

I love cricket, but I'm not sure I love it as much as Maurice Nona.

In January 2009, just after my retirement from Test cricket, I attended the Imparja Cup, an annual tournament for Australia's Indigenous cricket sides. The Community Shield – also for young Indigenous cricketers – is run in conjunction with the cup. Like me, Maurice Nona flew to Alice Springs for the tournament, but his journey was a little more eventful. He was so keen to play that he piloted a small tinnie for 42 kilometres from Badu Island to Thursday Island for the first leg of his journey. Wind and choppy seas threatened to sink the boat until he speared a dugong and put it in the front of the tinnie to add ballast, enabling him to plough a steady course. When Maurice told me his story, I was in awe of his commitment.

I was also taken by the story of Queensland batsman Trent Clemments, from flood-stricken Ingham, who dragged his cricket gear two and a half kilometres along a rail line in bare feet to catch a two-seater plane to Townsville. There's a widespread assumption that Indigenous cricketers don't have the same passion for the game as non-Indigenous folk. I wouldn't be telling that to Maurice Nona or Trent Clemments.

Indigenous culture has always fascinated me and, long before I arrived on the scene, it similarly fascinated my parents. Mum was one of nine children and was only four when her mother died. Her father hired an Aboriginal woman called Laura to help with the housework. My grandfather made it clear that Laura was to be treated with the utmost respect, which she was. Even now, Mum and Dad have some Aboriginal sculptures on their mantelpiece – they are a constant reminder of a national heritage which has at its core a deep reverence for the land. Our family can relate to that. To live off the land, whether it be coastal or bush, takes an enormous amount of skill and knowledge, which is passed down from one generation to the next.

Some of the children I have met in remote communities are the most beautiful people I have ever encountered, and such natural storytellers. Since retiring, I've become involved in work that aims to help Indigenous players enter Australia's mainstream cricket programs. I initially committed myself for three years but would consider myself a huge failure if that commitment waned over the next 30. At Cricket Australia I share the portfolio for Indigenous cricket with John Bannon, and am very much enjoying it.

Australian Rules football has done much to encourage Indigenous players. About one in 10 AFL footballers are of Indigenous origin, including some of the most brilliant and exciting players the game has seen. Think of Gavin Wanganeen, Michael Long, Adam Goodes, Maurice and Cyril Rioli – the list goes on. The contribution Indigenous players have made to the game is duly recognised by the annual AFL Dreamtime at the 'G match at the MCG between the Essendon and Richmond football clubs (the colours of these two clubs combine to form those of the Aboriginal flag).

Some very impressive people have also helped the cause of Indigenous cricketers along the way, but have received precious little recognition. One of them, Faith Thomas, was not only the first Aboriginal woman to play cricket for Australia, she was the first Aboriginal woman to represent Australia in *any* sport. Thomas played cricket, hockey and squash while training to be a nurse. She was one of the first Aboriginal nurses to graduate from the Royal Adelaide Hospital and went on to be the first to run a hospital. She was selected to play cricket for Australia in 1958 and, in her words, was seen as 'a curiosity'. In an interview in 2004, she said, 'I wasn't a cricketer, I was a native-nurse cricketer, you know?' It's my firm hope that we have moved on since then, and that budding Indigenous cricketers such as Maurice Nona and Trent Clemments will be appreciated not as a 'curiosities', but simply as talented cricketers whose passion is second to none.

As is becoming more widely known, the first organised group of Australian cricketers to travel overseas was the Australian Aboriginal cricket team, which toured England in 1868. It seems incongruous that, over 140 years later, Jason Gillespie is believed to be the only male with any Aboriginal ancestry to have represented Australia in cricket. It must change. It will change. And I can't wait to see it happen.

40

The Board Walk – ACA to CA

People sometimes think players' unions are all about getting more money. But money, while a prime concern, is only part of the story.

The night before a one-day game against Sri Lanka in Colombo, 2004, I found a local doctor playing darts at our team hotel – with my backside! I'd been struck down with food poisoning and felt desperately ill. A doctor I'd never seen before (or since) was called to my room, and he gave me several injections. I was worried. For a start, it didn't fix the problem. I wobbled out to the crease the next day, stopping to double over on the boundary fence, and somehow made 15 off 20 balls. But my main concern was how vulnerable I felt getting treatment from someone I didn't know. We all remember the New Zealand rugby team allegedly having their meals poisoned the night before the 1995 World Cup final against South Africa. How could I know the man I saw was in fact a doctor? Or aware which drugs were on the banned substances list? Or even aware that such a list existed?

This incident fortified my resolve to be part of the Australian Cricketers' Association executive and make a difference to player welfare. The ACA were chasing a long list of benefits enjoyed by workers in most other industries. Money was a key part of the negotiations, but I was interested in getting the structures and support systems right also.

Towards the end of my career I ran into the Brisbane Lions' coach, Michael Voss, several times during training at the Gabba, and I was in awe of the Lions' set-up there. It was much more sophisticated than that provided to the Australian cricket team. When I told Vossy about the Sri Lankan episode his jaw hit the ground – he couldn't believe we didn't have a doctor on tour with us. I always believed the Australian cricket team was under-resourced and still do.

The ACA was only formed in 1997, and that in itself was a great achievement. Over the years generations of players had wanted to form a players' association but didn't have the collective drive to pull it off. Ours did, and I'm proud of that. It enabled us to negotiate properly with a structure that was becoming more professional and more and more lucrative. My first contract with Cricket Australia was for $11 000. My last was over $600 000. Allan Border's last contract with Australia in 1994 was for $90 000. Compare that to the base fee of more than $1 million paid to Ricky Ponting in 2009–10.

Inaugural ACA chief executive Tim May did a great job riding bareback on an organisation that was just skin and bones. The bones were strong, from the seniors right down to players who'd just risen from grade cricket, but they were bones nonetheless. Grade cricketers were basically asked to support superstars like Glenn McGrath and Shane Warne, who were on seven-figure sums annually, when boys at the bottom of the chain were earning next to nothing. And they did so because they recognised it was fair in a game making much more money, and to stick by their mates. It was pretty inspiring.

I wasn't playing for Australia in late 1997, when cricketers around the country were ready to walk out. They weren't happy about the prospect of striking, because once you strike, you lose the support of the press, the public and sponsors, but nonetheless, strike action was so close that the national team even voted on it in a hotel room, with Greg Blewett pulling the votes out of a baggy green cap. It was 11 to one in favour of a strike. Just as the team was about to pass the point of no return, Maysie rang with the news that momentum had swung their way and to hold their horses.

A strike was averted at the 11th hour and the two warring parties found their way to the negotiating table where they nutted out a ground-breaking Memorandum of Understanding, which resulted in pay rises for first-class cricketers and improved conditions not only for the current generation but also for those who followed.

Maysie wasn't an ivory-tower sort of official. Because the ACA was so short-staffed, he was effectively our Minister for Everything. People criticised the ACA for bringing in heavy-duty negotiator James Erskine to negotiate our memorandum of understanding with Cricket Australia, but something had to be done. We needed high-level professional guidance and we didn't have the funds to fight a decent battle – the ACA was only receiving $6000 per year in fees, plus about $90 000 in memorabilia fees. Erskine promised to bankroll the ACA for five years and that secured our future. In many ways it was perfect timing, because Australia had become the number-one side in the world after the West Indies tour in 1995. You can't argue from a position of weakness. If we'd been plodding mid-table on the rankings, or lost the Ashes in the late 1990s, we could never have achieved what we did. We were lucky to have not only a strong, stable group of senior players like Shane Warne, Steve and Mark Waugh and Ian Healy, but also another group in Gilly, Justin, Punter and myself, who continued to support the cause strongly as time moved on.

There was no doubt that the voices agitating most loudly for players' rights paid a price for their involvement. I know there were reservations among some ACB members in supporting Stephen Waugh for the Australian captaincy in 1999, because of the perception that he was a strong union man. I felt the heat of my ACA role at every contract meeting I attended, but I never felt intimidated by my employer. I just promised myself I'd become so good it wouldn't matter.

The ACA made a provocative but shrewd move in hiring sacked ACB chief Graham Halbish as a key advisor. Who better to advise you than the man who used to manage the board's bank accounts and plot its key strategies? Graham certainly raised Stephen Waugh's eyebrows when he told him, 'They'll tell you they need money for a rainy day, but there is no rainy day.' Graham had used those precise words in contract talks with Stephen.

I came to serve on the ACA board, and after I left, chief executive Paul Marsh was generous enough to thank me publicly for my contribution. He said, 'Matthew was a driving force and was never afraid to voice his opinions, even if his views were different to the rest of the executive. Not long after the English

Cricket Board launched its Twenty20 competition we had an executive meeting in Melbourne and there were very mixed views about the future of Twenty20. Matthew was adamant it was going to be enormous and that we needed to be involved in its development. I'm not sure he convinced everyone, but how right he turned out to be. He never backed down on an issue he believed in and it didn't matter who was on the other side of the discussion. I would have loved to have been a fly on the wall during some of his contract meetings with Cricket Australia!'

So when I retired, I sensed some doors might open to me – but I never thought one of them would lead to the boardroom of Cricket Australia. In August 2009, I received a call from Queensland Cricket chief executive Graham Dixon asking whether I'd like to serve as a Queensland delegate on the Cricket Australia board. Queensland has two positions on the 14-member board, which includes former West Australian Test batsman Wally Edwards, former South Australian premier John Bannon, and former Test cricketer and Australian captain Mark Taylor.

The invitation certainly took me aback. I've always been a 'players' man' and proud of it. I'd been honoured to serve on the ACA executive and happy to be the man who said things that needed to be said, even if that tested my own personal position and relationships at times. It's been said that I was viewed as the shop steward of the Australian team, and that description is probably fair. So when this new invitation came, I felt interested, challenged and cautious all at once. Did I have the passion for it? Did I have the time for it? Kell had already been through 15 years of my commitment to the game. I took the call as I was returning from the Gold Coast, where I'd filmed a two-day shoot for the theme parks. It was my first winter as a retired Australian player and I'd never been busier, so I hesitated over making a decision. On the way to England to commentate on the 2009 Ashes series, I talked it over with Geoffrey Schuhkraft, executive director of my company The Hayden Way. I realised that I wanted to make a major contribution to the game of cricket at a very sensitive time in its development – and that this was a perfect way of doing it.

When I joined the board, I know many people were surprised. I can't blame them. I became cricket's version of Peter Garrett, campaigning for the Greens one week then joining the Labor Party the next. Nonetheless, I've enjoyed the challenge of Cricket Australia so far. It's like attending a university lecture every day, and I am now a very willing student. Importantly, I know that I can also bring the players' perspective to the board.

41

A Changing Game

During the 2009 Ashes series when I was touring England as a BBC guest commentator, I had an on-air chat with journalist Christopher Martin-Jenkins in which I highlighted areas of the game I was particularly concerned about. He immediately challenged me to offer some solutions, and fair enough, too. It's one thing to question the schedules, mismatches and meaningless series, but quite another to find answers.

Over the next few weeks I talked to lots of people, from some of the game's key figures to men and women on the street. Several times I found my views being shaped not so much by the game's movers and shakers but by the fans. And so, after listening to many cricket voices, great and small, I formed the Hayden blueprint for the future of cricket. Here it is.

Problem 1: Tests deserve a bigger audience

My solution: create a Test cricket world championship. If Test cricket is to be the number-one form of the game, the public, players and financial backers around the world must be engaged. Grounds are regularly almost empty, and not just for lesser internationals – when the two top teams in world cricket played each other, in Australia's tour of South Africa in 2009, the spectator figures were really poor.

The ICC's Future Tours Program just doesn't work. It creates too many meaningless matches, like England playing the West Indies at home when they've just toured the Caribbean. I propose the establishment of a World Series – a 'Test World Championship', if you like – which would be on a rolling calendar with finals every two years. And there'd be the iconic series that already exist – the Ashes, and India vs. Pakistan – that should remain as five-match series.

Aside from those iconic series, teams should be pooled in two groups, with everyone playing each other and scoring points for wins, draws and series wins, and picking up bonus points for stand-out batting and bowling performances. The leading two teams in each group would progress to semi-finals and a final; the others would enter a rankings play-off system.

This way, every game means something – even the dead rubber at the end of a series between two lesser sides. Every Test fits into a bigger picture that adds up to a championship. It gives players something to aim for, fans a format they can follow, and commercial stakeholders something that's compact and exciting and therefore more marketable, generating additional revenue. More revenue in the sport is good for everyone, including players, and for the development of the game.

Problem 2: Some Tests are just mismatches

My solution: Zimbabwe and Bangladesh have to drop out of

the top level. When a team like Australia plays a team like Bangladesh in a Test series, you've got problems. It can't be fun for the underdogs and it's no challenge for the favourites. Just as importantly, it's not a good spectacle. Discounting matches between Zimbabwe and Bangladesh, the former have won just four of 75 Tests, the last in 2001. The latter have won two from a total of 55 played – and both of them were against a West Indies team severely weakened by a players' strike. So in my Test World Championship, I've left them out. It won't be popular, but I believe it's necessary.

Problem 3: The conflicts between traditional cricket and expanded Twenty20 competitions can't go on

My solution: embrace the new wave. Franchise cricket, as played in the IPL, has revolutionised the game. Speaking as a player, there is nothing more exciting and challenging than the opportunity to play amongst the best players in the world. The Twenty20 format is high-impact, colourful and attractive. I truly believe the formula works and that the IPL, the world's premier franchise competition, is here to stay.

So how would the rest of the cricket world work within the competition to everyone's benefit? Scheduling is the main point of conflict between the IPL and the established game, particularly the clash of players' contracts. This could be avoided in the future by creating a two-month window each year – I'd make it March and April – when other forms of the game take a back seat. That is, no Tests, no World Cup cricket and so on. The IPL has the ability to generate international fan bases in the same way as English football's Premier League.

I believe some IPL matches should go on the road each year

and be played in other countries, to make it a global competition. The sooner the world of cricket embraces the IPL, the sooner everyone can find ways to benefit from its massive potential. I know there is no easy solution to this scheduling issue because I love the way the KFC Big Bash has taken off in Australia and would like to see a window for Australian players to play in it as well.

Problem 4: Where will all the crowds watch the games?
My solution: we need to rethink where we play the top matches. The issue's already in motion. Just look at the 2009 Ashes, starting in Cardiff – you don't always have to play games in the accepted, traditional grounds. Historical precedents, such as the MCG always staging the Boxing Day Test, should be just one factor among others such as crowd capacity, the quality of the playing area and pitch facilities. Why not stage cricket indoors, if the arena is big enough? There's no reason we couldn't play an indoor IPL game in the Millennium Dome, now known as the O2, or elsewhere, including the United States.

Problem 5: There are too many confusing one-day competitions
My solution: scrap the Champions Trophy, for starters. After the battle for the 2009 Ashes was settled, the Australian team played seven one-day games in a row against England – that's right, seven. Were fans glued to each and every one of those? Surely five is enough in any series.

Equally, there are too many confusing one-day trophies. World Cups are the key shop windows for international one-day cricket. They provide dramatic entertainment within a global 'event' inclusive of smaller nations, all factors which help promote cricket to new markets. They are also significant revenue-generators. Playing the World Twenty20 every other year is too much. And why have the Champions Trophy (a 50-over tournament) when you've already got a 50-over World Cup?

There are strong lessons to be learnt from the success achieved in other sports, such as the quadrennial cycle of football's World Cup and UEFA European Championships. Cricket should follow this with a similar cycle of the Twenty20 World Cup and the ODI World Cup. To maximise coverage, these should be played in odd-numbered years – since football's major competitions, and the Olympics, are in even-numbered years. In the alternate years we can stage qualifying competitions. This meets the challenge for our sport to create meaningful competition for developing nations in regional pools.

Problem 6: How do we keep track of it all?

The solution: let's all agree on a global calendar. Football fans know if they're in a World Cup year or Euro Champs year. They know when seasons start and when trophies are decided, give or take a few weeks. Not so in cricket. A universal calendar is fundamental to all the above solutions. Once this is in place, competitions for each of the different formats of the game can be settled on, and everyone – fans, broadcasters, sponsors and players – will know where they stand.

42

World XI – Champions of the Game

In 2005, Australia took on a World XI and beat them convincingly, but I'll give you a side that would have been a greater threat – the Hayden All-Stars. Part of the joy of playing international cricket is watching and appreciating the talents of players from other nations, and there were many to savour in my era. From the loose-wristed artistry of Brian Lara and the quirky genius of Muralitharan to the bottomless stamina of Courtney Walsh, I saw many legends from close range. I decided to put them together in my All-Star XI – the best players I confronted throughout my international career.

VIRENDER SEHWAG (India)

I'm not sure what Sehwag was expecting me to say to him the day I made a point of crossing his path in a drinks break during our 2004 tour of India. A sledge maybe? In fact, it was the opposite. 'Mate, I just want to tell you I love the way you play,' I said to him, and walked off as he looked at me quizzically, perhaps waiting for a harder-edged punchline (which never came). I meant it too. There's something magnetic about Sehwag. The core of his appeal to me is his natural aggression and his cool demeanour: he'll smoke one through the covers with imperious timing, then look up with total nonchalance as if to say, 'What was the big deal about that? I do it for a living, you know.' The crowd will be going crazy, yet he shows about as much emotion as a man who's just licked a stamp and put it on a letter.

A great player can suck you into bowling where they want you to, and Sehwag was always a very difficult man to plan for. On our 2004 tour of India we spent more time talking about him than any other player – Tendulkar included. We knew he could slaughter us outside off stump if his radar was working. We also knew it was where we were likeliest to get him out. Back and forth we'd go at team meetings without ever feeling comfortable with our plan . . . but the honours finished slightly our way with his relatively modest returns of 299 runs at 42 in the Test series.

Sehwag's weakness was that he could be a nervous starter and a feeler for the ball. In that, he differed from another Indian champion, Rahul Dravid. Dravid was a beautifully organised batsman with magnificent discretion. He'd drive you for four one ball, but not even think about offering a stroke to the next delivery if it was pitched three centimetres wider, and thus just outside his driving zone. But Sehwag's thinking was never quite as clear. Sehwag was also a better cutter than he was a puller, but you had to be careful because you could really get hurt if you got it wrong.

The Australian team spent a lot of time with our hands on our hips when he was batting. At times we paid the penalty for locking in to one strategy against him, which was banging it in around his head. It took an enormous amount of effort, was difficult to do precisely and was also a tactic he could prepare for. Alfie Langer always said, 'No batsman enjoys a good old-fashioned bouncer fest', but the strategy comes at a cost because nothing drains an attack like delivering wave after wave of bouncers. We'd also try to get Sehwag fishing outside off stump, always living with the fear that once he was away he could hurt us quickly and badly. In Melbourne in 2003 he scored 195 in less than a day, shredding an attack that was missing Brett Lee and Shane Warne.

GRAEME SMITH (South Africa)

The South African captain is a worthy choice at the top of the order. His mental toughness was admirable, and becoming captain of a young side at just 22 hardened him into an excellent leader. He grew as a man and as a batsman. It's an impressive package.

Initially, Smith's game was rigidly structured, but he has learnt to improvise and added some subtle touches. Deft deflections to third man are one such improvement. It was our strategy to go hard at him verbally because he was a new young captain, and he was seen as the man who unmasked Australia's sledging tactics, when we allegedly handed out a truckload of abuse in 2002 during his Test debut against Australia. In a magazine article published months after the tour, he detailed the list of sledges against him. But it wasn't a protest or a complaint, more a way of him saying, 'It was on for young and old that afternoon.' He seemed absorbed rather than offended by it.

I remember having a massive crack at his giant pads when he walked out for his Test debut. At least, I think they were pads. They'd have made great mattresses for the kids, they were so big. Seeing them for the first time, I remember saying, 'Mate, we're trying to get you lbw and you come out in those? Any chance you could give us a bigger target?' Warnie was in his element with that sort of stuff. When sledging a young Smith he was like a cat with a piece of string. We later saw what Smith had said about us in the press, but no one took offence. I certainly didn't. Occasionally I'd use that sort of stuff to sharpen my motivation, but what happened on the field generally stayed there.

Smith grew into leadership after having it thrust upon him, getting over an early habit of baiting opponents and deciding to beat them instead. He was a very good on-side player as well as being a fine cutter. I like the thought of Smith and Sehwag batting together. They mirror each others' strengths.

BRIAN LARA (West Indies)

Brian Lara was a chameleon of the crease. If you stacked the off-side field, he'd toy with you on the on side. If you switched plans, he would switch too, always staying one step ahead of you. Plenty of batsmen have a great technique, but very few have several great techniques – Lara did. He was renowned for his extravagantly high backlift, yet if he wanted to he could cut it to half the size and still be comfortable. He could trim his footwork to not go as far forward as he normally would, if it suited the pitch and the bowling. The key to his adaptability was his beautiful hands. Soft, quick and malleable, they would take him to the places he wanted to be. They were the best hands ever, I reckon, and they made him my favourite player by a street.

RAHUL DRAVID (India)

They called him 'the Wall', and he was well named. Great mental toughness, watchability and the capacity to inspire are basic prerequisites for selection in my side. Dravid had all these. Others might have quickened the pulse of spectators more, but with his textbook purity and great concentration Dravid was still absorbing to watch. And he was a great slipper. In my era, he was the Björn Borg of cricket, absolute ice under pressure, and when you played him he gave very little away. As the chaotic forces of Indian cricket swirled around him, he was a beacon of serenity, and must be especially admired for the way he handled the ongoing confusion around his one-day role. India struggled to house such a classical player in limited-over cricket. Up and down the order he would go. Sometimes he kept, other times he didn't. Only an individual as calm as Dravid could have stood it.

More than anything, Dravid had beautiful balance, in cricket and life. He has a much broader perspective than most athletes I've come across. His father worked in a jam factory and Dravid worked hard early in his career to get a commerce degree in case his cricket career didn't blossom as expected.

During the second season of the IPL, in South Africa, I met Dravid in a bookshop at the Sandton Sun complex in Johannesburg and we had a fascinating chat, which started with a laugh at how old-fashioned we both were. Two cricketers meeting in a bookshop? You wouldn't pick it these days. Why read a book when you can play with the latest gadget? We felt a bit like two old rock stars meeting in a shop that sold records. We chatted for a couple of hours and he was such absorbing company I could have stayed there all day.

In the course of our conversation, we talked about the future of the game and the possibility of setting up a cricket committee of players to send recommendations to the ICC. When I was playing I felt that I might have a lot in common with Dravid, but with the tension of competition it's difficult to let your guard down. I'm thankful for that meeting in the bookshop, which proved Dravid was the man I'd always sensed him to be.

SACHIN TENDULKAR (India)

How could you leave Sachin out? There were a lot of things I liked about him. One rarely mentioned but significant part of his game was his fierce body language. For a little man, he had a huge stature. And he exuded a cool nonchalance at the crease. He may have had the occasional crack, but generally he let his bat do the talking. He was so fearless and (ridiculously) skilful. He and Lara were the most skilful batsmen I have ever seen. Just the way they manipulated the field was fascinating to watch. Against spin Sachin was in complete control. He might get out to it occasionally, but there was never any strategy implemented by Warnie or another spinner against him which made me think, *Here we go . . . let's see how he handles this*.

Sachin is a quite a shy guy, and I can't claim to know him well at all. He kept his distance. But for Sachin to survive and thrive in international cricket for two full decades is extraordinary. He had to negotiate not only Warne and McGrath, but also Walsh and Ambrose and Waqar Younis and Wasim Akram. And he handled them all.

JACQUES KALLIS (South Africa)

Kallis provided tremendous stability, and radiated a dependability that made him one of the best players of his era and certainly the most prolific all-rounder. When you can average more than 50 as a Test batsman and also take more than 250 wickets, you qualify for selection in the best team not just of your era but of any era. He'd be the first person chosen in my side and, in different circumstances, I believe he could have been even better than he was. Had it not been up to him every time – every innings – we'd have seen him spread his wings a little more, and I'm sure we would have seen him go to even greater heights.

KUMAR SANGAKKARA (Sri Lanka)

There is no doubt Sangakkara, like a lot of keepers, loves his chirping from behind the stumps. But if you had to pick a guy to offer counsel on the game, he'd be among the first chosen, along with the likes of Dravid, Justin Langer, Steve Waugh and Michael Vaughan. Sangakkara had an exceptional understanding of the game, and his playing ability, charisma and personality made him a great package. He can speak three languages, is studying to be a lawyer and is an articulate, thoughtful character who not only plays the game well but also interprets it beautifully, as seen by some of his work as a part-time journalist for Cricinfo. He is a very debonair character and has a huge following. For many years Murali, Sanga and Mahela Jayawardene *were* the Sri Lankan cricket team.

With a batting average in the mid-fifties he is worthy of consideration as a batsman alone. To have kept wicket as well, often over the stumps in sapping conditions, makes him a stand-out choice. I am particularly impressed by the fact he averages around 50 in overseas Tests and to me he is a clear choice ahead of any rival, including South Africa's Mark Boucher.

MUTTIAH MURALITHARAN (Sri Lanka)

It's not just what Murali did, it's what he brought to the game. In his heart, Murali will stay 22 forever. His youthful exuberance for the game knows no bounds, and he loved talking about cricket so much that I took late-night phone calls from him during the IPL to chat about the game. I got the impression he'd exhausted everyone else in the team. Deep down, I think we all want to test the game and test ourselves, and Murali did that. The quirkiness of his action changed the way cricket is played. Only when I played with him in the IPL did I realise he has a real vulnerability behind that enthusiasm. Maybe it comes from all the obstacles he's encountered, which he's succeeded in overcoming.

HARBHAJAN SINGH (India)

Harbhajan gets the second spinner's spot ahead of India's Anil Kumble, New Zealand's Dan Vettori, and Pakistan's Saqlain Mushtaq. I've gone for the man who caused me the most trouble at the crease. Harbhajan was a very attacking bowler, and traditionally an attacking spinner normally means a teasing flight bowler. He definitely wasn't one of those. He was more of an into-the-wicket spinner, using the sharp revolutions he put on the ball to get bite off the wicket and cause problems.

Harbhajan brought an intensity and controversy to the contest that put bums on seats. There was a real 'game on' feel to anything he was involved with. He could be impetuous at times – and he could make you feel impetuous. His over-the-top celebrations – like doing a lap of the Gabba after getting Ricky Ponting out – were cringe-worthy. But I'd still pick Harbhajan for his superb skills. When he bowled his doosra – the ball that spins away from right-handed batsmen – to go with his conventional off spinner, like Murali, he lifted his game to a level beyond the reach of conventional off spinners. The doosra was a priceless weapon – it made his other balls so much more dangerous as well, as batsmen asked themselves whether or not to play.

WASIM AKRAM (Pakistan)

Wasim Akram was the prettiest bowler of all time, a true artist of his craft. Like Craig McDermott and Allan Donald, he'd almost charm you with his textbook action. I didn't face a lot of him, but when I did I'd often think, *Wow, that's perfect seam position.* You'd be convinced it was going to swing – and it did. Perfect. He bowled me a ball at the Gabba, when Queensland was playing Pakistan, which just missed my outside edge and, to the amazement of everyone on the ground, was taken by second slip. That's how much it moved in the air. Soap suds are expected to float like that. Cricket balls aren't. Wasim galloped down the wicket and expressed total bewilderment that I wasn't given out. I didn't feel any need to explain, but I could appreciate his thoughts. Balls that just miss the edge rarely go anywhere near first slip, never mind second – but I swear I didn't hit it.

Sir Donald Bradman once said that Wasim was the finest left-armed bowler he'd ever seen, and there can't be much higher praise than that. When Wasim was in his prime, Allan Border said he was the rival player he admired most. Wasim has a near perfect build for a fast bowler, with a giant backside that acted as a launching pad and a shock absorber. Left-armed quicks are famed for their volatility; Brendon Julian and Chris Matthews suffered agonising periods when their radar would scramble completely. Wasim experienced that too. In Kenya in 2002, he bowled an outrageously wide ball to Gilly, in the first ball of a one-day final, which went for three wides. Then he followed up with a couple more wild ones before – bang! – he curled a beauty straight through Gilly's defence – fourth ball of the innings – to rock his castle.

Wasim's arm action was so unnervingly quick, it enhanced his menace. Other express bowlers like Brett Lee had such flowing, rhythmical actions you were able to see the ball all the way through their action, and it was presented to you at precisely the moment you expected. But Wasim was different: a flash of his arm and it was over.

CURTLY AMBROSE (West Indies)

When asked who was the best bowler I faced my answer is always delivered without a moment's contemplation – Curtly gets the nod by a country mile. Others maybe have been quicker but he was quick enough, and his ability to hold his line and deck the ball away from left-handers made him an absolute menace. He didn't really swing the ball but he didn't need to, because he had everything else – bounce, consistency, endurance, seam, magnificent body language and a fierce will to win.

COURTNEY WALSH (West Indies) – 12th man

I have a real soft spot for Courtney. At the crease I spoke to him more than any other bowler I faced because he was such a nice person. Punter would occasionally get angry with me and say, 'What are you talking to him for?' But I couldn't help it.

For starters, Courtney used to laugh at whatever you said, so you instantly felt like the funniest guy on the planet. He was so nice it was a bit like having your dad bowling at you. It was almost impossible not to talk to him. I'll never forget Colin

Miller coming on to bowl at the SCG in a Test against the West Indies. When Funky took his hat off and revealed his newly dyed blue hair, Courtney, who was batting at the time, had to pull away because he was laughing so much.

Courtney would be the perfect foil for Curtly and Wasim in this team, and between the three of them they'd strangle you to death. Where would you score a run? Courtney was slightly easier to leave than Curtly, but a very cagey and consistent performer. He'd start the ball on a line outside leg stump, and it would just miss off stump. He was always hard to get forward to, but you never really felt comfortable going back because he was too close to you. You couldn't pull him because he was rarely short enough, so your prime option was letting him go, which never seemed like much of a victory, particularly if you wanted to keep the game moving forward. You could try batting out of your crease, but he had good pace and a scorching bouncer.

Off the field Courtney was endlessly sociable. He had his favourites such as Andrew Symonds, with whom he'd played at Gloucestershire, but I always felt a nice connection with him born of simple rapport and respect. He is universally regarded as a good man. When he took his 500th Test wicket in front of his home town in Jamaica, his mum was in the crowd and provided the most memorable quote of the day when she said, 'God only gave me one son, but he gave me a good one.'

Statistically, Courtney was a machine. When fast bowlers discussed workloads and longevity they didn't even bother mentioning him because his deeds were off the chart. He bowled more than 116 000 balls in his senior career. Freakish stuff.

43

IPL – the New World

Here is an inescapable fact about world cricket: Australia cannot thrive without India, but India doesn't need us to the same degree. This was reinforced to a group of Australian players in India in October 2007, when we met with dynamic Indian cricket administrator Lalit Modi to discuss cricket's great new adventure, the Indian Premier League. The IPL was hastily organised as a response to the rebel Indian Cricket League, but from the start its plans were shamelessly ambitious. Marquee players, massive sponsorships, the world's top players lured by more money than they had ever dreamed of . . . Cricket would never be the same.

Clearly the IPL was going ahead whether or not we were on board. The IPL needed Australian players but didn't need Australia as an entity. We wouldn't be running the show and Modi was fairly dismissive of any excessive demands. Michael Clarke found that out in a hurry. I remember him saying to Modi, 'I'm worth X amount of dollars.' Modi laughed at him.

Clarke, he explained, wasn't worth anything until he was signed at the auction. Clarke argued that he didn't have to go to auction because he already had several franchises lining up for his signature. 'You'll be going to auction if you want to play in the IPL,' said Modi. End of story. Later, Michael decided not to put himself in the auction and has never played in the tournament.

Australian cricket has seen its share of wealthy sporting benefactors over the years, but the IPL is a fair few rungs up. I'm talking serious cash, as one Victorian sponsorship manager found when he visited South Africa during the second season of the IPL. He was chasing Indian sponsorship for a stadium, and when one Indian billionaire asked him what he was looking for, he gave a six-figure reply. The Indian billionaire was intrigued. 'And how much to buy your stadium?' he asked. He wanted to buy the MCG!

The first-year auction was an interesting process. There were rumours around that Australia's senior players such as Ricky Ponting and me would be out of favour because of our roles in the Monkeygate affair. As it turned out, I went for US$350 000 and Ricky went for US$400 000. For two months' work it was a lot of money, but it was certainly under the odds when you consider Cameron White went for US$500 000, and other players who'd done far less went for a lot more. Regardless of the auction results, though, the money was certainly a first for cricket. My Chennai teammate, and later coach, Stephen Fleming, said the reaction in New Zealand was shock and amazement. Rugby union is, without doubt, New Zealand's number-one sport, yet the IPL payments dwarfed those received by the All Blacks. Apparently the nation's leading footballers were taken aback by the contract fees to IPL players.

I had some trepidation about joining the IPL. One of the advantages I had playing for Cricket Australia is that you have only one employer, and for better or worse, you know where you stand. In the IPL I'd be answering to more than one boss, and I also felt I'd been undervalued at the auction. Entering the IPL was a leap of faith because the competition had no history, and you had no idea which franchise you would end up at. But cricket was turning a fresh page and I wanted to be part of it. I had always loved the entertainment side of the game and felt that IPL cricket would be played like Australian cricket. And I got lucky: I was bought by a great franchise, the Super Kings.

Chennai, my new home ground, held so many beautiful memories for me. Every time I went to the MA Chidambaram Stadium, my mind drifted back to the specialist spin clinic I'd flown over for 10 years before, a watershed in my career. And then, in 2001, there was the famous Third Test in which I made 203. I felt a strong connection with the place.

What's more, the Super Kings have a strong, rational, hierarchical structure I have confidence in. They are owned by India Cements, whose managing director, N. Srinivasan, is also secretary of the BCCI and the boss of Tamil Nadu cricket. It was a bit like joining a Melbourne franchise run by James Sutherland – a cricket franchise run by cricket people. I heard one story about a franchise owner, shattered by his side's form, calling them to a meeting at 2 a.m. Players were summoned from their sleep for a crisis meeting after they'd lost a series of games. That would never happen at the Super Kings, though you could certainly feel the tournament pressure rise quickly after a few losses. In our second year, when we were beaten in the semi-final, our owners were absolutely shattered, but never irrational. They understood cricket and were always very proud of their team.

As much as I enjoyed the IPL, it frustrated me that Australia was stranded back at the docks holding the broken streamers while the Twenty20 boat left harbour to tackle the high seas. I can understand why it happened. Australia had helped build the great brand of 50-over cricket, and because we'd made it what it was, we embraced it with enthusiasm. We knew it was a major cash cow for cricket, and the Twenty20 game was seen as cannibalising the profits. But for all that, I still think we've been too conservative and missed the chance to leave the dock with the boat. That's the bad news. The good news is that I don't think it will matter too much, because we are not India and would never have been able to create a tournament to match the IPL.

What we can do is become the best Twenty20 side in the world, and trade off that ranking. It struck me that cricket will lose out as franchises emerge around the world, because the franchises will take what they need to be successful without feeling the need to give much back. I'm as passionate about players' rights as anyone, but the players can consider themselves fortunate to still have 12-month Cricket Australia contracts while they are playing in the IPL. If a window is found for players to play two months a year in the IPL, then Cricket Australia contracts should only be for 10 months of the year. The first year of the IPL contained the cream of Australian cricket, yet the flow-on effect to Australia, to the states and the clubs who have produced those players, was zero. That's where our administrators have been slow to react.

In our first year, the Super Kings were coached by Kepler Wessels and I enjoyed the experience of playing under him. He was my first catch in my first Test in 1994 and was just leaving the game as I started making a mark. We had a lot in common – we were both left-handed opening batsmen who'd played with Valleys, Queensland and Australia – and enjoyed an immediate rapport. Like me, he loved Queensland but felt that the state outfits at the end of his career and the start of mine were a bit too sloppy. His standards were well ahead of his time and a striking contrast to those of many men he played with in the mid-1980s.

His record at club level in Brisbane for Valleys – where he scored nine centuries from 32 games and averaged 87.5 – said everything about his commitment to the game at all levels. There was no such thing as a game of social cricket to Kepler, nor one which could be taken at less than maximum intensity. He was a hardcore professional, who achieved what he deserved because he worked hard at his game. In the mid-1980s, when there was a push to axe Kepler from the Australian side, selector Greg Chappell, who knew Kepler well from their World Series days, said, 'Don't do it . . . I know how tough he is – he'll be back.' And of course he was. The scars of playing for Australia in the turbulent years of the mid-1980s took their toll on Kepler in the same way as they did with Allan Border – that brutal era traumatised both men. Neither could relax watching cricket. Whack a set of pads on them and put them in the middle and you'd have two men as hard as a bitumen road, yet in the dressing-room they were cats on a hot tin roof.

I understand that Kepler and AB had a major falling out when Kepler left Australia and returned to South Africa, but before that they'd been the greatest of mates. I can see why, because they had a similar and committed work ethic. As a coach, however, Kepler was always worrying about the worst-case scenario. It'd get to the stage where I'd say to him, 'Mate, just relax . . . it'll be what it's going to be, you know?' No doubt he was also a bit shell-shocked by how the game had changed.

Kepler played at a time when you were considered favourites to win a 50-over game if you put 225 on the board. Now he was watching teams make 180 in 20 overs. Scoring rates had gone from *Driving Miss Daisy* pace to Formula One. Understandably, he struggled to inspire the men under him to play such a freewheeling game. Kepler also found out that you can't coach the one quality that bankrolls Twenty20 cricket – instinct. He was a very structured man with a structured game, and he coached in a structured way. Unfortunately, he wasn't very popular among the Indian players. He could say what he liked to me without offending me, but it wasn't the same with the Indians. He might say, 'That was a dreadful shot, mate,' and I'd think, *You're right*, but same line would cause the more sensitive Indians to recoil in horror.

Kepler did well: we were beaten off the final ball in the first IPL final. But his replacement, Stephen Fleming, was a breath of fresh air. Being a player in the side in the first year undoubtedly helped him, because the other players already knew him and could relate to him. Also, he was humble enough to ask for feedback, and sometimes it was simple stuff that made a difference. The Indian players asked him to talk slower at team meetings so they could understand him. (That was a lesson to all of the non-Indians, actually.) I like Flem's style and have admired him for as long as I've known him. When he captained New Zealand, I was always impressed by the team's planning. They knew they could never match us on resources, but they planned more meticulously than any team we faced. Marto used to get frustrated by their strategy of feeding him short balls outside off stump in Test matches in the hope he'd glide one to a packed gully region. They attacked his strength and tried to turn it into a weakness. He didn't enjoy it, but he grudgingly respected it.

The IPL had advertising banners that read, *Who would you support?* with photos of national teammates facing off against each other – Ganguly from the Kolkata Knight Riders against Tendulkar from the Mumbai Indians, or Graeme Smith from the Rajasthan Royals against Jacques Kallis from the Royal Challengers Bangalore. The battles extended on-field as well. The Australian players of my era knew each other so well that there were fascinating moments great and small in our clashes.

In the past I'd learnt to expect the most from Adam Gilchrist when he quietly tapped the batting crease while facing up for the first over rather than smashing the ground like an axeman at the Royal Easter Show. One day during the second season of the IPL in Kingsmead, Durban, when I was standing at gully as he came to the crease, I immediately feared the worst: he stood there, totally poised with beautifully still hands, tapping rather than thumping his bat. As I squatted into position, a premonition of doom flashed through my mind – *We are in big trouble here* – and so it proved as he made 44 runs off just 19 balls. By the time he departed in the sixth over, the game felt almost gone.

Some elements of the franchise system are terrific for players, such as the 'can do' philosophy that creates such positive vibes. When my family came over for the preseason camp at the start of the season in South Africa, I needed a bigger room and initially swapped with Flem, who had a superior suite. But it had only one bed in it and I needed something bigger, so I asked our manager Russell Radhakrishnan if a further change could be arranged.

He found two rooms connected to each other. While the move also involved shifting Parthiv Patel, the manager arranged it effortlessly and even picked up the tab for the extra room. 'So long as my players are happy, I'm happy,' he said. If I'd tried to do that while playing for Australia, it would have been deemed outside team rules and have triggered an enormous bunfight.

The IPL is the future and the master of Twenty20 cricket. There may be other leagues, but I believe the IPL will always be superior, because it remains the league most likely to be able to afford the game's next superstar.

I once heard that when New Zealander John Wright was asked about the challenges of coaching India, he simply pulled an Indian banknote out of his pocket and pointed to it. There's one sentence on the note that is explained in India's 15 languages, from Bengali to Nepali to Tamil and a dozen others.

I visited India many times as a player for Australia, but I must confess to being largely ignorant of the nuances of its different cultures, languages and dialects, and the fact that they could change every few hundred kilometres. I didn't realise there was no quintessential India or Indian, that in the one Indian dressing-room there could be Hindus, Muslims, Christians and Sikhs, some very religious, others less so. Some who ate meat, others who didn't. Some who preferred rice, others wheat. And that on any given day there could be eight different languages apart from English spoken in the Indian dressing-room. But I'm now much more aware of Indian culture in all its diversity.

My re-education often came in subtle ways. There were times when I'd be watching television with four or five Indian teammates in our team room in Chennai, and one of them would start laughing at something said on television. 'What's he laughing at?' I'd say to one of the others, and he'd shrug and say, 'Don't know . . . not sure what dialect it is. We can't understand it either.'

The IPL has been a great vehicle for international cricketers to learn more about each other's cultures. I'm not just talking about players in the same franchise either. My great friend Mike Young was fielding coach at the Deccan Chargers, where New Zealand's Scott Styris said to him one day, 'Youngy, I can cop most Australians but the one I really hate is Matthew Hayden.' Youngy stood up for me and the two had a chat about it. A few minutes later, Scott took a call from my Super Kings teammate Jacob Oram, and said to him, 'I was just telling Youngy how much I can't stand Hayden. How do you find him?' Jake was apparently quite gracious about me, which prompted Scott to go back to Youngy and say, 'This is doing my head in.' I'm not sure what Scott thinks of me now, but the point is that those sorts of exchanges can only be good for international cricket. In the IPL opinions are challenged and barriers are broken down naturally, simply by the force of familiarity. With the days of the shared dressing-room beer fading, perhaps the IPL will provide a new path to friendships between rivals.

The cultural crossovers triggered some offbeat scenes in the IPL. Australians have always loved the singing of our cricketing anthem, 'Beneath the Southern Cross', the highpoint of our post-match celebrations, and New Zealanders have a victory poem, but many nations, India included, do nothing. One day on the Super Kings team bus, Tasmanian batsman George Bailey got together with Stephen Fleming and penned a victory song, which did a lot for team harmony. It was based on the 1970s hit 'Living Next Door to Alice'. The real song has a line, 'Now I've got to get used to not living next door to Alice,' which was changed to, 'Now you've got to get used to being beaten by the boys from Chennai.'

We started a tradition that the man of the match had to lead the chorus. In the same way that you hear a mighty 'Ooooohhhhhhhhh' echoing around the dressing-room as AFL teams rock back and forth in their victory huddle before bursting into the club song, it was up to the man of the match to get the show rolling.

One of George's little treasures is a video of our Indian teammate Subramaniam Badrinath starting the song with a seriously squeaky voice. At first we thought his falsetto tones were going to soar off into a tribal chant, but eventually the rest of the boys joined in and we went into our little homespun ditty. Badrinath had been tentative at first, but he really got into the song and, not surprisingly, so did the world's greatest cricket nuffy, Murali, who's always up for anything to do with bonding, fun and, of course, cricket.

The most fascinating character at the Super Kings is the Indian captain and superstar, M.S. Dhoni. He's India's Ricky Ponting, an unpretentious working-class boy with simple, clear thoughts on the game and a love of rolling up his sleeves and getting into it. Like Punter, he thrives at training. One minute he's batting, next he's throwing the stumps down, next he's onto something else. If a training drill needs an extra hand, he's there. Dhoni is very direct, another quality I like, though I wonder whether his pointy-ended messages are a translation thing. During our training camp in Durban in 2009, he said to me,

'I feel I can talk to you now . . . that means I am comfortable with you.' I thought, *Mate, I've been comfortable with you for a long time. I haven't studied your language but I've studied the way you go about your business.*

I related to Dhoni on several levels, including his ability to enjoy life outside the game and see cricket as a vehicle to pursue other passions. I know he's never read a book on cricket, for instance. Growing up, he loved books on war, tanks, guns and motorbikes, and still does. He's an all-action sort of character, in every way. When we were playing in Kimberley in South Africa, he was the one Indian player who came on an outback excursion with us (organised by Albie Morkel). I stayed only one night because I wanted to get back to surf, so I missed an epic clay pigeon shootout between Dhoni and Glenn McGrath, who'd done a lot of shooting and – here's a surprise – fancied himself as a crack shot. Dhoni apparently beat him easily, shooting down clay pigeons everywhere, and in so doing he took down the biggest Pigeon of all.

It didn't surprise me. Dhoni loves having a shoot, and I can only imagine the assistance he gets from the cricket-mad military in India. This may sound strange given how seriously the Indians take their cricket, but it's very much a game to Dhoni. It's almost as if his philosophy is, 'Yeah, I know we hit balls, but it's not really that tough, you know.' He can be an elusive character. I've never once got him on the phone, and at times I think he likes to hide from the madhouse world in his hotel room, as well as getting out and doing his own thing.

My Indian teammates in the Super Kings side are very endearing characters. They have an forthrightness I put down to growing up in a country of one billion people – if you don't speak up for yourself, then life just whizzes by without you. When I had my first decent chat with my opening partner, Parthiv Patel (the former Test keeper), one of the first things he said was, 'Do you remember that day when we clashed?' I thought, *Oh no, what have I done?* He then recounted the time when, as a young 12th man at the Gabba, he'd jogged past me with a smile on his face and I erupted, saying, 'What are you smiling at, you infant?' With those little glasses and that baby face, he certainly looked as if he'd snuck out of a local boarding school in the lunch break to see his cricketing heroes. And he *was* young. When he chirped Steve Waugh in Steve's last Test at the SCG, Steve shot back, 'What are you talking about – you were in school when I started, so just shut up!'

Parthiv is a great bloke. He's softly spoken, very well educated and a real family man, always accompanied by his wife. He also has some endearing superstitions. One of them is to touch bats and do little 'shazzams' or glove punches when you meet in the middle of the pitch. When we were first paired together, I initially said, 'No, mate, not for me,' but then he stood to attention – all three foot of him! – and gave me a look which seemed to say, 'We are doing it . . . and I won't repeat myself again.' So out of respect for him, we did it. For years, Australian teams had taken the rise out of the glove-touching fad, and to the mirth of the boys, Ricky Ponting became the first to do it when he batted with Brian Lara in the tsunami game at the MCG. Brian raised his gloves and Ricky had nowhere to go. He knew he'd cop it from the rest of us, and he wasn't disappointed. 'Right, then, so you'll do it with Lara and the rest of us get brushed – is that the deal?' we said.

Like Parthiv and the other Indians, Murali was also

disarmingly direct. Sometimes he'd ring me late at night in my room and say, 'Haydos, what are you *doing*? How can you get out to that bloke – he doesn't even spin the ball.' Our unofficial team mascot was Murali's son Naren. He came on tour in South Africa with us and would dart around the place at a million miles an hour, until someone like Makhaya Ntini would sweep him up and carry him around like a little trophy.

Ntini was our Merv Hughes, a serial pest who loved a stage and a captive audience. When the IPL was transferred to South Africa, Ntini's homeland, he barely got a game for the entire tournament, yet every time you saw him walking through a hotel foyer, he'd be high-fiving someone he knew or laughing or generally carrying on. You often heard him before you saw him. On every plane flight he'd try to wind someone up or just create a little bit of fun and mischief. Then eventually it would be open slather and everyone would be into it. The Australian side thought he was a bit mad – in a nice way – when we played him, and I saw nothing in my time with the IPL to disprove the theory. I still remember facing him one day in a Test when he was repeatedly directing these bizarre ramblings at me, which I simply couldn't decipher. I said, 'You're a goose, mate. What are you yelling about?' He just kept saying, 'Mangoes . . . man goes . . . mangoes.' I should've ignored it, but curiosity got the better of me and I finally said, 'What's all this rubbish about mangoes?' He replied, 'Wherever woman goes . . . mangoes.' Go figure.

I have the deepest respect for Makhaya as a bowler. I have to – he got me out nine times in Tests. Before he was a fast bowler he was a shepherd, and I wonder if that accounts for his amazing endurance. It's become a cliché to say of stout-hearted fast bowlers that they can go all day, but he literally could, his pace barely dropping. I always felt he was better with the old ball than the new one, because his angles were subtly threatening rather than being hugely pronounced.

When Makhaya heard I was writing a book, he mentioned he planned to pen one himself and had already settled on the title – *Ubulongwe* – which means 'cow dung' in Xhosa, his native tongue. As a youngster herding goats in his home village of Mdingi, on the Eastern Cape, he'd keep his feet warm by placing them in cow dung, and he insists that's where his life's journey began.

Getting to understand rival cultures is one of the great things about the IPL, but getting reacquainted with your old mates as you fly around the country is another genuine bonus. Kell has a special connection with Glenn McGrath, who was playing with the Delhi Daredevils, and one day I was walking through the Sandton Sun complex in Johannesburg, on the phone to Kell in Australia, and she asked me if I'd seen the big fella. Amazingly, at that very moment he appeared around the corner in front of me and I simply said, 'Here he is now. I'll put him on.'

44

Surfing the Wave

In March 2009, news came through that the Indian Premier League would be switched from India to South Africa. I was rapt. I enjoyed playing in India, but I adore South Africa, where I have many great friends from my playing days, and surf, sun and sand abound.

For those two months in South Africa, I batted on pure instinct. I didn't have a single net session throughout the tournament – the boys were outraged that I could play so well with such minimal preparation. I took home the orange cap for the most runs in the tournament, with 572 from 12 games. When I was speaking to former Queensland coach Terry Oliver on my return to Australia, I told him that for once I'd found a balance between work and play that liberated my mind and let my natural ability flow. He swore that he wouldn't drop a word of it to Queensland's young players in case it sent the wrong message.

I didn't want him to tell them either, because it was really only half the story. The sole reason I could play so well without training was because I'd spent the previous two decades hitting more balls in the nets than anyone else. Occasionally you'll hear a well-known songwriter say they wrote a famous song in 15 minutes. But I reckon the only reason they could do that is because they've been writing songs for the previous 20 years.

My unofficial motto for the tournament was, 'Just don't think.' Twenty20 cricket is pretty freestyle, and I felt completely unburdened. The less I thought about my batting, the better it flowed. I just saw the ball and hit it. Even in the previous IPL season in India, I'd been a bit weighed down by complex thought processes. Now I was thinking, *It's time to just relax and play*. In the past, I had lamented how cricket got in the way of a good tour. It always frustrated me that we'd visit the most exotic locations on the planet, yet often see nothing more than a hotel and cricket ground. On the IPL's South African safari, it was time to change that.

You know you're enjoying life if you can enjoy a drug test, and that's what happened to me in Port Elizabeth, where a post-match test – traditionally one of the least appealing aspects of our sport – became one of the favourite nights of my cricket career. I was chosen for the drug test and the rest of the boys were heading off when Freddie Flintoff realised I'd be stranded by myself, and decided to keep me company. It was like having a front-row seat at a West End comedy. Freddie kept a tub of beers beside us and proceeded to relate some of the funny things that have happened in his life, from being stalked by the tabloid press to the infamous pedalo incident in the West Indies when he fell out of one of the little boats during the 2007 World Cup. I laughed so much it hurt. I love Freddie. He was bloody hard to compete against, and would be an invaluable player for any side.

The third season of the IPL in 2010 was back in India. It wasn't a great one for me personally – I struck a lean patch – but it was memorable for the Super Kings because we won the tournament! We came good at the right time after quietly lobbing along mid-table for most of the tournament in a congested pack. I realised how lucky we were as a team to have owners who were cricket-savvy. We never felt heat from them to upgrade our performance, and I never felt pressured to lift my own game.

At times winning the tournament seemed as difficult as climbing Everest, so it was fitting that the turning point came in a match in Dharamasala, in the foothills of the Himalayas, home of the Dalai Lama. We got to meet the Tibetan spiritual leader before the game, and some of the players asked him to bless them. Maybe that helped – we clawed out of deep trouble to notch a stunning win, thanks to a great innings by M. S. Dhoni.

But it was the journey from Dharamasala to Chennai that I found especially uplifting. The morning after the match we arrived at the airport to find our 10 a.m. flight had been moved to 12.30 p.m. Then it suddenly disappeared from the schedule altogether. So off we went by bus through the Himalayas to Chandigarh, in the hope of catching a flight to Chennai. Unfortunately, by the time we reached Chandigarh our flight had gone. We ended up having a 28-hour plane, train and automobile adventure on our way to Chennai.

In the three weeks leading up to that journey I had felt suffocated by the intensity of life in India. From despair at the poverty to amazement at the unique scenery to the isolation of my small hotel room, it was overwhelming me. On that trip, though, I just surrendered to my environment and thought, *Whatever*. Suddenly I could breathe again. We called into a street market, and it was incredible to see this isolated little community roar to life as word swept the region that M.S. Dhoni was in town for the first (and perhaps last) time in his career.

Chennai became a second home for me during the IPL, and I developed such a good relationship with the staff at the ITC Sheraton Park Hotel & Towers that when I rang for room service they would guess my order before I made it.

During my third IPL experience I also had a wonderful day taking the boys out on Chennai Harbour in a Riviera boat. I loved the Riviera boat company in Australia and had once promised their executives that I would help them sell a boat or two in India. Eventually I arranged for a few of the executives to meet a great friend of mine in Chennai, Reggie Aban. They clicked, and Reggie bought the first Riviera boat to be shipped to India, a 48-footer. Taking some of the Chennai Super Kings out on the harbour was the icing on the cake, and a lot of fun. Whenever you go anywhere with M.S. Dhoni, you're sure to attract a crowd, and M.S. George Bailey, Suresh Raina, Parthiv Patel and his wife, Justin Kemp, Albie Morkel, Michael Kasprowicz, my dear friend Neil Honan and I were mobbed on the way to the harbour, but it was all worth it.

By 2010 the IPL had grown so much that cinemas around India were screening live IPL games instead of Bollywood movies. Local producers wisely reckoned that there was no point in taking on the IPL, so there were no major releases during the competition. Sachin Tendulkar was behind the push to get the

IPL into cinemas. He bought the first ticket, which was later auctioned off and raised several thousand dollars for charity.

Beating a Tendulkar-led Mumbai in the final that year was a fantastic moment, but I'm not even sure our franchise owners attended the game because they were so superstitious and feared they might jinx us if they did. In our second-last home game in Chennai, the room attendants had been so worried about my form that they suggested I sit in a different spot in the dressing-room. And earlier in the tournament, we'd changed dressing-rooms after losing a few games, a move which concerned me so much that I said to our manager, 'What happens if we keep losing? Where do we go to change then?' I considered switching my spot but had a rethink on the bus when it hit me that the player sitting beside me, batsman Suresh Raina, was in the form of his life. Why unsettle him by moving away?

The shocking postscript to the tournament was the suspension of the man who was the face and force of the IPL: Lalit Modi. The charges against Modi include rigging IPL bids, holding proxy stakes in teams, taking money from companies in return for broadcasting rights and having a dictatorial management style.

I know nothing of these activities, but what I can say of Modi is that he had incredible drive. He reminded me of Kerry Packer in that he was brave enough to see that the game had to be ushered into a new era, and bold enough to do it.

The IPL certainly is an ambitious venture, especially when you think of the enormous potential issues – of communication and culture – that arise when you mix players from around the world. I was given a humorous insight into the communication gap between the various cultures when during the 2010 tournament I decided it was time, as a senior player, to give the side a serious spray. It concerned me that some of the younger players were letting their standards slip by having a few late nights, so I gave them my best tub-thumping, expletive-laden address. I could tell I was hitting the mark by how they were nodding along with me. Or so I thought.

When George Bailey asked our Sri Lankan signing, Thilan Thushara, what he thought of my spray, he said, 'I could understand the F words but apart from that . . . nothing.' Oh well, I tried. It was just one of many sweet memories from a great journey. But in spite of all of my fondness for Chennai and India, my first cricketing home will always be the Gabba.

Although my cricketing days in Australia were over, I had returned to the Gabba in 2010 to do a television commercial, and the ground that had been a pulsating mass of goodwill on the night of my retirement was empty.

It had changed a lot since I'd first played there almost 20 years before, with Gaz sitting up somewhere behind the bowler's arm and urging me with hand messages to play straight. Gone was the old Cricketers' Club, along with the aroma of sizzling steaks that used to waft invitingly over the oval while we were batting or fielding. I could still recall the sound of the wires gently tinkling against the metal flagpoles on top of the clubhouse as we took the field. But my affection for the place was undiminished, and I felt not a single pang of regret. Instead I was filled with a contented desire to take my children to a Test match and see the game through their eyes.

I'd squeezed every ounce of potential from my game. I know

most of the guys from my era feel the same. We miss singing the team song and we miss each other, but our careers have been happily put to bed. We have willingly moved on to a broad range of new challenges, satisfied with what we achieved.

As the TV crew broke up after the filming, I took one last look around the Gabba. My mind drifted back to the first time I'd sat alone on the wicket block the day before my first Sheffield Shield match, how I'd closed my eyes and conjured images of success, conditioning my mind for all the sounds and sights that would greet me the next day. It was a ritual I followed throughout my career.

I thought, *You've been a great old ground. You've housed my family, my Test wins, our first Sheffield Shield win . . .* So many wonderful memories came back to me. I felt grateful to the ground and to cricket itself, for the wonderful life I've had. Two simple words came in to my head: *Thank you.*

Life with Matt

BY KELLIE HAYDEN

It was only an old rocking chair but what made it special was the lady who used to sit in it – Katherine Mary Hayden, Matt's grandmother, who had recently passed away. When I sat down in our lounge room to watch Matt play his first innings of the Indian Test tour in 2001, there was no other choice – I had to sit in that chair. That would be my connection to him. And knowing how much he loved his grandmother and was missing her, it felt like a strong one. So I sat there and rocked . . . and rocked, and rocked. I could not leave the chair. By the time I got up, Matthew had made the Test century that revived his career.

I firmly believe that in life nothing happens by chance: it is all preordained. And this belief was reaffirmed by the events leading up to my beautiful friend Jane McGrath's final battle with cancer after her long illness.

It was in 2008, when Matt was on tour in the West Indies. When I look back at Matt's sensational career, I think it's amazing he never had to come home from tour until that one, 15 years after his first. Gracie and I were going to go over to spend 10 days with him, but the day before we were due to leave he rang to say he was coming home. The medical people couldn't manage his injury properly over there for want of basic necessities such as imaging equipment.

Matt had only been home one night when Glenn called to say Jane had taken a turn for the worse. I left immediately for Sydney, and on the way there all I could think was, *Thank goodness I wasn't overseas when my friend needed me, and that Matt is home for our kids.* It was meant to be, and I was able to spend the next week in Sydney and share some precious time with Jane, Glenn, James and Holly.

I treasure many things about my time as a member of the Australian cricket family, but none more so than my special friendship with the incomparable Jane McGrath. I'm so proud to have called myself her friend. Jane was the real deal: funny, warm, caring, fun-loving, nurturing and beautiful. We spent a lot of time together, chatting about everything from world affairs to our kids' progress and the dilemma of what to wear to the Allan Border Medal. Sometimes we take those little conversations for granted, and we really shouldn't. During the 2005 Ashes tour in England, Jane took me and the kids to see where she'd grown up as a little girl. I felt very privileged to share that experience with her. Jane is godmother to our youngest child, Thomas, and it is really no surprise to us that he has her beautiful gift of making people laugh.

Sadly, Jane died in June 2008. I will always miss her dearly. She was an inspiration to me. She always found the energy to help others even at the height of her illness. I promised her I would remain a part of her family's life, something I love doing.

I grew up on an acreage property on the south side of Brisbane, the much-loved daughter in a family of three children. We had a wonderful, carefree childhood. As a little girl growing up with two sport-crazed brothers, I was often called on to make up the numbers in their games of tennis, football and cricket, but after I had a bat I'd find something else I'd rather be doing. Cricket just wasn't my thing. Matt says that with that attitude I would never have been allowed to play with him and Gary. It is a little ironic now, as I have probably watched as many cricket matches as the most devoted of fans, and certainly have grown to love and respect cricket culture.

I was 17 when I first met Matt at Silks restaurant at Albion Park in around January 1993. I was there with my parents and my brother, as my mum trained a few greyhounds back then and had a dog racing that night. Twenty-one-year-old Matt was there with his aunty Lorna, his brother Gary and his uncle Father Pat Jones, who was down from North Queensland visiting his family. My parents knew Father Pat very well, since he had supported them in Cairns when my brother was dying after a road accident.

Father Pat had taken a shine to me on the few times we had met before, and Mum sent me over to say hello. That night Matthew asked me if I'd like to come to the cricket some time, and I told him, no thanks, I didn't really like cricket. Matt still remembers what I was wearing that night – an electric-blue dress – and never lets me forget it.

A few weeks later, after returning from travelling with the Queensland team, he got my phone number from his uncle and called me up to ask me out for dinner. Back then he lived in a little unit on the north side of town with Gary. After dinner together we saw each other when we could, and became great friends. I was finishing Year 12 and Matt had just been selected to tour for the 1993 Ashes series, so we only talked once every few weeks, but it was enough to cement our relationship. He says he knew it had to be love when the country boy from Kingaroy was happy to drive from the north side of Brisbane over the Gateway Bridge, paying $1.20 each way, to pick me up on the south side of town – dating me cost him a fortune, he claims.

I wrote Matt letters when he was on that first tour, and sprayed them with my favourite perfume before posting them. Years later I still left little notes in his bag or sent packages of his favourite things over with Trevor Hohns or someone else I knew who might have been going on tour halfway through. I was working in those early years so I didn't travel a lot with him.

Matt was home for the births of all our children, which was a blessing, and we have a different story and memory for each of them. My first big overseas trip was with our eldest daughter, Grace, who was eight months at the time. Matt had been in South Africa for the World Cup for three months, then came home for a few days before heading off to the West Indies. Gracie and I didn't go to South Africa as she was only a few months old and had not been well, so Matt and I decided that the West Indies was it.

The boys were away a lot that year, so quite a few of the wives and children were going over. Most of us agreed to travel together and fly out of Sydney, but that meant flying through America and it wasn't that long after September 11. We knew the security would be tough with babies and prams, etc., but there was a warning out about the bird flu throughout Asia so we thought America was the best way to go. I think the flight went from Brisbane to Sydney to LA to Miami to Santo Domingo and finally Barbados. Sometimes when I say to Matt, 'I feel tired today,' he says to me, 'I have never seen you look more tired than when I met you and Gracie in Barbados.' The West Indians were never short on a party and when we arrived at the hotel they partied all night long. How we got Grace to sleep I will never know. But it was a wonderful trip and a beautiful place to experience, and the people were very welcoming.

On the way home we made it to LA but then there were problems with our flight out. It had been due to leave at 10 p.m., but we waited until 4 a.m. and it still hadn't left. The kids were given little cardboard boxes to sleep in. We got buses to a hotel in LA for a few hours sleep and had to be back at the airport at 8 a.m. to get our flight the next day. By the time we arrived in Sydney we had missed our flight home to Brisbane, so ended up in a Sydney hotel overnight. Even though it was probably the hardest trip I'd made over all the years, it didn't deter me from jumping at the chance to travel again, even when we had three kids, so we could be together as a family wherever the Australian team was playing.

Matt started playing in an era when cricket time was considered work time and there was not a lot of post-match mingling with the families. But that changed when Steve Waugh became captain, and we all enjoyed being more of a part of things, seeing the players straight after a Test win and being able to celebrate with them. Just as Matt considers himself fortunate to have played with such a great group of players, I feel the same about their wives. I remember being very nervous as a 20-year-old, mixing with the likes of Lynette Waugh, Sue Porter (Mark Waugh's former partner), Helen Healy and Steff Slater. But they were all great, and as Matt's relationship with Steve Waugh grew, so too did my bond with Lynette. She is great at picking up the phone and calling when she senses things aren't going too well, because she knows the pressure that can quickly descend upon the family unit. The most obvious question – 'Gee, Matt's under pressure, are you worried he might get dropped?' – never actually gets mentioned. You talk around it, but it doesn't matter because you both know what the call means. It's about support.

Something Lynette said proved the catalyst for my decision to make an impromptu return to England for the last Ashes Test at the Oval in 2005. She told me, 'Always remember you are a wife as well as a mother.' It was a reminder that, for all your important duties at home with the children, there were times when you might be needed on the road by your partner even more. When Stephen retired, Lynette told me, 'I had a lot of support and didn't always use it and I have some regrets – I don't want you to have those regrets.' Her words struck a chord with me. Near the end of the 2005 tour, Matt was struggling and I wanted to be with him. On the phone he was saying, 'Everything's great . . . I'm fine.' But I knew it wasn't. I was there when he started. I intended to be there if it ended.

I wanted to surprise him, but given what he was going through, it almost broke my heart to say I was off to Stradbroke Island for a couple of days and might be difficult to contact by phone. For once it was Matt and not one of his fish who swallowed the bait. He was totally shocked to receive an early-morning knock on the door and find me standing before him with our newborn baby, Joshua. I was bleary-eyed but so happy I'd made the trip.

As low-key as I'd tried to be, my arrival caused waves almost as soon as I reached the hotel. Sue Langer was so shocked to see me she started screaming in the breakfast room, and Adam and Mel Gilchrist looked as if they had seen a ghost – only a few weeks earlier they'd farewelled me from the tour. Sue and I were together when Matt and Justin had opened together for the first time at the Oval four years before, and here we were again. The boys had been through a lot since then, and Sue and I had become very close as well.

The funny thing was that even though I flew from one side of the world to the other to be with Matt, I never actually saw him make his century in that tour. When I went to the ground with Josh in a sling, I had beer cans raining down around me and it was baking in the sun. I had done my job as a wife – now it was time to be a mum again. I left, made sure Josh was happy and went shopping. The first I knew about Matt scoring a century was when texts arrived from Mel Gilchrist saying, *WOW . . . well done.*

The close partnership I formed with Sue Langer (or The Sue Langers, as Grace likes to call her) continues to this day. Rarely a week goes by that we don't talk, and to have that bond when your husbands have also shared a unique journey is so lovely. I'm so proud to be godmother to adorable little Grace Langer, it is one of the most blessed treasures a friend can bestow upon you.

Matt never brought his cricket home with him. I remember one day he got out for a low score on just about the last ball of the day for Queensland, and I wondered what sort of mood he'd be in when he got home. But he was fine. And there were never any hard feelings against someone who'd taken his spot. We had a party at our place one Valentine's Day and as we partied, Simon Katich, who had just taken Matt's place, scored a century. Straightaway Matt texted Simon a *Well done* message. If Matt did have a problem, he would always confront that person face-to-face and give them a chance to tell their side of the story.

The Matt I see is different to the one the cricket world may know. People say, 'Oh, he's fiery, isn't he?' I have trouble relating to that because at home he barely ever raises his voice. In fact, the one time he did, I think Grace and I both started crying out of shock. Matt can certainly be a softie where the kids are concerned. When he goes out boating for the day it doesn't matter what sort of colour his guests turn as our boat churns through the ocean – he never turns back. Yet I remember one day when he went out in choppy weather and Grace started to get upset pretty soon after they left port. He turned to her and said, 'Do you want to turn back, darling?' She nodded, and they did.

His adventurous instincts have definitely been passed on. Sometimes at Stradbroke Island, Matt and the kids swim miles out from shore and Grace will suddenly appear and say, 'Mum, we just swam over a bull shark!' – not the sort of comment Mum likes to hear. Matt and Grace are very much alike and read each other well. Matt tells the story of facing up in a Test match in Cairns and realising he could hear Grace crying as the bowler was running in to bowl. She'd just taken a tiny tumble down the terraces and his paternal radar picked up her cry, even though he was in full combat mode.

Matt and I have a lot to thank our parents for. Laurie and Moya Hayden invested so much time in Matt and Gary, and every bit of it was worthwhile. They learnt many precious skills: snorkelling, boating, hunting, fishing, shooting, cooking, farming, woodwork – you name it, they were taught it. And taught it well. Moya always says, 'If you're going to do something, don't be half-hearted.' Matt still says that to the kids when they make their beds.

When I look up at the giant surrounds of the MCG, I'm amazed that anyone could be brave enough to overcome the aura of the place and do well, but there is no doubt Moya's theatrical side has given Matt a love of the big stage, the big event, the big opponent. It was always easier for him to get motivated against the major opponents than the lesser sides.

Matt is a beautiful man who gives so much love, support and kindness. People who meet him often feel like they can tell him anything, and sometimes they do! I don't know if it's his big blue eyes or the huge cuddly bear hugs he greets everyone with. I love him with all my heart, and feel so blessed to have such a loving husband and three beautiful children.

When I think back on our journey through cricket, I am so thankful for everything we have experienced. Even though the kids were young and might not remember a lot of it, they have learnt some great skills as a result of their experiences: things like being able to sleep anywhere and just going with the flow.

It was a really great life. It still is.

Key Innings

Playing for the Bulls: first class debut

QUEENSLAND VS. SOUTH AUSTRALIA

At Brisbane Cricket Ground, Woolloongabba, Brisbane, 1, 2, 3, 4 November 1991. Match drawn.
Toss: South Australia. **First-Class Match Debut:** ML Hayden. **Umpires:** MD Ralston, CD Timmins.

Queensland

TJ Barsby	c Siddons b Hickey	4	c Nielsen b Hickey	12
ML Hayden	c Bishop b Faull	149	lbw b Scuderi	5
DM Wellham	c Nielsen b Scuderi	80	not out	63
AR Border	run out (Faull)	196	not out	39
SG Law	c Blewett b Scuderi	64	c Hilditch b Hickey	22
GM Ritchie	not out	53	c Faull b George	6
†IA Healy			b George	48
PL Taylor			run out (George/Nielsen)	12
CJ McDermott				
GJ Rowell				
*CG Rackemann				
	l-b 16, n-b 26	42	l-b 4, n-b 22, w 6	32
	(139.3 overs, 527 mins) (5 wickets dec)	**588**	**(55 overs, 222 minutes)**	**239**
	Fall: 8 217 275 432 588		Fall: 14 38 47 91 101 148	

Bowling: First Innings – Hickey 28.3-1-129-1; Scuderi 33-6-143-2; George 20-3-72-0; May 43-5-151-0; Faull 4-1-22-1; Hookes 9-2-33-0; Blewett 2-0-22-0. Second Innings – Hickey 15-1-73-2; Scuderi 17-7-40-1; George 10-0-57-2; May 5-1-30-0; Blewett 7-2-23-0; Hilditch 1-0-12-0.

South Australia

GS Blewett	c Border b Rowell	18
AMJ Hilditch	lbw b McDermott	4
MP Faull	run out (Wellham)	51
JD Siddons	c Border b McDermott	149
GA Bishop	c Rackemann b McDermott	64
DW Hookes	c Wellham b Rackemann	26
TJ Nielsen	c Healy b McDermott	88
JC Scuderi	c Law b McDermott	37
TBA May	lbw b McDermott	33
DJ Hickey	run out (Wellham)	6
SP George	not out	0
	b 1, l-b 16, n-b 60, w 1	78
	(171.1 overs, 674 mins)	**554**
	Fall: 9 29 178 311 361 367 441 533 554 554	

Bowling: First Innings – McDermott 45-7-150-6; Rowell 31-8-89-1; Rackemann 34-5-124-1; Taylor 42.1-14-122-0; Border 19-6-52-0.

Playing for Australia: Test debut

SOUTH AFRICA VS. AUSTRALIA, FIRST TEST (TEST 1252)

At New Wanderers Stadium, Johannesburg, 4, 5, 6, 7, 8 March 1994. South Africa won by 197 runs.
Toss: South Africa. **Player of the Match:** WJ Cronje. **Umpires:** SB Lambson and DR Shepherd.

South Africa

AC Hudson	c Healy b McDermott	17	b Warne	60
G Kirsten	b Hughes	47	c Hughes b May	35
WJ Cronje	c Border b SR Waugh	21	c SR Waugh b Hughes	122
*KC Wessels	c Hayden b Hughes	18	c Border b Warne	50
PN Kirsten	b May	12	c Boon b May	53
JN Rhodes	c ME Waugh b McDermott	69	c Healy b SR Waugh	14
BM McMillan	c Boon b May	0	b Warne	24
†DJ Richardson	lbw b Warne	31	c Border b Warne	20
CR Matthews	c Boon b Hughes	6	not out	31
PS de Villiers	b McDermott	16	b McDermott	4
AA Donald	not out	0	not out	15
	b 1, l-b 10, n-b 3	14	b 13, l-b 4, n-b 5	22
	(80.2 overs, 323 mins)	**251**	**(159.5 overs, 618 mins) (9 wickets dec)**	**450**
	Fall: 21 70 103 116 126 126 194 203 249 251		Fall: 76 123 258 289 324 343 366 403 406	

Bowling: First Innings – McDermott 15.2-3-63-3; Hughes 20-6-59-3; May 22-5-62-2; SR Waugh 9-2-14-1; Warne 14-4-42-1. Second Innings – McDermott 35-3-112-1; Hughes 25-5-86-1; May 39-11-107-2; SR Waugh 10-3-28-1; ME Waugh 6-2-14-0; Warne 44.5-14-86-4.

Australia

MJ Slater	c Hudson b de Villiers	26	b de Villiers	41
ML Hayden	c Richardson b Donald	15	b de Villiers	5
DC Boon	c de Villiers b Donald	17	b Matthews	83
ME Waugh	run out	42	c Richardson b Donald	28
*AR Border	run out	34	c G Kirsten b McMillan	14
SR Waugh	not out	45	c Richardson b Matthews	0
†IA Healy	b Matthews	11	c & b Donald	30
MG Hughes	c G Kirsten b McMillan	7	not out	26
SK Warne	lbw b Matthews	15	lbw b McMillan	1
CJ McDermott	lbw b Donald	31	b McMillan	10
TBA May	lbw b de Villiers	2	c G Kirsten b Cronje	11
	b 1, l-b 1, n-b 1	3	l-b 5, n-b 2	7
	(67.3 overs, 303 mins)	**248**	**(96.3 overs)**	**256**
	Fall: 35 56 70 136 142 169 170 201 245 248		Fall: 18 95 136 164 164 191 219 225 235 256	

Bowling: First Innings – Donald 19-0-86-3; de Villiers 19.3-1-74-2; McMillan 14-3-46-1; Matthews 15-4-40-2. Second Innings – Donald 23-3-71-2; de Villiers 30-11-70-2; McMillan 19-2-61-3; Matthews 20-6-42-2; G Kirsten 4-0-7-0; Cronje 0.3-0-0-1.

Frank Worrell Trophy: First Test century

AUSTRALIA VS. WEST INDIES, FOURTH TEST (TEST 1352)

At Adelaide Oval, Adelaide, 25, 26, 27, 28 January 1997. Australian won by an innings and 183 runs.
Toss: West Indies. **Player of the Match:** MG Bevan. **Umpires:** SG Randell and DR Shepherd.

West Indies

SL Campbell	c Healy b McGrath	0	c Taylor b Bevan	24
AFG Griffith	lbw b Bichel	13	c SR Waugh b McGrath	1
S Chanderpaul	c Taylor b Warne	20	c Taylor b Bevan	8
BC Lara	c Blewett b Warne	9	c Healy b Warne	78
CL Hooper	c ME Waugh b McGrath	17	lbw b Warne	45
JC Adams	c & b Warne	10	c ME Waugh b Bevan	0
†JR Murray	c Blewett b Bevan	34	c Taylor b Bevan	25
IR Bishop	c Healy b Bevan	1	c Bevan b Warne	0
*CA Walsh	c Healy b Bevan	2	c SR Waugh b Bevan	1
CE Cuffy	c Healy b Bevan	2	not out	3
PIC Thompson	not out	10	c Hayden b Bevan	6
	b 4, l-b 1, n-b 9	14	b 2, l-b 5, n-b 6	13
	(47.5 overs, 195 mins)	**130**	**(69.4 overs, 260 mins)**	**204**
	Fall: 11 22 45 58 72 113 117 117 119 130		Fall: 6 22 42 138 145 154 181 192 196 204	

Bowling: First Innings – McGrath 12-4-21-2; Bichel 10-1-31-1; Bevan 9.5-2-31-4; Warne 16-4-42-3. Second Innings – McGrath 17-4-31-1; Bichel 8-4-16-0; Bevan 22.4-3-82-6; Warne 20-4-68-3; Blewett 2-2-0-0.

Australia

*MA Taylor	lbw b Bishop	11
ML Hayden	st Murray b Hooper	125
JL Langer	c Murray b Cuffy	19
ME Waugh	c Murray b Hooper	82
SR Waugh	c Hooper b Chanderpaul	26
GS Blewett	b Cuffy	99
MG Bevan	not out	85
†IA Healy	c Lara b Thompson	12
SK Warne	c Hooper b Bishop	9
AJ Bichel	c Lara b Walsh	7
GD McGrath	b Walsh	1
	b 2, l-b 15, w 4, n-b 20	41
	(162.3 overs, 685 mins)	**517**
	Fall: 35 78 242 288 288 453 475 494 507 517	

Bowling: First Innings – Walsh 37.3-6-101-2; Bishop 34-6-92-2; Cuffy 33-4-116-2; Thompson 16-0-80-1; Hooper 31-7-86-2; Adams 8-0-23-0; Chanderpaul 3-1-2-1.

Border-Gavaskar Trophy: taking on Harbhajan Singh

INDIA VS. AUSTRALIA, FIRST TEST (TEST 1531)

At Wankhede Stadium, Mumbai, 27, 28 February, 1 March 2001. Australia won by 10 wickets.
Toss: Australia. **Player of the Match:** AC Gilchrist. **Umpires:** DR Shepherd and S Venkataraghavan.

India

SS Das	c Hayden b Gillespie	14	c SR Waugh b Gillespie	7
S Ramesh	c Gilchrist b McGrath	2	c Ponting b McGrath	44
R Dravid	c Gilchrist b Fleming	9	b Warne	39
SR Tendulkar	c Gilchrist b McGrath	76	c Ponting b ME Waugh	65
*SC Ganguly	c Hayden b Warne	8	run out (Slater/Warne)	1
VVS Laxman	c Ponting b McGrath	20	c Gilchrist b ME Waugh	12
†NR Mongia	not out	26	c Gilchrist b Gillespie	28
AB Agarkar	c & b Warne	0	b ME Waugh	0
J Srinath	c ME Waugh b Warne	12	b McGrath	0
Harbhajan Singh	c SR Waugh b Warne	0	not out	17
RL Sanghvi	c Gilchrist b Gillespie	2	b Gillespie	0
	b 2, l-b 3, w 1, n-b 1	7	b 4, l-b 1, n-b 1	6
	(71.3 overs)	**176**	**(94.1 overs)**	**219**
	Fall: 7 25 31 55 130 139 140 165 166 176		Fall: 33 57 58* 154 156 174 174 193 210 216 219	

Bowling: First Innings – McGrath 19-13-19-3; Fleming 15-3-55-1; Gillespie 15.3-4-50-2; Warne 22-7-47-4. Second Innings – McGrath 17.1-9-25-2; Fleming 15-1-44-0; Warne 28-11-60-1; Gillespie 19-8-45-3; ME Waugh 15-5-40-3.

Australia

MJ Slater	b Agarkar	10	not out	19
ML Hayden	c Mongia b Srinath	119	not out	28
JL Langer	c Dravid b Harbhajan Singh	19		
ME Waugh	c Ganguly b Harbhajan Singh	0		
*SR Waugh	c Dravid b Sanghvi	15		
RT Ponting	c Das b Harbhajan Singh	0		
†AC Gilchrist	st Mongia b Harbhajan Singh	122		
SK Warne	c Tendulkar b Sanghvi	39		
JN Gillespie	c Mongia b Srinath	0		
DW Fleming	c Srinath b Agarkar	6		
GD McGrath	not out	0		
	b 9, l-b 7, n-b 3	19		0
	(73.2 overs)	**349**	**(7 overs, 25 mins)**	**47**
	Fall: 21 71 71 98 99 296 326 327 349 349			

Bowling: First Innings – Srinath 16-3-60-2; Agarkar 12-1-50-2; Harbhajan Singh 28-3-121-4; Sanghvi 10.2-2-67-2; Tendulkar 7-1-35-0. Second Innings – Srinath 2-0-17-0; Agarkar 1-0-8-0; Harbhajan Singh 2-0-11-0; Sanghvi 2-1-11-0.

Border-Gavaskar Trophy: a double ton

INDIA VS. AUSTRALIA, THIRD TEST (TEST 1539)

At MA Chidambaram Stadium, Chennai, 18, 19, 20, 21, 22 March 2001. India won by two wickets.
Toss: Australia. **Player of the Match:** Harbhajan Singh and ML Hayden. **Umpires:** AV Jayaprakash and RE Koertzen.

Australia

MJ Slater	c Laxman b Khan	4	c Laxman b Harbhajan Singh	48
ML Hayden	c Ganguly b Harbhajan Singh	203	c Khan b Kulkarni	35
JL Langer	c Dravid b Harbhajan Singh	35	c Laxman b Bahutule	21
ME Waugh	c sub (HK Badani) b Bahutule	70	c Dravid b Harbhajan Singh	57
*SR Waugh	handled the ball	47	c Das b Harbhajan Singh	47
RT Ponting	st Dighe b Harbhajan Singh	0	c Dravid b Harbhajan Singh	11
†AC Gilchrist	lbw b Harbhajan Singh	1	lbw b Harbhajan Singh	1
SK Warne	c Das b Harbhajan Singh	0	lbw b Harbhajan Singh	11
JN Gillespie	c Ganguly b Harbhajan Singh	0	c Dravid b Harbhajan Singh	2
CR Miller	c Bahutule b Harbhajan Singh	0	lbw b Harbhajan Singh	2
GD McGrath	not out	3	not out	11
	b 8, l-b 10, n-b 10	28	b 8, l-b 6, n-b 4	18
	(115.2 overs, 474 mins)	**391**	**(97.5 overs, 373 mins)**	**264**
	Fall: 4 67 217 340 340 344 374 376 385 391		Fall: 82 84 93 141 193 211 241 246 251 264	

Bowling: First Innings – Khan 15-5-57-1; Ganguly 2-1-11-0; Harbhajan Singh 38.2-6-133-7; Kulkarni 23-5-67-0; Bahutule 21-3-70-1; Tendulkar 16-1-35-0. Second Innings – Khan 4-0-13-0; Ganguly 1-0-8-0; Harbhajan Singh 41.5-20-84-8; Kulkarni 30-11-70-1; Tendulkar 12-0-43-0; Bahutule 9-0-32-1.

India

SS Das	lbw b McGrath	84	c & b McGrath	9
S Ramesh	c Ponting b Warne	61	run out (Ponting/Gilchrist)	25
VVS Laxman	c ME Waugh b McGrath	65	c ME Waugh b Miller	66
SR Tendulkar	c Gilchrist b Gillespie	126	c ME Waugh b Gillespie	17
*SC Ganguly	c Gilchrist b McGrath	22	c ME Waugh b Gillespie	4
R Dravid	c Gilchrist b Gillespie	81	c SR Waugh b Miller	4
†SS Dighe	lbw b Warne	4	not out	22
SV Bahutule	not out	21	c Warne b Miller	0
Z Khan	c & b Miller	4	c ME Waugh b McGrath	0
Harbhajan Singh	c ME Waugh b Miller	2	not out	3
NM Kulkarni	lbw b Miller	4		
	b 19 l-b 2, w 1, n-b 5	27	l-b 3, n-b 2	5
	(165 overs, 697 mins)	**501**	**(41.1 overs, 219 mins)**	**155**
	Fall: 123 211 237 284 453 468 470 475 477 501		Fall: 18 76 101 117 122 135 135 151	

Bowling: First Innings – McGrath 36-15-75-3; Gillespie 35-11-88-2; Miller 46-6-160-3; Warne 42-7-140-2; Ponting 2-1-2-0; ME Waugh 3-0-8-0; Hayden 1-0-7-0. Second Innings – McGrath 11.1-3-21-2; Gillespie 15-2-49-2; Miller 9-1-41-3; Warne 6-0-41-0.

South Africa in Australia: man of the series

AUSTRALIA VS. SOUTH AFRICA, THIRD TEST (TEST 1582)

At Sydney Cricket Ground, Sydney, 2, 3, 4, 5 January 2002. Australia won by 10 wickets.
Toss: Australia. **Player of the Match:** ML Hayden and JL Langer. **Umpires:** DJ Harper and DR Shepherd.

Australia

JL Langer	c McKenzie b Boje	126	not out	30
ML Hayden	c Kallis b Pollock	105	not out	21
RT Ponting	run out (Ontong/Boucher)	14		
ME Waugh	c Boucher b Donald	19		
*SR Waugh	b Pollock	30		
DR Martyn	c McKenzie b Boje	117		
†AC Gilchrist	c Boucher b Kallis	34		
SK Warne	b Pollock	37		
B Lee	b Boje	29		
SCG MacGill	c Henderson b Boje	20		
GD McGrath	not out	1		
	b 4, l-b 8, w 1, n-b 9	22	l-b 2, n-b 1	3
	(144.2 overs, 554 mins)	**554**	**(10.1 overs, 44 mins)**	**54**
	Fall: 219 247 253 302 308 356 439 502 542 554			

Bowling: First Innings – Donald 31-6-119-1; Pollock 37-11-109-3; Kallis 22-1-129-1; Henderson 27-3-112-0; Boje 25.2-6-63-4; Ontong 2-0-10-0. Second Innings – Donald 3-0-12-0; Pollock 3-1-11-0; Boje 2.1-0-15-0; Henderson 2-0-14-0.

South Africa

HH Gibbs	c ME Waugh b MacGill	32	b Lee	10
G Kirsten	c Ponting b McGrath	18	b MacGill	153
HH Dippenaar	b McGrath	3	c Ponting b MacGill	74
JH Kallis	c Gilchrist b MacGill	4	c Gilchrist b Warne	34
ND McKenzie	b Warne	20	c MacGill b Lee	38
JL Ontong	lbw b Warne	9	lbw b Warne	32
†MV Boucher	c Ponting b Warne	35	c Gilchrist b McGrath	27
*SM Pollock	c Martyn b McGrath	6	not out	61
N Boje	run out (Langer/McGrath)	7	b MacGill	1
CW Henderson	c McGrath b MacGill	9	b MacGill	2
AA Donald	not out	2	c Lee b Warne	2
	l-b 8, n-b 1	9	b 8, l-b 7, n-b 3	18
	(62.2 overs, 241 mins)	**154**	**(141.5 overs, 525 mins)**	**452**
	Fall: 37 43 56 77 93 98 111 121 148 154		Fall: 17 166 211 282 356 372 392 393 403 452	

Bowling: First Innings – McGrath 17-6-35-3; Lee 6-2-13-0; MacGill 20.2-6-51-3; Warne 19-5-47-3. Second Innings – McGrath 28-5-95-1; Warne 42.5-8-132-3; Lee 19-5-62-2; MacGill 45-13-123-4; ME Waugh 6-1-14-0; Ponting 1-0-11-0.

Sharjah: taking on Shoaib Akhtar

AUSTRALIA VS. PAKISTAN, SECOND TEST (TEST 1617)

At Sharjah Cricket Association Stadium, 11, 12 October 2002. Australia won by an innings and 198 runs.
Toss: Pakistan. **Player of the Match:** ML Hayden. **Umpires:** SA Bucknor and S Venkataraghavan.
Close of play: First day, Australia (1) 191/4 (Hayden 74, Martyn 19); Second day, Pakistan (2) 53 – end of match.

Pakistan

Imran Nazir	c Warne b McGrath	0	c Gilchrist b Warne	16
Taufeeq Umar	b Lee	0	run out (Ponting/McGrath)	0
Abdul Razzaq	c Martyn b Warne	21	retired hurt	4
Younis Khan	c Bichel b McGrath	5	lbw b McGrath	0
Misbah-ul-Haq	c ME Waugh b Bichel	2	c SR Waugh b Bichel	12
Faisal Iqbal	lbw b Warne	4	c ME Waugh b Warne	7
†Rashid Latif	not out	4	c ME Waugh b Bichel	0
Saqlain Mushtaq	lbw b Warne	0	c Warne b Lee	9
Shoaib Akhtar	c Gilchrist b Bichel	1	c SR Waugh b Warne	2
*Waqar Younis	lbw b Warne	0	lbw b Warne	0
Danish Kaneria	b Lee	8	not out	1
	b 8, l-b 2, n-b 4	14	n-b 2	2
	(31.5 overs, 148 mins)	**59**	**(24.5 overs, 121 mins)**	**53**
	Fall: 0 1 8 23 41 46 46 49 50 59		Fall: 0 11* 13 32 34 36 50 52 52 53	

Bowling: First Innings – McGrath 7-4-10-2; Lee 7.5-1-15-2; Bichel 6-2-13-2; Warne 11-4-11-4. Second Innings – McGrath 6-2-5-1; Lee 5-2-16-1; Bichel 7-1-19-2; Warne 6.5-2-13-4.

Australia

JL Langer	run out (Danish Kaneria)	37
ML Hayden	c Imran Nazir b Saqlain Mushtaq	119
RT Ponting	lbw b Danish Kaneria	44
ME Waugh	lbw b Saqlain Mushtaq	2
*SR Waugh	c sub (Imran Farhat) b Saqlain Mushtaq	0
DR Martyn	c Taufeeq Umar b Abdul Razzaq	34
†AC Gilchrist	c Taufeeq Umar b Shoaib Akhtar	17
SK Warne	c Younis Khan b Saqlain Mushtaq	19
B Lee	lbw b Abdul Razzaq	12
AJ Bichel	not out	2
GD McGrath	lbw b Abdul Razzaq	0
	b 15, l-b 7, n-b 2	24
	(92.1 overs, 438 mins)	**310**
	Fall: 55 145 148 148 224 252 285 304 310 310	

Bowling: First Innings – Waqar Younis 8-2-25-0; Shoaib Akhtar 14-3-42-1; Danish Kaneria 26-2-116-1; Abdul Razzaq 10.1-3-22-3; Saqlain Mushtaq 34-2-83-4.

A Pinnacle in Perth: Test record high score

50 PARTNERSHIP HAYDEN - GILCHRIST IN 31 MIN
100 " " " " 65 "
150 " " " " 94 "

200 PARTNERSHIP HAYDEN/GILCHRIST IN 119 MIN

CRICKET AUSTRALIA

LUNCH SCORES: 1-93 - HAYDEN - 31, PONTING - 31 | 5-524 - HAYDEN - 271, GILCHRIST - 13

TEA SCORES: 3-203 - HAYDEN - 76, WAUGH - 4 | 5-731 - HAYDEN - 376, GILCHRIST - 113

STUMPS SCORES: 3-372 - HAYDEN - 183, WAUGH - 61

MATCH AUSTRALIA v ZIMBABWE

AT W.A.C.A. PERTH ON 9-13 OCTOBER 2003

1ST INNINGS OF AUSTRALIA

COMPETITION FIRST TEST. DATE 9 OCTOBER / 10 "

UMPIRES P. WILLEY - S. VENKAT

3rd UMP. S. DAVIS REF VISWANATH

CAPTAINS S. WAUGH - H. STREAK

WKT-KEEPERS A. GILCHRIST - T. TAIBU

12th MEN B. WILLIAMS -

TOSS WON BY ZIMBABWE

TEAM BATTING FIRST AUSTRALIA

SCORERS C. BULL - S. WHEELER

TIME IN	TIME OUT	MINS	50	100	150		BATSMEN	RUNS AS SCORED	HOW OUT	BOWLER	RUNS	BALLS	4's	6's
10.00	10.42	42				1	LANGER. J.L	4111444241	BOWLED	ERVINE	26	38	5	-
10.00	3.04	622	164	303	243	2	HAYDEN. M.L	[illegible]	C CARLISLE	GRIPPER	380	438	38	11
10.44	12.35	91				3	PONTING. R.T	41414 4224111 42	LBW	ERVINE	37	65	6	-
12.57	2.33	96	89			4	MARTYN. D.R	34442244121444241421	C WISHART	GRIPPER	53	75	9	-
2.35	10.39	182	133			5	WAUGH. S.R	[illegible]	C & B	ERVINE	78	124	10	1
10.41	11.42	61				6	LEHMANN. D.S	32614211441	C & B	ERVINE	30	48	3	1
11.44	3.04	140	63	121		7	GILCHRIST. A.C	[illegible]	NOT OUT		113	95	12	4
						8								
						9								
						10								
						11								
						12	HAYDEN. (CONT'D)	[illegible]						

BYES 4 LEG-BYES 442 WIDES 1 NO BALLS 111 TOTAL SUNDRIES 18

	1	2	3	4	5	6	7	8	9	10
FALL OF WICKET	43	102	199	406	502	735				
BATSMEN OUT	1	3	4	5	6	2				
BATSMEN N.O.	2 (16)	2 (33)	2 (76)	2 (200)	2 (266)	7 (113)				
PARTNERSHIP	43	59	97	207	96	233				
MINS/BALLS	42	91	96	182	61	140				

TOTAL 6/735 DECL'D

INNINGS TIME 622 MINS

HOURS	1	2	3	4	5	6	7	8	9	10	11
OVERS	13	15	13	15	15	14	14	14	13	14	
RUNS	54	39	55	55	39	101	63	96	89	106	

PENALTY EXTRAS: HAYDEN 200 / 250 (MIN 412 / 463); 292 / 323; 263 / 297; 300 / 350 (MIN 524 / 588); 364 / 404; 338

50 PARTNERSHIP HAYDEN - PONTING IN 76 MIN
50 " " - MARTYN " 49 "
50 " " - WAUGH " 75 "
100 " " " " 98 "
150 " " " " 127 "

200 PARTNERSHIP HAYDEN - WAUGH IN 173 MIN
50 " " - LEHMANN " 34 "

The Ashes 2005: changing tactics in a difficult series

ENGLAND VS. AUSTRALIA, FIFTH TEST (TEST 1763)

At Kennington Oval, London, 8, 9, 10, 11, 12 September 2005. Match drawn.
Toss: England. **Player of the Match:** KP Pietersen. **Umpires:** BF Bowden and RE Koertzen.

England

ME Trescothick	c Hayden b Warne	43	lbw b Warne	33
AJ Strauss	c Katich b Warne	129	c Katich b Warne	1
*MP Vaughan	c Clarke b Warne	11	c Gilchrist b McGrath	45
IR Bell	lbw b Warne	0	c Warne b McGrath	0
KP Pietersen	b Warne	14	b McGrath	158
A Flintoff	c Warne b McGrath	72	c & b Warne	8
PD Collingwood	lbw b Tait	7	c Ponting b Warne	10
†GO Jones	b Lee	25	b Tait	1
AF Giles	lbw b Warne	32	b Warne	59
MJ Hoggard	c Martyn b McGrath	2	not out	4
SJ Harmison	not out	20	c Hayden b Warne	0
	b 4, l-b 6, w 1, n-b 7	18	b 4, w 7, n-b 5	16
	(105.3 overs, 471 mins)	**373**	**91.3 overs, 432 mins)**	**335**
	Fall: 82 102 104 131 274 289 297 325 345 373		Fall: 2 67 67 109 126 186 199 308 335 335	

Bowling: First Innings – McGrath 27-5-72-2; Lee 23-3-94-1; Tait 15-1-61-1; Warne 37.3-5-122-6; Katich 3-0-14-0. Second Innings – McGrath 26-3-85-3; Lee 20-4-88-0; Warne 38.3-3-124-6; Clarke 2-0-6-0; Tait 5-0-28-1.

Australia

JL Langer	b Harmison	105	not out	0
ML Hayden	lbw b Flintoff	138	not out	0
*RT Ponting	c Strauss b Flintoff	35		
DR Martyn	c Collingwood b Flintoff	10		
MJ Clarke	lbw b Hoggard	25		
SM Katich	lbw b Flintoff	1		
†AC Gilchrist	lbw b Hoggard	23		
SK Warne	c Vaughan b Flintoff	0		
B Lee	c Giles b Hoggard	6		
GD McGrath	c Strauss b Hoggard	0		
SW Tait	not out	1		
	b 4, l-b 8, w 2, n-b 9	23	l-b 4	4
	(107.1 overs, 494 mins)	**367**	**0.4 overs, 3 mins)**	**4**
	Fall: 185 264 281 323 329 356 359 363 363 367			

Bowling: First Innings – Harmison 22-2-87-1; Hoggard 24.1-2-97-4; Flintoff 34-10-78-5; Giles 23-1-76-0; Collingwood 4-0-17-0. Second Innings – Harmison 0.4-0-0-0.

The Ashes 2006–07: an epic win

AUSTRALIA VS. ENGLAND, SECOND TEST (TEST 1819)

At Adelaide Oval, Adelaide, 1, 2, 3, 4, 5 December 2006. Australia won by six wickets.
Toss: England. **Player of the Match:** RT Ponting. **Umpires:** SA Bucknor and RE Koertzen.

England

AJ Strauss	c Martyn b Clark	14	c Hussey b Warne	34
AN Cook	c Gilchrist b Clark	27	c Gilchrist b Clark	9
IR Bell	c & b Lee	60	run out (Clarke/Warne)	26
PD Collingwood	c Gilchrist b Clark	206	not out	22
KP Pietersen	run out (Ponting)	158	b Warne	2
*A Flintoff	not out	38	c Gilchrist b Lee	2
†GO Jones	c Martyn b Warne	1	c Hayden b Lee	10
AF Giles	not out	27	c Hayden b Warne	0
MJ Hoggard			b Warne	4
SJ Harmison			lbw b McGrath	8
JM Anderson			lbw b McGrath	1
	l-b 10, w 2, n-b 8	20	b 3, l-b 5, w 1, n-b 2	11
	(168 overs, 707 mins) (6 wickets dec)	**551**	**(73 overs, 324 mins)**	**129**
	Fall: 32 45 158 468 489 491		Fall: 31 69 70 73 77 94 97 105 119 129	

Bowling: First Innings – Lee 34-1-139-1; McGrath 30-5-107-0; Clark 34-6-75-3; Warne 53-9-167-1; Clarke 17-2-53-0. Second Innings – Lee 18-3-35-2; McGrath 10-6-15-2; Warne 32-12-49-4; Clark 13-4-22-1.

Australia

JL Langer	c Pietersen b Flintoff	4	c Bell b Hoggard	7
ML Hayden	c Jones b Hoggard	12	c Collingwood b Flintoff	18
*RT Ponting	c Jones b Hoggard	142	c Strauss b Giles	49
DR Martyn	c Bell b Hoggard	11	c Strauss b Flintoff	5
MEK Hussey	b Hoggard	91	not out	61
MJ Clarke	c Giles b Hoggard	124	not out	21
†AC Gilchrist	c Bell b Giles	64		
SK Warne	lbw b Hoggard	43		
B Lee	not out	7		
SR Clark	b Hoggard	0		
GD McGrath	c Jones b Anderson	1		
	b 4, l-b 2, w l, n-b 7	14	b 2, l-b 2, w 1, n-b 2	7
	(165.3 overs, 718 mins)	**513**	**(32.5 overs, 161 mins)**	**168**
	Fall: 8 35 65 257 286 384 502 505 507 513		Fall: 14 33 116 121	

Bowling: First Innings – Hoggard 42-6-109-7; Flintoff 26-5-82-1; Harmison 25-5-96-0; Anderson 21.3-3-85-1; Giles 42-7-103-1; Pietersen 9-0-32-0. Second Innings – Hoggard 4-0-29-1; Flintoff 9-0-44-2; Giles 10-0-46-1; Harmison 4-0-15-0; Anderson 3.5-0-23-0; Pietersen 2-0-7-0.

The Ashes 2006–07: a memorable partnership

AUSTRALIA VS. ENGLAND, FOURTH TEST (TEST 1824)

At Melbourne Cricket Ground, Melbourne, 26, 27, 28 December 2006. Australia won by an innings and 99 runs.
Toss: England. **Player of the Match:** SK Warne. **Umpires:** Aleem Dar and RE Koertzen.

England

AJ Strauss	b Warne	50	c Gilchrist b Lee	31
AN Cook	c Gilchrist b Lee	11	b Clark	20
IR Bell	lbw b Clark	7	lbw b McGrath	2
PD Collingwood	c Ponting b Lee	28	c Langer b Lee	16
KP Pietersen	c Symonds b Warne	21	b Clark	1
*A Flintoff	c Warne b Clark	13	lbw b Clark	25
†CMW Read	c Ponting b Warne	3	not out	26
SI Mahmood	c Gilchrist b McGrath	0	lbw b Warne	0
SJ Harmison	c Clarke b Warne	7	lbw b Warne	4
MS Panesar	c Symonds b Warne	4	c Clarke b Lee	14
MJ Hoggard	not out	9	b Lee	5
	b 2, l-b 1, n-b 3	6	l-b 12, w 1, n-b 4	17
	(74.2 overs, 324 mins)	**159**	**(65.5 overs, 301 mins)**	**161**
	Fall: 23 44 101 101 122 135 136 145 146 159		Fall: 41 48 49 75 90 108 109 127 146 161	

Bowling: First Innings – Lee 13-4-36-2; McGrath 20-8-37-1; Clark 17-6-27-2; Symonds 7-2-17-0; Warne 17.2-4-39-5. Second Innings – Lee 18.5-6-47-4; McGrath 12-2-26-1; Clark 16-6-30-3; Warne 19-3-46-2.

Australia

JL Langer	c Read b Flintoff	27
ML Hayden	c Read b Mahmood	153
B Lee	c Read b Flintoff	0
*RT Ponting	c Cook b Flintoff	7
MEK Hussey	b Hoggard	6
MJ Clarke	c Read b Harmison	5
A Symonds	c Read b Harmison	156
†AC Gilchrist	c Collingwood b Mahmood	1
SK Warne	not out	40
SR Clark	c Read b Mahmood	8
GD McGrath	c Bell b Mahmood	0
	l-b 6, w 1, n-b 9	16
	(108.3 overs, 505 mins)	**419**
	Fall: 44 44 62 79 84 363 365 383 417 419	

Bowling: First Innings – Hoggard 21-6-82-1; Flintoff 22-1-77-3; Harmison 28-6-69-2; Mahmood 21.3-1-100-4; Panesar 12-1-52-0; Collingwood 3-0-20-0; Pietersen 1-0-13-0.

The Ashes 2006–07: farewell to Alfie, Pigeon, Warnie and Buck

AUSTRALIA VS. ENGLAND, FIFTH TEST (TEST 1826)

At Sydney Cricket Ground, Sydney, 2, 3, 4, 5 January 2007. Australia won by 10 wickets.
Toss: England. **Player of the Match:** SR Clark. **Umpires:** Aleem Dar and BF Bowden.

England

AJ Strauss	c Gilchrist b Lee	29	lbw b Clark	24
AN Cook	c Gilchrist b Clark	20	c Gilchrist b Lee	4
IR Bell	b McGrath	71	c Gilchrist b Lee	28
KP Pietersen	c Hussey b McGrath	41	c Gilchrist b McGrath	29
PD Collingwood	c Gilchrist b McGrath	27	c Hayden b Clark	17
*A Flintoff	c Gilchrist b Clark	89	st Gilchrist b Warne	7
†CMW Read	c Gilchrist b Lee	2	c Ponting b Lee	4
SI Mahmood	c Hayden b Lee	0	b McGrath	4
SJ Harmison	lbw b Clark	2	not out	16
MS Panesar	lbw b Warne	0	run out (Symonds)	0
JM Anderson	not out	0	c Hussey b McGrath	5
	l-b 5, w 3, n-b 2	10	b 2, l-b 3, w 1, n-b 3	9
	(103.4 overs, 462 mins)	**291**	**(58 overs, 278 mins)**	**147**
	Fall: 45 58 166 167 245 258 258 282 291 291		Fall: 5 55 64 96 113 114 114 122 123 147	

Bowling: First Innings – McGrath 29-8-67-3; Lee 22-5-75-3; Clark 24-6-62-3; Warne 22.4-1-69-1; Symonds 6-2-13-0. Second Innings – Lee 14-5-39-3; McGrath 21-11-38-3; Clark 12-4-29-2; Warne 6-1-23-1; Symonds 5-2-13-0.

Australia

JL Langer	c Read b Anderson	26	not out	20
ML Hayden	c Collingwood b Harmison	33	not out	23
*RT Ponting	run out (Anderson)	45		
MEK Hussey	c Read b Anderson	37		
MJ Clarke	c Read b Harmison	11		
A Symonds	b Panesar	48		
†AC Gilchrist	c Read b Anderson	62		
SK Warne	st Read b Panesar	71		
B Lee	c Read b Flintoff	5		
SR Clark	c Pietersen b Mahmood	35		
GD McGrath	not out	0		
	l-b 10, w 4, n-b 6	20	l-b 3	3
	(96.3 overs, 432 mins)	**393**	**(10.5 overs, 44 mins)**	**46**
	Fall: 34 100 118 155 190 260 318 325 393 393			

Bowling: First Innings – Flintoff 17-2-56-1; Anderson 26-8-98-3; Harmison 23-5-80-2; Mahmood 11-1-59-1; Panesar 19.3-0-90-2. Second Innings – Anderson 4-0-12-0; Harmison 5-1-13-0; Mahmood 1.5-0-18-0.

South Africa in Australia: the last Test

AUSTRALIA VS. SOUTH AFRICA, THIRD TEST (TEST 1904)

At Sydney Cricket Ground, Sydney, 3, 4, 5, 6, 7 January 2009. Australia won by 103 runs.
Toss: Australia. **Player of the Match:** PM Siddle. **Umpires:** BF Bowden, EAR de Silva.

Australia

ML Hayden	b Steyn	31	b Morkel	39
SM Katich	c de Villiers b Kallis	47	lbw b Steyn	61
*RT Ponting	c Boucher b Morkel	0	b Morkel	53
MEK Hussey	c Kallis b Harris	30	not out	45
MJ Clarke	c & b Duminy	138	c Amla b Harris	41
AB McDonald	c Boucher b Ntini	15		
†BJ Haddin	b Steyn	38		
MG Johnson	c Smith b Steyn	64		
NM Hauritz	c Duminy b Harris	41		
PM Siddle	lbw b Harris	23		
DE Bollinger	not out	0		
	l-b 7, w 3, n-b 8	18	b 8, l-b 9, n-b 1	18
	(136.2 overs, 583 mins)	**445**	**(67.3 overs, 289 mins) (4 wickets dec)**	**257**
	Fall: 62 63 109 130 162 237 379 381 440 445		Fall: 62 134 181 257	

Bowling: First Innings – Steyn 27-5-95-3; Ntini 29-5-102-1; Morkel 27-3-89-1; Kallis 20-6-54-1; Harris 29.2-6-84-3; Duminy 4-0-14-1. Second Innings – Steyn 13-1-60-1; Ntini 12-1-66-0; Morkel 12-2-38-2; Kallis 10-5-13-0; Harris 20.3-1-63-1.

South Africa

ND McKenzie	lbw b Siddle	23	c Hussey b Bollinger	27
*GC Smith	retired hurt	30	b Johnson	3
HM Amla	lbw b McDonald	51	c Katich b Hauritz	59
JH Kallis	c Hayden b Johnson	37	c & b McDonald	4
AB de Villiers	run out (Johnson)	11	b Siddle	56
JP Duminy	lbw b Johnson	13	lbw b Johnson	16
†MV Boucher	b Siddle	89	lbw b Siddle	4
M Morkel	b Siddle	40	c Johnson b Bollinger	0
PL Harris	lbw b Siddle	2	lbw b Siddle	6
DW Steyn	b Siddle	6	lbw b McDonald	28
M Ntini	not out	0	not out	28
	l-b 12, w 9, n-b 4	25	b 12, l-b 18, w 4, n-b 2, pen 5	41
	(120.5 overs, 486 mins)	**327**	**(114.2 overs, 442 mins)**	**272**
	Fall: 35* 76 131 161 166 193 308 310 316 327		Fall: 2 68 91 110 166 172 190 202 257 272	

Bowling: First Innings – Siddle 27.5-11-59-5; Bollinger 23-4-78-0; Johnson 28-6-69-2; McDonald 22-8-41-1; Hauritz 20-4-68-0. Second Innings – Siddle 27-12-54-3; Bollinger 21-5-53-2; Johnson 23.2-7-49-2; McDonald 13-6-32-2; Hauritz 28-10-47-1.

Chappell-Hadlee Trophy: Australian record high score

NEW ZEALAND VS. AUSTRALIA, THIRD ONE DAY INTERNATIONAL (ODI 2527)

At Seddon Park, Hamilton, 20 February 2007. New Zealand won by one wicket (with three balls remaining).
Toss: Australia. **Player of the Match:** ML Hayden. **Umpires:** Aleem Dar and GAV Baxter.

Australia

ML Hayden	not out	181
SR Watson	lbw b Patel	68
†BJ Haddin	c Vincent b Tuffey	38
BJ Hodge	b Patel	12
*MEK Hussey	c McCullum b Gillespie	13
CL White	c Styris b Gillespie	13
AC Voges	not out	16
	b 1, l-b 1, w 1, n-b 2	5
	(50 overs, 227 mins)	**346**
	Fall: 122 210 251 279 302	

Did not bat: GB Hogg, NW Bracken, SW Tait, MG Johnson
Bowling: Tuffey 10-0-68-1; Franklin 10-0-43-0; Gillespie 10-0-83-2; Patel 10-0-70-2; Styris 8-0-52-0; McMillan 2-0-28-0.

New Zealand

L Vincent	c Hogg b Tait	11
*SP Fleming	c Hodge b Tait	9
LR Taylor	c & b Bracken	11
SB Styris	c Haddin b Johnson	0
PG Fulton	c Hussey b Watson	51
CD McMillan	b Watson	117
†BB McCullum	not out	86
JEC Franklin	c Voges b Johnson	2
DR Tuffey	c Haddin b Johnson	8
MR Gillespie	run out (Voges)	28
JS Patel	not out	0
	l-b 4, w 22, n-b 1	27
	(49.3 overs, 230 mins)	**350**
	Fall: 23 34 38 41 116 281 285 303 339	

Bowling: Bracken 9.3-0-44-1; Tait 10-0-60-2; Johnson 10-0-81-3; Watson 10-0-88-2; Hogg 7-0-40-0; Voges 3-0-33-0.

ICC World Cup: form explosion

22ND MATCH, AUSTRALIA VS. SOUTH AFRICA (ODI 2552)

At Warner Park, Basseterre, St Kitts, 24 March 2007. Australia won by 83 runs.
Toss: South Africa. **Player of the Match:** ML Hayden. **Umpires:** MR Benson and SA Bucknor.

Australia

†AC Gilchrist	c Gibbs b Langeveldt	42
ML Hayden	c Gibbs b Kallis	101
*RT Ponting	c de Villiers b Ntini	91
MJ Clarke	run out (Pollock/Langeveldt)	92
A Symonds	b Hall	18
MEK Hussey	c Kallis b Hall	5
SR Watson	not out	14
	l-b 4, w 9, n-b 1	14
	(50 overs)	**377**
	Fall: 106 167 328 347 353 377	

Did not bat: GB Hogg, NW Bracken, SW Tait, GD McGrath
Bowling: Pollock 10-0-83-0; Ntini 9-0-68-1; Langeveldt 10-0-82-1; Hall 10-0-60-2; Smith 2-0-14-0; Kallis 9-0-66-1.

South Africa

*GC Smith	c Gilchrist b Hogg	74
AB de Villiers	run out (Watson)	92
JH Kallis	c Clarke b Hogg	48
HH Gibbs	st Gilchrist b Hogg	17
AG Prince	c Hayden b McGrath	1
†MV Boucher	b Tait	22
JM Kemp	lbw b Tait	1
SM Pollock	b Watson	7
AJ Hall	not out	8
CK Langeveldt	b Bracken	0
M Ntini	b Bracken	7
	w 11, n-b 1, pen 5	17
	(48 overs)	**294**
	Fall: 160 184* 220 223 256 264 277 279 280 294	

Bowling: Bracken 9-0-40-2; Tait 10-0-61-2; McGrath 9-0-62-1; Watson 8-1-46-1; Hogg 10-0-61-3; Symonds 2-0-19-0.

Crunching The Numbers

Test Career Batting and Fielding

	M	I	NO	Runs	HS	Ave	100	50	SRate	Ct
Australia	103	184	14	8625	380	50.73	30	29	60.09	128

Test Career Bowling

	Balls	Mdns	Runs	Wkts	BB	Ave	5wI	10wM	SRate	Econ
Australia	54	0	40	0	0-7					4.44

First-Class Career Batting and Fielding

	M	I	NO	Runs	HS	Ave	100	50	Ct
Overall	295	515	47	24603	380	52.57	79	100	296

First-Class Career Bowling

	Balls	Mdns	Runs	Wkts	BB	Ave	5wI	10wM	SRate	Econ
Overall	1097	25	671	17	3-10	39.47	0	0	64.52	3.67

One-Day International Career Batting and Fielding

	M	I	NO	Runs	HS	Ave	100	50	SRate	Ct
Australia	160	154	15	6131	181*	44.10	10	36	78.98	68
ICC World XI	1	1	0	2	2	2.00	0	0	40.00	0
Overall	161	155	15	6133	181*	43.80	10	36	78.96	68

One-Day International Career Bowling

	Balls	Mdns	Runs	Wkts	BB	Ave	4wI	5wI	SRate	Econ
Australia	6	0	18	0	0-18					18.00

One-Day Career Batting and Fielding

	M	I	NO	Runs	HS	Ave	100	50	Ct
Overall	308	299	29	12051	181*	44.63	27	67	129

One-Day Career Bowling

	Balls	Mdns	Runs	Wkts	BB	Ave	4wI	5wI	SRate	Econ
Overall	339	0	358	10	2-16	35.80	0	0	33.90	6.33

International Twenty20 Career Batting and Fielding

	M	I	NO	Runs	HS	Ave	100	50	SRate	Ct
Australia	9	9	3	308	73*	51.33	0	4	143.92	1

Twenty20 Career Batting and Fielding

	M	I	NO	Runs	HS	Ave	100	50	SRate	Ct
Overall	41	41	5	1415	93	39.30	0	12	138.86	12

Test Career Batting/Fielding Performance by Opponent

Versus	M	Inns	NO	50s	100s	HS	Runs	Avg	Ca	St
Bangladesh	4	5	0	2	0	72	168	33.60	7	0
England	20	35	3	2	5	197	1461	45.66	29	0
ICC World XI	1	2	0	1	1	111	188	94.00	3	0
India	18	35	3	8	6	203	1888	59.00	23	0
New Zealand	11	18	0	5	1	136	658	36.56	5	0
Pakistan	6	10	2	2	1	119	374	46.75	3	0
South Africa	19	36	2	5	6	138	1486	43.71	22	0
Sri Lanka	7	13	0	1	3	132	664	51.08	9	0
West Indies	15	27	3	3	5	177	1237	51.54	23	0
Zimbabwe	2	3	1	0	2	380	501	250.50	4	0
Overall (10)	103	184	14	29	30	380	8625	50.74	128	0

Acknowledgements

It takes courage to do something different. I am deeply appreciative of the help I had from Penguin Australia, who were happy to wait until 2010 to publish this book, thereby giving me crucial extra time to gain a post-retirement perspective. Like the opening of a good wine, it gave my story a little time to breathe.

Special thanks to Penguin CEO Gabrielle Coyne, who had an instant connection to me and my story, and to Ben Ball and Belinda Byrne for their encouragement, wise counsel and endless patience as I tested their deadlines. We got there!

Thank you to Robert Craddock for the hours and days of work on this project. It has been a lot of fun telling yarns across the airwaves, in planes, in hotels, in cars, in separate countries in any countless number of destinations. Heck, we even learnt how to use Skype! It's all been worth it. Thanks for your devotion and commitment to get the job right. For over two decades, we've worked together from opposite sides of the fence, and this speaks volumes about our mutual respect. Good on you, mate!

Thanks to Elysa Craddock for her editorial assistance and flawless dedication in researching and transcribing – and for being the organised one in her family.

Andrew Dawson and Gideon Haigh were silent forces in the book. Hearty thanks to them and to the *Courier-Mail* for doing all it could to support the project.

I greatly appeciated the following people's help with interviews, advice and other aspects of the book: Greg Chappell, Stephen Waugh, Jimmy Maher, Michael Kasprowicz, Peter Parker, Stephen Gray, John Buchanan, Brian Lara, the late Father Pat Jones, Gwen McLaughlan, John Eales, Andrew Symonds, Chris Holding, Paul Jackson, Bob Simpson, Carl Rackemann, Trevor Barsby, Ian Healy, Allan Border, Barry Richards, Matthew Mott, Michael Slater, Trevor Hohns and Adam Gilchrist.

Special thanks to Andrew Flintoff. I have always respected you as a player and I consider it a huge bonus to have got to know you after the curtain was drawn on our international careers. Your contribution to the book brings a rare glimpse from behind enemy lines – and let's not worry about the fishing and surfing talk, mate; a couple of mango seasons in Queensland should sort that out!

To my beautiful wife Kellie and our three adorable children, Grace, Joshua and Thomas – thank you. Your infinite love, affection and wisdom through the best and the worst times have provided incredible support and strength. I admire each of your individual spirits. I am so proud to be the husband who loves his wife and the father who writes cookbooks and gets his hands dirty with any kind of outside activity in our beautiful country.

Thank you Mum and Dad, for your commitment to me as your son in providing such moral fabric and remarkable examples. There was never one moment when I felt alone in life – I felt secure and loved.

To dearest Gary and Alex Hayden and their three children, Ellie, Billy and Tim – I am blessed to have such a special brother with such a great family. Your energy and passion for life is simply addictive and was a huge source of strength and support in my formative years. Thank you for also being a great brother-in-law to Kellie – just knowing that you were looking out for her made it that little bit easier to remain away as long as I did.

Thank you to Gary Jones and my late aunt Lorna Jones for cataloguing 19 years of newspaper clippings, which proved to be an outstanding resource throughout this project. And thank you for being my Brisbane parents while I was at Marist College Ashgrove; the same can be said of you as can be said of my own parents.

Thank you to Bernie, Maureen and Tony Culey – since the moment I met Kellie in 1993 I have felt supported by you all as if you were my own family. Thank you for your amazing contribution to our lives. My late uncle, Father Pat Jones, said it best as a prelude to our first meeting: 'Matt, you have to meet some friends of mine – they simply are special people. Oh, and by the way, their daughter is lovely – her name is Kellie.' Good call, Pat!

I would like to thank Neil and Jenny Honan, Guy and Jenny Reynolds, Geoffrey Schuhkraft, Lindar Butler, Pam and Joanna Jones, Trevor and Jenny O'Hoy, John and Kerrie Dunphy, Pierre Tostee, Mick, Nola, Seb, Bart and Julian Wilson, Chris White, Allan Jones, Justin and Sue Langer, Leanne Walker, Bronwen McLauchlan, Karen Henley and Andrew Symonds – you have all been our 'away' family, providing such a terrific grounding as pillars of support. Thank you for your fantastic mentoring and contribution to our lives.

Finally, thank you to Graham Dixon and all his staff at Queensland Cricket and to the members of Valleys District Cricket Club for providing the start a young man with a big dream needed. It has been an honour and a privilege to represent you all around the world. I hope I have done you proud.

PICTURE CREDITS

Unless otherwise credited, photographs are from Matthew Hayden's private collection. While every attempt has been made to contact copyright owners, the publisher would be happy to hear of any omissions so that we can correct these in future editions.

Section 1

p. 8 Both photographs by Newspix/Michael Thomas
p. 9 Newspix/Michael Thomas
p. 14 Newspix/Paul Wager
p. 15 Top: Newspix/Anthony Weate
p. 12 Top: Newspix/Phil Hillyard
p. 13 Reuters
p. 14 Both photographs by Reuters
p. 15 Both photographs by Newspix/Phil Hillyard
p. 16 Newspix/Phil Hillyard

Section 2

p. 1 Newspix
p. 2 Both photographs by Newspix
p. 3 Newspix
p. 4 Both photographs by Newspix
p. 5 Top: Newspix/Anthony Weate; bottom: Newspix/Bob Fenney
p. 7 Top: Getty; bottom: Newspix/Phil Hillyard
p. 8 Top: Getty; bottom: Newspix/Phil Hillyard
p. 9 Newspix
p. 10 Top: Reuters; bottom: Newspix/Phil Hillyard
p. 11 Top: Newspix/Anthony Weate; bottom: Newspix/David Kapernick

Section 3

p. 3 Bottom: Newspix/Paul Riley
p. 4 Top: Newspix/Phil Hillyard
p. 5 Both photographs by Getty
p. 6 Newspix/Phil Hillyard
p. 7 Top: Newspix/Gregg Porteous; bottom: Newspix
p. 8 Getty
p. 9 Top: Getty; bottom left: Reuters; bottom right: Newspix/Colleen Petch
p. 10 Bottom: Newspix/Jon Hargest
p. 11 Top: Getty/Mark Kolbe
p. 12 Associated Press
p. 13 Top: Newspix/Darren England

INDEX